Classics to Read Aloud to Your Children

WILLIAM F. RUSSELL

Classics to Read Aloud to Your Children

Crown Publishers, Inc.
New York

Published by Crown Publishers, Inc., One Park Avenue, New York, New York 10016, and simultaneously in Canada by General Publishing Company Limited

Manufactured in the United States of America

Library of Congress Cataloging in Publication Data

Russell, William F., 1945–
  Classics to read aloud to your children.

  Summary: Selections, including some rewritten for reading aloud, from poems, novels, and plays by Homer, Mallory, Shakespeare, Dickens, Hawthorne, Twain, and other well-known authors.
  1. Children's literature.   2. Oral reading. [1. Literature—Collections]   I. Title.
PZ5.R87C 1984   808.8'99282   84-7033
ISBN 0-517-55404-6

10 9 8 7 6 5 4 3 2 1

First Edition

For Brantley,
whose world now is filled with wonder,
in the hope that this will always be so

Contents

Classics to
Read Aloud
to Your
Children

Some Questions and Answers about Reading to Your Children

Reading *to* your children may be the single, most powerful contribution that you, as a parent, can make toward their success in school. Although teachers and school administrators emphasize the importance of providing quiet study time and space within the home, a child who has difficulty in reading and writing simply will not be able to make productive use of even the most advantageous study conditions. It is only when children enjoy reading and truly appreciate the benefits that artful use of language can have that they pursue their studies with vigor. Children who have a good command of the language—the good readers, those with large vocabularies, those who can convey their ideas clearly both orally and in writing—consistently achieve academic success in math, science, and social studies as well as in English classes.

This is not mere coincidence, nor can it be explained by the all-too-commonly accepted notion that "gifted" children are inherently more capable in all areas of study. The ability to understand story problems in mathematics, the ability to answer essay questions on a history test, and the ability and willingness to respond when called upon for an answer in a biology class all depend on fluency with language. Grades and scores only partially reflect one's knowledge of a subject—the manner in which an idea is phrased can change the content of that idea, either for good or ill, as any politician or used-car salesman can attest, and that requires a subtle understanding of language. Add to this the fact that children who find reading, writing, and speaking difficult and tiresome will not eagerly pursue their studies in *any* subject (for the acquisition of knowledge in all school subjects is, has been, and will be primarily dependent upon reading) and you will, I think, begin to agree with me that developing a child's interest and skills in language could be the most important task facing any parent.

Granted, you may say, that competence and ease in reading, writing, and speaking are requisite for success in school, but it is *the child's* ability to use language—not the ability of the parents—that contributes to academic achievement; why then should parents concentrate on reading *to* their children instead of encouraging children to read for themselves? A fair question, and one commonly asked. The answer is that reading *to* your children is absolutely the best way to develop their ability to read for themselves and by themselves. Studies have shown that the one common factor found in all children who learned to read without being formally taught how was not high IQ, not high family income, not parents who had college degrees; rather, the one factor was that all these children were read to by their parents regularly, frequently, and from whatever materials happened to be at hand—newspapers, road signs, even packing labels. Reading to your children not only allows them to become aware of relationships between printed words, spoken words, and the meaning of words but also allows them to hear a galaxy of words that they do not, as yet, use in their own speech, to realize that these words can be used in conveying ideas, and to become accustomed to the pattern of complete sentences.

Although many parents do read simple stories, nursery rhymes, and picture books to their preschool children, they commonly make one unfortunate mistake: They stop reading aloud once the children begin to read for themselves. It is my belief that parents should continue to read *to* their children throughout their children's elementary school years and into early adolescence. A preschooler profits from a parent's oral reading by being exposed to a level of language that he or she will someday adopt; a ten-year-old can profit equally from a parent's oral reading of language that is an increment beyond that child's reading level. The complexity, subtlety, and vocabulary of a work that an eighth-grader finds difficult to read can be understood and appreciated when that child hears the work read aloud. Then, too, the social benefits that parents find in reading to their children—the affection and togetherness that are developed during oral reading sessions—need not be curtailed simply because the child has learned to read, nor are they benefits that are prized only by parents. Children, too, find happiness in having a parent devote uninterrupted time in which they can be together. Even teenagers, when questioned outside the presence and pressure of their peers, say that they would enjoy being read to—especially if the reader could be one of their parents.

Parents who acknowledge the benefits of reading to their children face a series of vexing questions as to how it is best done. Their inability to answer these questions sends many into retreat, rekindling their former notions that perhaps reading should be left to schools and teachers after all. To these parents, I offer the following suggestions.

WHAT should I read?

A parent who is used to reading nursery stories to a preschooler is faced with two pressing oral reading problems after the child begins school: What stories will the child be interested in hearing, and what stories will the parent be interested in reading? Don't give this second question short shrift—it is probably more important than the first. Every parent knows that preschoolers have an almost insatiable appetite for hearing their favorite stories read over and over again. Parents' interest in reading a particular story wanes very quickly, but they persevere not only because their child wishes them to do so but also because they do not have any new selections immediately at hand. But if a parent is not honestly entertained while reading a story, this lack of interest is very subtly communicated to the child during the reading. The resulting message is that reading is a tiresome, laborious, even boring task.

I have selected for this volume works that I believe will be interesting for children to hear and for parents to read. They are truly "classics" in that they represent some of the best works of some of the best writers of the Western world. They are works that many parents will recall having read for themselves during their school days; others parents may know about, but have never actually read. Each story and poem, however, is valuable both for the tale it tells and for the artful language it employs. You will not find in these works the street slang and the slovenly usages that cascade from the lips of television characters and, consequently, become adopted into the general speech and writing of American children (and adults). But you will soon discover that the use of complete sentences and precise vocabulary in no way diminishes the excitement, the impact, or the beauty of the tale being told. Even when a work employs a nonstandard dialect to reflect the actual speech of a character, the sentences are still complete and well crafted, qualities not often found in the speech of our television and sports heroes.

Not all classics, of course, are suitable to read to all children, and so I have grouped these works into three categories. The selections in the first category (Listening Level I) are intended for children who are aged 5 and up. The vocabulary in these selections is admittedly—and by design—beyond the reading vocabulary of many of these children. But it is not beyond their *listening* vocabulary; that is, they will be able to understand the meaning of words they would not recognize by sight because they will have heard the words before, and they will understand the context in which they now hear them being used. Remember that although a first-grader's reading primer in school is written with a controlled vocabulary of approximately 350 words, the *listening* vocabulary of most first-graders approaches 10,000 words! Most of the works in Listening Level I are also somewhat shorter than those in the next higher category, and the subjects that they deal with are not as emotionally provocative. These stories and poems are typically brief, light, fanciful pieces that should spark the child's imagination and appeal to the child's sense of wonder.

The second category, Listening Level II, is designed for listeners aged 8 and up. It includes works that are a bit longer, more complex, and cover a wider emotional range than those in the previous group.

Listening Level III is the most demanding in that it employs an adult vocabulary, and, in some cases, it deals with topics that only older children are likely to be emotionally prepared to handle. These more lengthy stories are intended for children aged 11 and up, but, as with the other levels, this is merely a suggested age range, and you must decide for yourself whether any particular work is suitable for your particular child —and for you.

WHO should do the reading?

Keep in mind that this is not a book that children are expected to be able to read for themselves. It is, instead, a book that a child should be able to ask you to read aloud, without ever feeling embarrassed or ashamed about wanting to listen rather than to read. After all, the child's motive in asking may not be to hear a story read aloud; the request may instead be the child's way of asking to spend some time with you. Or, you might be the one to suggest a reading session to allow you to spend some quiet time with your child. In any event, the book is intended for both of you, so always try to let it be an instrument of joint pleasure. This is not to say that a child, especially a younger child, should be discouraged from thumbing through the pages or pretending to be reading alone. In fact, such occasions may themselves be subtle requests for your presence and may profitably be followed up by your suggesting that you'd like to read aloud for a while.

Reading aloud to children should not be the responsibility of one parent alone; children need private reading sessions with their fathers just as much as with their mothers. Single parents should actively seek adult role models of the opposite sex— grandparents, neighbors, friends, etc.—to read. Fathers (and adult males in general) have a special responsibility as oral readers since children all too frequently see reading skill as a feminine characteristic, perhaps because a majority of their teachers in school are women. This is particularly apparent in the reading of poetry: Children, especially boys, do not see writing or reading poetry as a masculine activity, and so they grow up believing that the enjoyment of poetry is not a "manly" pursuit. If school-aged children could hear their fathers read poetry aloud, if they could witness adult men receiving pleasure from the beauty of well-written verse, they would be better able to resist prevailing cultural stereotypes and to choose for themselves the type of writing that pleases them to hear or read or even write.

HOW should the works be read?

Oral reading is more difficult than silent reading. You have to pronounce each word when you read aloud, and you cannot as easily overcome your errors. Each mistake, subsequent retreat, and rereading diminishes the impact of the passage for the listener and lessens the listener's enjoyment of the work being read. Yes, the task is more difficult, but with practice the process becomes so enjoyable for listener and reader alike that many readers find the pleasure greatest when the work is shared with someone else.

I have tried to anticipate the pronunciation problems that you will encounter in each work by giving the standard pronunciations for any troublesome words and names at the beginning of each selection. You should look over these words and pronunciations by yourself before beginning an oral reading. I have also provided some brief definitions in case the usage of a word is unfamiliar to you or in case your child should ask you what the word means. As an additional aid I have shown the pronunciations again, inside brackets, where the word first appears in the selection itself.

I have suggested a Listening Level (I, II, or III) for each selection, as a very general indication of the emotional and linguistic difficulty of the work. You will also find an Approximate Reading Time listed, and you should use this to help you select which works you can read in the time you have available. Unless some unexpected emergency arises, you should not end your reading session partway through a story (or partway through a chapter of a longer work). Always try to allow enough time to ask your child a question or two about the work you have just read. What would he or she have done if faced by the same situation that occurred in the story? What did the characters in the story learn from what happened? Why do you think the author wanted people to read this story? Questions like these are open-ended, requiring the child to respond with more than a simple, one-word answer. Open-ended questions are much more thought-provoking than those that only call for factual information from the story or those that can be answered by a simple yes or no.

Let me caution you about asking the child whether he or she knows the meaning of specific words used in the story. While certain words are crucial to understanding what is taking place, most of these meanings will be understood in the context of the story and may be difficult to phrase as specific definitions. In time, as your child hears various words used repeatedly, their meanings will become clear and eventually may even be adopted as part of his or her speaking vocabulary.

Your child may never adopt some words, however, because the original language of these tales has been left intact whenever possible, and that language can be challenging even to a highly educated, adult vocabulary. Indeed, each time I have faced the troublesome choice of retaining or altering the original language of these works, I have imagined their authors leering over my shoulder, and the chance of their reproach caused me to favor leaving the works intact.

A special mention should be made of how to read poetry aloud. When there is a punctuation mark at the end of a line of a poem, the author is indicating that the reader should pause —briefly for a comma, longer for a semicolon or a period. When there is no punctuation at the end of a line, there should be no pause, and the reader should continue right on into the beginning of the following line. For example, in the stanza below (from Coleridge's "The Rime of the Ancient Mariner"), the fourth line should be read as though it were attached to the end of the third line:

> *Day after day, day after day,*
> *We stuck, nor breath nor motion;*
> *As idle as a painted ship*
> *Upon a painted ocean.*

You will answer for yourselves the questions of when and where to read to your children as you discover your children's particular preferences as well as your own. Some children enjoy bedtime stories (even many adolescents), while others demand a reading session before they set off for school in the morning. Some parents prefer to schedule a specific time for oral reading in the evening, while others opt to be more flexible, reading aloud when they feel like doing so or their children request it. There is no one right way, and the only wrong way is to avoid reading aloud altogether. There is a whole world of good writing, good reading, and good listening awaiting your children—a world that you can open up to them and one that they will enjoy for the rest of their lives. What better gift can there possibly be?

Listening Level I

(Ages 5 and up)

Children who are in the dawn of their schooling actually began their education years ago, and they acquired the idea during that time that reading was enjoyable for adults and that being read to stirred the imagination and caused them to wonder. Just because they have now reached school age, why on earth should we allow them to think any differently about these matters?

The wonder that is excited by an outcast duckling's transformation into a swan, or by the tale of a boy who becomes King of all England, or by the idea that objects can be changed to gold at the touch of a finger—such wonders cannot be put off until children can read well enough to learn of them on their own. The stories in this section have in common a brevity and this sense of wonder; both characteristics should be kept in mind when choosing other oral reading materials for this age group.

"The Ugly Duckling"

by

HANS CHRISTIAN ANDERSEN

About the story:

> *Originally written in Danish, this story about an out-*
> *cast duckling who is transformed into a beautiful swan*
> *has been translated into every language in the world.*
> *Andersen's tales were intended to be read to children,*
> *rather than by children. If your younger ones find this*
> *story appealing, you will be happy to know that there*
> *are many collections of similar tales by Hans Christian*
> *Andersen to be found in the local library, collections that*
> *include such classics as "The Fir Tree," "The Emperor's*
> *New Clothes," and "The Princess and the Pea."*

Approximate reading time: 9 minutes
Pronunciation and vocabulary guide:
   burdock [BURR-dock]: an herb with prickly leaves

A pleasant old farmhouse stood close by a river, and from the house down to the bank of the river there grew great burdock [BURR-dock] leaves. These were so high that a child could stand under the tallest, and they grew so close together that they looked like a little forest.

In a snug place under one of these burdock leaves, a duck sat on her nest waiting for her young brood to hatch. She was becoming very tired, for the little ones were a long time in coming out of their shells, and she did not often have company. The neighbor ducks liked better to swim about in the river than to climb its slippery banks and sit under the burdocks gossiping.

After a while one shell cracked, then another, and another, and from each egg came a fluffy little yellow creature that lifted its head and cried, "Peep! peep!"

"Quack! quack!" said the mother, and then they all quacked as well as they could.

After a little while they came out from under their mother's wings and looked about them. "What a great world this is," said the young ducks, "so very much larger than the eggshell." "Do you think that this is the whole world?" asked their mother. "Wait until you have seen the farmyard, the garden, and the pasture.

"Are you all out?" she asked, rising. "No, I declare, the largest egg lies there still. I wonder how much longer I must stay here; I am very tired of this," and she sat down again on the nest.

"Well, how are you getting along?" asked an old duck who called just then.

"Very well," said the mother. "All the eggs are hatched but one; and are not these little ones the prettiest ducklings you ever saw?"

"They are very pretty," said the visitor. "But just let me see that egg that will not hatch. It must be a turkey's egg. I hatched some once, and after all my care and trouble the young ones were afraid of the water. I quacked and coaxed, but it did no good. I never could get one of them into the water. Yes, that is a turkey's egg. Now, if I were in your place, I would leave it where it is, and teach the other children to swim."

"I think I will sit on it a little while longer," said the duck. "I have been here so long that a few days more will not matter."

"Well, do as you please," said the old duck, and she waddled away.

At last the large egg broke, and the young one crept out crying, "Peep! peep!" The mother duck stared at it and said, "What a large duckling! and it is not at all like the others. I wonder if it really is a turkey. We shall soon find out when we go to the water. It shall go in, if I have to push it in myself."

On the next day the sun shone brightly on the burdock leaves, so the mother took her brood and waddled off down to the river. When they came to the water, the mother duck jumped in with a splash. "Quack! quack!" she cried, and one after another the little ducklings jumped in after their mother. They swam about quite prettily, with their legs paddling under them as though they had been born in the water, and the ugly brother was there with the others.

"Oh," said the mother, "that is not a turkey; how well he

uses his legs and how gracefully he holds his body. He is my own child and I do not think he is very ugly. Quack! quack! Come with me now, children; I will take you to a place where there are many fine people, but you must keep close to me or you may be stepped on, and above all, look out for the cat."

Then they climbed the slippery bank of the river, and waddled after their mother. When they came to the farmyard fence, the mother stopped and said, "Come now, my children, see how well you can behave. Don't turn in your toes. A duckling who is well brought up spreads his feet wide apart just as his mother does—so, do you see? Now bend your necks and say 'quack,' " and the young ducks did just as their mother told them to do.

An old duck who saw the new brood coming stared at them and said, "Do look; here is another brood, as if there were not enough of us already; and what a queer-looking fellow one of them is; we do not want him here," and then she flew at him and bit him in the neck.

"Let him alone," said the mother, "he is doing no harm."

"Yes, but he is so big and ugly that he must be turned out," said the hateful duck.

A very grand old duck said, "They are very pretty children, all but that one. I wish his mother would fix him up a little."

"I cannot do that," said the mother. "He is not pretty, but he is kind and good and swims even better than the others. I think he will become pretty," and then she stroked his neck and smoothed his feathers.

The little ducks made themselves at home in the farmyard, but the poor ugly duckling had not one minute's peace. The turkey gobbler puffed himself out and flew at the poor little duckling, and became very red in the head with anger. The ducks pecked him, the children chased him, and the girl who fed the poultry kicked him. Even his brothers and sisters were unkind to him, and would say, "Oh, you ugly creature, I wish the cat would get you," and his mother said, "I wish he had never come from the shell."

At last he could endure it no longer, so he ran away, frightening the little birds in the hedge as he flew over it. "They are afraid of me because I am so ugly," he said. Then he closed his eyes and ran on and on until he came to a swamp, where the wild geese lived. He stayed here all night, feeling very tired and sad.

In the morning, two wild geese flew over him. When they saw him they began to make fun of him. Just then "pop! pop!" went a gun, and the two fell dead among the rushes, coloring the water with their blood. "Pop! pop!" was heard all around, and whole flocks of wild geese flew up from the rushes.

The blue smoke from the guns rose like a dark cloud over the trees, and a number of dogs bounded in among the rushes. How frightened the poor duckling was! He turned away his head to hide it under his wing when a large terrible dog passed quite near him. The dog's mouth was open, his tongue hung from his mouth, and his eyes looked very fierce. He thrust his nose close to the duckling, showing his sharp teeth, and then "splash! splash!" he went into the water without touching him.

"How glad I am that I am so ugly. Even a dog will not bite me," said the duckling.

So he lay quite still, while the shot rattled through the rushes, as gun after gun was fired over him. It was late in the day before it became quiet, and then the poor young thing did not dare to move. He waited quietly for several hours and, after looking carefully around him, he flew away from the swamp as fast as he could go.

The next morning, just as the sun arose, he came to a stream of water. Here he could swim and dive, but all the animals kept away from him, he was so ugly; so he was very lonely.

Autumn came, and the leaves in the forest turned to orange, red, and gold; and then as winter drew near the wind caught them and whirled them in the cold air.

The weather grew colder and colder. Winter was here, and the poor duck had to swim about in the water to keep from freezing, but each night the place on which he swam became smaller. After a while he grew weak and tired and lay still and helpless, frozen fast in the ice.

Early in the morning, a farmer who was passing saw what had happened. He broke the ice in pieces and carried the duckling home to his wife. The poor creature felt better after getting warm, but when the children wanted to play with him, the duckling thought they were going to hurt him, so he started up, frightened, fluttered into the milk pan, and splashed the milk about the room.

Then the woman clapped her hands, which frightened him still more. He flew first into the jar of butter, then into the flour barrel and out again. What a bad fix he was in! The woman screamed and struck at him with a poker; the children laughed and screamed and tumbled over each other trying to catch him, but finally he got away. The door was open a little way and he slipped out and flew down among some bushes. Here he lay, tired out, in the newly fallen snow.

After he had rested himself, he flew to a swamp, where all winter long he suffered from hunger and cold. When winter had passed, and he was lying one morning among the rushes, he felt that his wings were strong, so he flapped them against his sides and rose high into the air. They carried him on and on, until he found himself in a large garden. Everything was beautiful there. From the bushes, close by, swam three white swans, rustling their feathers as they moved over the smooth water.

"I will fly to these birds," he said, "and they will kill me because I am so ugly and dare to come near them; but it makes no difference. It is better to be killed by these beautiful birds than to be pecked by the ducks, chased by the hens, kicked about by the girl who feeds the poultry, or starved and frozen in the winter."

Then he flew to the water and swam toward the fine swans. The moment they saw him they hurried to meet him with outstretched wings. "Kill me," said the poor bird, and he bent down his head, waiting for them to take his life. But what do you think he saw as he looked down into the water? His own likeness, but how changed! He was no longer a dark, gray bird, ugly to look at, but a beautiful swan. The other swans swam around the newcomer and stroked his neck with their beaks.

Soon after, some little children came into the garden and threw bread and cake into the water.

"Oh, see," cried the youngest child, "there is a new one!"

How happy they all were to see the new swan. They ran to call their father and mother to come and see him.

Then they threw bread and cake into the water for the new

bird, and they said, "This is the finest of all, he is so young and graceful."

The poor swan was so happy he did not know what to do, but he was not at all proud. He had been hated for being ugly, and now he heard them say that he was the most beautiful of all the birds. He rustled his feathers and curved his slender neck, and said, "Now, when people see me they will not be angry, they will be glad. I never dreamed of such happiness when I was an ugly duckling."

"Androcles and the Lion"

from
Aesop's Fables

About the story:
   *The fables of Aesop need not be presented to young chil-
   dren as being instructive or their animal characters as
   having human qualities. If you choose to read selections
   of* **Aesop's Fables** *to your child, just let them stand as
   entertaining stories; you will have ample opportunity to
   draw upon their wisdom as your child becomes more
   capable of seeing their parallels to daily life.*

Approximate reading time: 5 minutes
Pronunciation and vocabulary guide:
   Androcles [ANN-droe-kleez]
   coliseum [kahl-uh-SEE-um]: a large stadium

There was once, in the days of ancient Rome, a certain
young slave named Androcles [ANN-droe-kleez], who
was so ill treated by his master that his life became
unbearable. Finding no remedy for what he suffered, he said
to himself, "It is better to die than to continue to live in such
hardship and misery as I am forced to suffer. Therefore, I must
run away from my master. If I am captured and brought back,
I know that I shall be punished with a cruel death, but it is
better to die at once than to live in misery. If I am to escape, I
must head into the deserts and woods, which are inhabited
only by beasts, but they cannot treat me any more cruelly than
I have been used by humans; therefore, it is better that I trust
myself with them than to continue to be a miserable slave."

Having formed this resolution, he took an opportunity of
leaving his master's house and hid himself in a thick forest that
was some miles outside the city. But here the unhappy young
man found that he had escaped from one kind of misery only
to experience another. He wandered about all day through a

vast and trackless wood, where his flesh was continually torn by thorns and brambles; he grew hungry, but could find no food in this dreary solitude. Soon he was ready to die with fatigue and lay down in despair in a large cavern which he had found by accident.

He had not lain long in the cavern before he heard a dreadful noise, which seemed to be the roar of some wild beast, and which terrified him very much. He bolted up with the intention of escaping and had already reached the mouth of the cave when he saw coming toward him a lion of immense size that prevented any possibility of retreat. Androcles now believed his death to be inevitable; but, to his great astonishment, the beast advanced toward him at a gentle pace, without any sign of hostility or rage, and uttered a kind of mournful wail, as if he wanted the assistance of the man.

Androcles, who had always had a bold disposition, took courage from this and decided to examine his strange guest. He saw, as the lion approached him, that he seemed to limp upon one of his legs and that the foot was extremely swollen, as if it had been wounded. Acquiring still more fortitude from the gentle manner of the beast, he went up to him and took hold of the wounded paw as a surgeon would examine a patient. He then perceived that a thorn of great size had penetrated the ball of the foot and was the cause of the swelling and lameness that he had observed. Androcles found that the beast, far from resenting his familiarity, received it with the greatest gentleness and seemed to invite him to proceed. He therefore extracted the thorn, and, pressing the swelling, forced out a quantity of liquid that had built up in the paw and had been the cause of so much pain.

As soon as the beast felt himself thus relieved, he began to show his joy and gratitude by every expression within his power: He jumped about like a spaniel, wagged his enormous tail, and licked the feet and hands of his physician. Nor was he contented with these demonstrations of kindness. From this moment Androcles became his guest; the lion never went forth in quest of prey without bringing home what he caught and sharing it with his friend. In this savage state of hospitality, Androcles continued to live for several months. In time, however, wandering through the woods, he met with a company of soldiers sent out to apprehend him and was taken prisoner by them and led back to his master. The laws of that time being very severe against slaves, he was tried and found guilty of having fled from his master, and, as a punishment for his crime, he was sentenced to the arena where he would face, unarmed, a ferocious wild animal that had been kept many days without food, and so be torn to pieces.

When the fatal day arrived, Androcles found himself in a spacious coliseum [kahl-uh-SEE-um], enclosed on every side, round which many thousands of people were assembled to view the mournful spectacle. Soon a dreadful yell was heard, which struck the spectators with horror; and a monstrous lion rushed out of an opened gate and darted forward with erected mane and flaming eyes, and jaws that gaped like an open tomb. A mournful silence instantly fell over the crowd. All eyes were directly turned upon the victim, whose destruction now appeared inevitable. But the pity of the multitude was soon converted into astonishment when they beheld the lion, instead of destroying his defenseless prey, crouch submissively at his feet, fawn upon him as a faithful dog would do upon his master, and rejoice over him as a mother that unexpectedly recovers her child. The governor of the province, who was present, then called out with a loud voice and ordered Androcles to explain to them this mystery. Androcles then related to the assembly everything that happened on his adventures in the woods and concluded by saying that the very lion which now stood before them had been his friend and host in the woods. All the persons present were astonished and delighted with the story, to find that even the fiercest beasts are capable of being softened by gratitude and moved by humanity; and they all asked for the governor to pardon Androcles for his crime. This was immediately granted, and the governor also made the young man a present of the lion, that had in this manner twice saved the life of Androcles.

"The Early Days of Black Beauty"

from *Black Beauty*
by
ANNA SEWELL

About the story:
Anna Sewell's classic tale about the education of a horse into the world of humans is told from the point of view of the horse, Black Beauty. Although the scenes presented here relate happenings that occurred while the horse was just a colt, the book itself follows Black Beauty through the time he is full-grown. Parents, especially those whose children are fond of horses, will find the entire book to be as enjoyable to read aloud as is the selection that follows.

Approximate reading time: 11 minutes
Pronunciation and vocabulary guide:
   crupper: a leather loop that passes under a horse's tail and is buckled to the saddle
   breeching: part of the harness
   chaise [SHAZE]: a small, two-wheeled carriage
   fortnight: two weeks

The first place that I can well remember was a large pleasant meadow with a pond of clear water in it. Some shady trees leaned over it, and rushes and water lilies grew at the deep end. Over the hedge on one side we looked into a plowed field, and on the other we looked over a gate at our master's house, which stood by the roadside; at the top of the meadow was a grove of fir trees, and at the bottom a running brook overhung by a steep bank.

While I was young, I lived upon my mother's milk, as I could not eat grass. In the daytime I ran by her side, and at night I lay down close by her. When it was hot, we used to stand by the pond in the shade of the trees, and when it was cold, we had a nice warm shed near the grove.

As soon as I was old enough to eat grass, my mother used to go out to work in the daytime and come back in the evening.

There were six young colts in the meadow besides me; they were older than I was; some were nearly as large as grown-up horses. I used to run with them and had great fun; we used to gallop all together round and round the field as hard as we could go. Sometimes we had rather rough play, for they would frequently bite and kick as well as gallop.

One day, when there was a good deal of kicking, my mother whinnied to me to come to her, and then she said:

"I wish you to pay attention to what I am going to say to you. The colts who live here are very good colts, but they are carthorse colts, and of course they have not learned manners. You have been well bred and well born; your father has a great name in these parts, and your grandfather won the cup two years at the Newmarket races; your grandmother had the sweetest temper of any horse I ever knew, and I think you have never seen me kick or bite. I hope you will grow up gentle and good and never learn bad ways; do your work with a good will, lift your feet up well when you trot, and never bite or kick even in play."

I have never forgotten my mother's advice; I knew she was a wise old horse, and our master thought a great deal of her. Her name was Duchess, but he often called her Pet.

Our master was a good, kind man. He gave us good food, good lodging, and kind words; he spoke as kindly to us as he did to his little children. We were all fond of him, and my mother loved him very much. When she saw him at the gate, she would neigh with joy and trot up to him. He would pat and stroke her and say, "Well, old Pet, and how is your little Darkie?" I was a dull black, so he called me Darkie; then he would give me a piece of bread, which was very good, and sometimes he brought a carrot for my mother. All the horses would come to him, but I think we were his favorites. My mother always took him to the town on market day in a light buggy.

There was a plowboy, Dick, who sometimes came into our field to pluck blackberries from the hedge. When he had eaten all he wanted, he would have what he called fun with the colts, throwing stones and sticks at them to make them gallop. We did not much mind him, for we could gallop off; but sometimes a stone would hit and hurt us.

One day he was at this game and did not know that the master was in the next field, but he was there, watching what was going on; over the hedge he jumped in a snap, and catching Dick by the arm, he gave him such a box on the ear as made him roar with the pain and surprise. As soon as we saw the master, we trotted up nearer to see what went on.

"Bad boy!" he said, "bad boy! to chase the colts. This is not the first time, nor the second, but it shall be the last. There— take your money and go home; I shall not want you on my farm again." So we never saw Dick anymore. Old Daniel, the man who looked after the horses, was just as gentle as our master, so we were well off.

Before I was two years old, a circumstance happened that I have never forgotten. It was early in the spring; there had been a little frost in the night, and a light mist still hung over the woods and meadows. I and the other colts were feeding at the lower part of the field when we heard, quite in the distance, what sounded like the cry of dogs. The oldest of the colts raised his head, pricked his ears, and said, "There are the hounds!" and immediately cantered off, followed by the rest of us to the upper part of the field, where we could look over the hedge and see several fields beyond. My mother and an old riding horse of our master's were also standing near and seemed to know all about it.

"They have found a hare," said my mother, "and if they come this way we shall see the hunt."

And soon the dogs were all tearing down the field of young wheat next to ours. I never heard such a noise as they made. They did not bark, nor howl, nor whine, but kept on a "yo! yo, o, o! yo! yo, o, o!" at the top of their voices. After them came a number of men on horseback, some of them in green coats, all galloping as fast as they could. The old horse snorted and looked eagerly after them, and we young colts wanted to be galloping with them, but they were soon away into the fields lower down; here it seemed as if they had come to a stand; the dogs left off barking and ran about every way with their noses to the ground.

"They have lost the scent," said the old horse; "perhaps the hare will get off."

"What hare?" I said.

"Oh, I don't know *what* hare; likely enough it may be one of our own hares out of the woods; any hare they can find will do for the dogs and men to run after"; and before long the dogs began their "yo! yo, o, o!" again, and back they came all together at full speed, making straight for our meadow at the part where the high bank and hedge overhung the brook.

"Now we shall see the hare," said my mother; and just then a hare wild with fright rushed by and made for the woods. On came the dogs; they burst over the bank, leaped the stream, and came dashing across the field, followed by the huntsmen. Six or eight men leaped their horses clean over, close upon the dogs. The hare tried to get through the fence; it was too thick, and she turned sharp round to make for the road, but it was too late; the dogs were upon her with their wild cries; we heard one shriek, and that was the end of her. One of the huntsmen rode up and whipped off the dogs, who would soon have torn her to pieces. He held her up by the leg torn and bleeding, and all the gentlemen seemed well pleased.

As for me, I was so astonished that I did not at first see what was going on by the brook, but when I did look, there was a sad sight; two fine horses were down, one was struggling in the stream, and the other was groaning on the grass. One of the riders was getting out of the water covered with mud, the other lay quite still.

"His neck is broken," said my mother.

"And it serves him right, too," said one of the colts.

"Well, no," she said, "you must not say that; but though I am an old horse, and have seen and heard a great deal, I never yet could make out why men are so fond of this sport; they often hurt themselves, often spoil good horses, and tear up the fields, and all for a hare, or a fox, or a stag, that they could get more easily some other way; but we are only horses and don't know. . . ."

I was now beginning to grow handsome; my coat had grown fine and soft and was bright black. I had one white foot and a pretty white star on my forehead. I was thought very handsome; my master would not sell me till I was four years old. He said lads ought not to work like men, and colts ought not to work like horses till they were quite grown up.

When I was four years old, Squire Gordon came to look at me. He examined my eyes, my mouth, and my legs; he felt them all down, and then I had to walk and trot and gallop before him; he seemed to like me, and said, "When he has been well broken in, he will do very well." My master said he would break me in himself, as he should not like me to be frightened or hurt, and he lost no time about it, for the next day he began.

Everyone may not know what breaking in is, therefore I will describe it. It means to teach a horse to wear a saddle and bridle and to carry on his back a man, woman, or child; to go just the way they wish, and to go quietly. Besides this, he has to learn to wear a collar, a crupper, and a breeching, and to stand still while they are put on; then to have a cart or a chaise [SHAZE] fixed behind, so that he cannot walk or trot without dragging it after him; and he must go fast or slow, just as his driver wishes. He must never start at what he sees, nor speak to other horses, nor bite, nor kick, nor have any will of his own; but always do his master's will, even though he may be very tired or hungry; but the worst of all is, when his harness is once on, he may neither jump for joy nor lie down for weariness. So you see this breaking in is a great thing.

I had of course long been used to a halter and a headstall and to be led about in the field and lanes quietly, but now I was to have a bit and bridle; my master gave me some oats as usual, and after a good deal of coaxing he got the bit into my mouth and the bridle fixed, but it was a nasty thing! Those who have never had a bit in their mouths cannot think how bad it feels; a great piece of cold hard steel as thick as a man's finger to be pushed into one's mouth, between one's teeth, and over one's tongue, with the ends coming out at the corner of your mouth, and held fast there by straps over your head, under your throat, round your nose, and under your chin; so that no way in the world can you get rid of the nasty hard thing; it is very bad! yes, very bad! at least I thought so; but I knew my mother always wore one when she went out, and all horses did when they were grown up; and so, what with the nice oats, and what with my master's pats, kind words, and gentle ways, I got to wear my bit and bridle.

Next came the saddle, but that was not half so bad; my master put it on my back very gently, while old Daniel held my head; he then made the girths fast under my body, patting and talking to me all the time; then I had a few oats, then a little leading about; and this he did every day till I began to look for the oats and the saddle. At length, one morning, my master got on my back and rode me round the meadow on the soft grass. It certainly did feel queer; but I must say I felt rather proud to carry my master, and as he continued to ride me a little every day, I soon became accustomed to it.

The next unpleasant business was putting on the iron shoes; that, too, was very hard at first. My master went with me to the smith's forge, to see that I was not hurt or got any fright. The blacksmith took my feet in his hand, one after the other, and cut away some of the hoof. It did not pain me, so I stood still on three legs till he had done them all. Then he took a piece of iron the shape of my foot, and clapped it on, and drove some nails through the shoe quite into my hoof, so that the shoe was firmly on. My feet felt very stiff and heavy, but in time I got used to it.

And now having got so far, my master went on to break me to harness; there were more new things to wear. First, a stiff heavy collar just on my neck, and a bridle with great side pieces against my eyes called blinkers, and blinkers indeed they were, for I could not see on either side, but only straight in front of me; next, there was a small saddle with a nasty stiff strap that went right under my tail; that was the crupper. I hated the crupper—to have my long tail doubled up and poked through that strap was almost as bad as the bit. I never felt more like kicking, but of course I could not kick such a good master, and so in time I got used to everything and could do my work as well as my mother.

I must not forget to mention one part of my training, which I have always considered a very great advantage. My master sent me for a fortnight to a neighboring farmer, who had a meadow which was skirted on one side by the railway. Here were some sheep and cows, and I was turned in among them.

I shall never forget the first train that ran by. I was feeding quietly near the fence which separated the meadow from the railway, when I heard a strange sound at a distance, and before I knew whence it came—with a rush and a clatter, and a puffing out of smoke—a long black train of something flew by and was gone almost before I could draw my breath. I turned and galloped to the farther side of the meadow as fast as I could go, and there I stood snorting with astonishment and fear. In the course of the day many other trains went by, some more slowly; these drew up at the station close by and sometimes made an awful shriek and groan before they stopped. I thought it very dreadful, but the cows went on eating very quietly and hardly raised their heads as the black frightful thing came puffing and grinding past.

For the first few days I could not feed in peace; but as I found that this terrible creature never came into the field, or did me any harm, I began to disregard it, and very soon I cared as little about the passing of a train as the cows and sheep did.

Since then I have seen many horses much alarmed and restive at the sight or sound of a steam engine; but thanks to my good master's care, I am as fearless at railway stations as in my own stable.

Now if anyone wants to break in a young horse well, that is the way.

My master often drove me in double harness with my mother, because she was steady and could teach me how to go better than a strange horse. She told me the better I behaved the better I should be treated and that it was wisest always to do my best to please my master. "But," said she, "there are a great many kinds of men; there are good, thoughtful men like our master, whom any horse may be proud to serve; and there are bad, cruel men, who never ought to have a horse or dog to call their own. Besides, there are a great many foolish men, vain, ignorant, and careless, who never trouble themselves to think; these spoil more horses than all, just for want of sense; they don't mean it, but they do it for all that. I hope you will fall into good hands; but a horse never knows who may buy him, or who may drive him; it is all a chance for us; but still I say, do your best whatever it is, and keep up your good name."

"Robin Hood and the Merry Little Old Woman"

by
EVA MARCH TAPPAN

About the story:

> There are many versions of the roguish outlaw of Sherwood Forest, but this one will serve as a worthy introduction to Robin Hood, Little John, Friar Tuck, and the rest of the Merry Men. In the children's section of the library, you will find collections of Robin's adventures, most of which are suitable for reading aloud. Each tale, however, like the one presented here, shows Robin Hood to be a good-hearted scoundrel, quick of wit and kind to every unfortunate and downtrodden creature in the realm.

Approximate reading time: 14 minutes
Vocabulary and pronunciation guide:
   mantle: a loose, sleeveless jacket
   treadle [TREDD-uhl]: a foot pedal that operates the spinning wheel
   ere [AIR]: before

> "Monday I wash and Tuesday I iron,
> Wednesday I cook and I mend;
> Thursday I brew and Friday I sweep,
> And baking day brings the end."

So sang the merry little old woman as she sat at her wheel and spun; but when she came to the last line she really could not help pushing back the flax wheel and springing to her feet. Then she held out her skirt and danced a gay little jig as she sang:

"Hey down, down, and a down!"

She curtsied to one side of the room and then to another, and before she knew it she was curtsying to a man who stood in the open door.

"Oh, oh, oh!" cried the merry little old woman. "Whatever shall I do? An old woman ought to sit and spin and not be dancing like a young girl. Oh, but it's Master Robin! Glad am I to set eyes on you, Master Robin. Come in, and I'll throw my best cloak over the little stool for a cushion. Don't be long standing on the threshold, Master Robin."

"It may come to pass that I'll wish I had something to stand on," said Robin, grimly, "for the proud bishop is in the forest, and he's after me with all his men. It's night and day that he's been following me, and now he's caught me surely. You've no meal chest, have you, or a featherbed that will hide me? I see only this one wee little room, and there's not even a mouse-hole."

The little woman's heart beat fast. What could she do?

"I remember very well a Saturday night," she said, "when I'd but little firewood and it was bitter cold; then you and your good men brought me such fine logs as the great folk at the hall don't have; then you came in yourself and gave me a pair of shoes and some brand-new stockings, all soft and fine and woolly—I don't believe the king himself has such a pair—oh, Master Robin, I've thought of something. Give me your mantle of green and your fine gray tunic, and you put on my skirt and jacket and tie my red and blue kerchief over your head—you gave it to me yourself, you did, one Easter morning—and then you sit down at the wheel and spin. See, you put your foot on the treadle [TREDD-uhl] *so*, to turn the wheel, and you twist the flax with your fingers *so*. Don't you get up, but just turn the wheel and grumble and mumble to yourself."

It was not long before the bishop and all his men came riding up to the little old woman's house. The bishop thrust open the door and called:

"Old woman, what have you done with Robin Hood?" but Robin sat grumbling and mumbling at the wheel and answered never a word to the bishop.

"She's probably daft," said one of the bishop's men. "We'll

soon find him"; and in a minute he had looked up the chimney and behind the dresser and under the wooden bedstead. Then he turned to the corner cupboard.

"You're daft yourself," said the bishop, "to look in that little place for a strong man like Robin." And all the time the spinner at the wheel sat grumbling and mumbling. It was a very strange thread that was wound on the spool, but no one thought of that. It was Robin they wanted, and they cared little what kind of thread an old woman in a cottage was spinning.

"He's here, your Reverence," called the man who had opened the lower door of the corner cupboard.

"Bring him out and set him on the horse," ordered the bishop, "and see to it that you treat him like a wax candle in the church. The king's ordered that the thief and outlaw be brought to him, and I well know he'll hang the rogue on a gallows so high that it will show over the whole kingdom; but he has given orders that no one shall have the reward if the rascal has but a bruise on his finger, save that it came in a fair fight."

So the merry little old woman in Robin's tunic and Robin's green cloak was set gently on a milk-white steed. The bishop himself mounted a dapple-gray, and down the road they went.

It was the cheeriest party that one can imagine. The bishop went laughing all the way for pure delight that he had caught Robin Hood. He told more stories than one could make up in an age of leap years, and they were all about where he went and what he did in the days before he became a bishop. The men were so happy at the thought of having the great reward the king had offered that they laughed at the bishop's stories louder than anyone had ever laughed at them before. And as for the merry little old woman, she had the gayest time of all, though she had to keep her face muffled in her hood, and couldn't laugh aloud the least bit, and couldn't jump down from the great white horse and dance the gay little jig that her feet were fairly aching to try.

While the merry little old woman was riding off with the bishop and his men, Robin sat at the flax wheel and spun and spun till he could no longer hear the beat of the horses' hooves on the hard ground. No time had he to take off the skirt and jacket and the kerchief of red and·blue, for no one knew when

the proud bishop might find out that he had the wrong prisoner and would come galloping back to the cottage on the
border of the forest.

"If I can only get back to my own good men!" thought Robin;
and he sprang up from the little flax wheel and ran out the
open door.

All the long day had Robin been away from his bowmen,
and as the twilight time drew near, they were more and more
fearful of what might have befallen him. They went to the edge
of the forest, and there they sat with troubled faces.

"I've heard that the sheriff was seen but two days ago on the
eastern side of the wood," said Much, the miller's son.

"And the proud bishop's not in his palace," muttered William Scarlet. "Where he's gone I know not, but may the saints
keep Master Robin from meeting him. He hates us men of the
greenwood worse than the sheriff does, and he'd hang any
one of us to the nearest oak."

"He'd not hang Master Robin," declared Much, the miller's
son, "for the bishop likes gold, and the king's offered a great
reward for him alive and unhurt." The others laughed, but in
a moment they were grave again and peered anxiously through
the trees in one way and then in another, while nearer came
the twilight.

"There are folk who say the forest is haunted," said Little
John. "I never saw anything, but one night when I was close
to the little black pond that lies to the westward, I heard a cry
that wasn't from bird or beast, I know that."

"And you didn't see anything?" asked Much, the miller's
son.

"No," answered Little John, "but where there's a cry, there's
something to make the cry, and it wasn't bird or beast; I'm as
sure of that as I am that my name's Little John."

"But it isn't," declared Friar Tuck. "You were christened
John Little." No one smiled, for they were too much troubled
about Robin.

"When I was a youngster," said William Scarlet, "I had an
old nurse, and she told me that a first cousin of hers knew a
woman whose husband was going through the forest by night,
and he saw a witch carrying a round bundle under her arm. It
was wrapped up in a brown kerchief; and while he looked, the

wind blew the kerchief away, and he saw that the round bundle was a man's head. The mouth of it opened and called, 'Help! help!' He shot an arrow through the old witch, and then he said to the head, 'Where do you want to go? Whose head are you?' The head answered, 'I'm your head, and I want to go on your shoulders.' Then he put up his hand, and, sure enough, his own head was gone, and there it lay on the ground beside the dead witch with the arrow sticking through her. He took up the head and set it on his shoulders. This was the story that he told when he came back in the morning, but no one really knew whether to believe it all or not. After that night he always carried his head a bit to one side, and some said it was because he hadn't set it back quite straight; but there are some folk that won't believe anything unless they see it themselves, and they said he had had a drink or two more than he should and then he took cold in his neck from sleeping with his head on the wet moss."

"Everybody knows there are witches," said William Scarlet, "and folks say that wherever they may be through the day, they run to the forest when the sun begins to sink, and while they're running they can't say any magic words to hurt a man if he shoots them."

"What's that?" whispered Much, the miller's son, softly, and he fitted an arrow to the string.

"Wait, make a cross on it first," said Little John.

Something was flitting over the little moor. The soft gray mist hid the lower part of it, but the men could see what looked like the upper part of a woman's body, scurrying along through the fog in some mysterious fashion. Its arms were tossing wildly about, and it seemed to be beckoning. The head was covered with what might have been a kerchief, but it was too dusky to see clearly.

"Don't shoot till it's nearer," whispered William Scarlet. "They say if you hurt a witch and don't kill her outright, you'll go mad forever after."

Nearer came the witch, but still Much, the miller's son, waited with his bow bent and the arrow aimed. The witch ran under the low bough of a tree, the kerchief was caught on a broken limb, and—

"Why, it's Master Robin!" shouted Much, the miller's son.

"It's Master Robin himself"; and so it was. No time had he taken to throw off the gray skirt and the black jacket and the blue and red kerchief about his head; for as soon as he could no longer hear the tramp of the horses' hooves, he had run to the shelter of the good greenwood and the help of his own faithful men.

Meanwhile the bishop was still telling stories of what he did before he was a bishop, and the men were laughing at them, and the merry little old woman was having the gayest time of all, even though she dared not laugh out loud.

Now that the bishop had caught Robin Hood, he had no fear of the greenwood outlaws, and as the forest road was much nearer than the highway, down the forest road the happy company went. The merry little old woman had sometimes sat on a pillow and ridden a farm beast from the plow; but to be on a great horse like this, one that held his head so high and stepped so carefully where it was rough and galloped so lightly and easily where it was smooth—why, she had never even dreamed of such a magnificent ride. Not a word did she speak, not even when the bishop began to tell her that no gallows would be high enough to hang such a wicked outlaw. "You've stolen gold from the knights," said he. "You've stolen from the Sheriff of Nottingham, and you've even stolen from me. Glad am I to see Robin Hood—but what's that?" the bishop cried. "Who are those men, and who is their leader? And who are you?" he demanded of the merry little old woman.

Now the little woman had been taught to order herself lowly and reverently to all her betters, so before she answered the bishop, she slipped down from the tall white horse and made a deep curtsy to the great man.

"If you please, sir," said she, "I think it's Robin Hood and his men."

"And who are you?" he demanded again.

"Oh, I'm nobody but a little old woman that lives in a cottage alone and spins," and then she sang in a lightsome chirrup of a voice:

> "Monday I wash and Tuesday I iron,
> Wednesday I cook and I mend;
> Thursday I brew and Friday I sweep,
> And baking day brings the end."

I fear that the bishop did not hear the little song, for the arrows were flying thick and fast. The little old woman slipped behind a big tree and there she danced her

"Hey down, down, and a down!"

to her heart's content, while the fighting went on.

It was not long before the great bishop was Robin's prisoner, and ere [AIR] he could go free, he had to open his strong leather wallet and count out more gold than the moon had shone on in the forest for many and many a night. He laid down the gold pieces one by one, and at every piece he gave a groan that seemed to come from the very bottom of his boots.

"That's for all the world like the cry I heard from the little black pond to the westward," said Little John. "It wasn't like bird and it wasn't like beast, and now I know what it was; it was the soul of a stingy man, and he had to count over and over the money that he ought to have given away when he was alive."

As for the merry little old woman, she was a prisoner, too, and such a time she had! First there was a bigger feast than she had ever dreamed of before, and every man of Robin's followers was bound that she should eat the bit that he thought was nicest. They made her a little throne of soft green moss, and on it they laid their hunting cloaks. They built a shelter of fresh boughs over her head, and then they sang songs to her. They set up great torches all round about the glade. They played every game that could be played by torchlight, and it was all to please the kind little woman who had saved the life of their master.

The merry little woman sat and clapped her hands at all their feats, and she laughed until she cried. Then she wiped her eyes and sang them her one little song.

The men shouted and cheered, and cheered and shouted, and the woods echoed so long and so loud that one would have thought they, too, were trying to shout.

By and by the company all set out together to carry the little old woman to her cottage. She was put upon their very best and safest horse, and Robin Hood would have none lead it but himself. After the horse came a long line of good bowmen and true. One carried a new cloak of the finest wool. Another bore a whole armful of silken kerchiefs to make up for the one that

Robin had worn away. There were shoes and stockings, and there was cloth of scarlet and blue, and there were soft, warm blankets for her bed. There were so many things that when they were all piled up in the little cottage, there was no chance for one-tenth of the men to get into the room. Those that were outside pushed up to the window and stretched their heads in at the door; and they tried their best to pile up the great heap of things so she could have room to go to bed that night and to cook her breakfast in the morning.

"And tomorrow's sweeping day," cried Robin. " 'Thursday I brew and Friday I sweep,' and how will she sweep if she has no floor?"

"We'll have to make her a floor," declared Friar Tuck.

"So we will," said Robin. "There's a good man not far away who can work in wood, and he shall come in the morning and build her another room."

"Oh, oh!" cried the merry little old woman with delight, "I never thought I should have a house with two rooms; but I'll always care for this room the most, for there's just where Master Robin stood when he came in at the door, and there's where he sat when he was spinning the flax. But, Master Robin, Master Robin, did anyone ever see such a thread as you've left on the spool!"

It was so funny that the merry little old woman really couldn't help jumping up and dancing:

"Hey down, down, and a down!"

And then the brave men and true all said good night and went back to the forest.

"How Arthur Was Crowned King"

from *Morte d'Arthur*
by
SIR THOMAS MALORY

About the story:

> *There are many versions of the King Arthur legend, and those that you find in the children's section of the library are probably quite good for reading aloud. What is important is for youngsters to become acquainted with such characters as Arthur, Merlin, Sir Lancelot, and the rest, and with the images of Camelot, the Round Table, and the sword in the stone presented here.*

Approximate reading time: 10 minutes

Pronunciation and vocabulary guide:

> **Uther** [YOU-thur]
> **malady** [MAL-uh-dee]: a disease or illness

When Uther Pendragon, King of England, died, the country for a long while stood in great danger, for every lord that was mighty gathered his forces, and many wished to be king. For King Uther's own son, Prince Arthur, who should have succeeded him, was but a child, and Merlin, the mighty magician, had hidden him away.

Now a strange thing had happened at Arthur's birth, and this was how it was.

Some time before, Merlin had done Uther a great service, on condition that the king should grant him whatever he wished for. This the king swore a solemn oath to do. Then Merlin made him promise that when his child was born it should be delivered to Merlin to bring up as he chose, for this would be to the child's own great advantage. The king had given his promise, so he was obliged to agree. Then Merlin said he knew a very true and faithful man, one of King Uther's lords, by name Sir Ector, who had large possessions in many parts of England and Wales, and that the child should be given to him to bring up.

On the night the baby was born, while it was still unchristened, King Uther commanded two knights and two ladies to take it, wrapped in a cloth of gold, and deliver it to a poor man whom they would find waiting at the gate of the castle. The poor man was Merlin in disguise, although they did not know it. So the child was delivered unto Merlin, and he carried him to Sir Ector, and made a holy man christen him, and named him Arthur; and Sir Ector's wife cherished him as her own child.

Within two years King Uther fell sick of a great malady [MAL-uh-dee], and for three days and three nights he was speechless. All the barons were in much sorrow and asked Merlin what was best to be done.

"There is no remedy," said Merlin. "God will have His will. But look ye all, barons, come before King Uther tomorrow, and God will make him speak."

So the next day Merlin and all the barons came before the king, and Merlin said aloud to king Uther:

"Sir, after your days shall your son Arthur be king of this realm and all that belongs to it?"

Then Uther Pendragon turned to him and said so that all could hear:

"I give my son Arthur God's blessing and mine, and bid him pray for my soul, and righteously and honorably claim the Crown, or he shall forfeit my blessing."

And with that, King Uther died.

But Arthur was still only a baby, not two years old, and Merlin knew it would be no use yet to proclaim him king. For there were many powerful nobles in England in those days, who were all trying to get the kingdom for themselves, and perhaps they would kill the little prince. So there was much strife and debate in the land for a long time.

When several years had passed, Merlin went to the Archbishop of Canterbury and counseled him to send for all the lords of the realm, and all the gentlemen of arms, that they should come to London at Christmas, and for this cause—that a miracle would show who should be rightly king of the realm. So all the lords and gentlemen made themselves ready, and came to London, and long before dawn on Christmas Day they were all gathered in the great church of St. Paul's to pray.

When the first service was over, there was seen in the churchyard a large stone, foursquare, like marble, and in the midst of it was an anvil of steel, a foot high. In this was stuck by the point a beautiful sword, with naked blade, and there were letters written on gold about the sword, which said thus: **"Whoso pulleth this sword out of this stone and anvil is rightly King of all England."**

Then the people marveled, and told it to the archbishop.

"I command," said the archbishop, "that you keep within the church, and pray unto God still; and that no man touch the sword till the service is over."

So when the prayers in church were over, all the lords went to behold the stone and the sword; and when they read the writing some of them—such as wished to be king—tried to pull the sword out of the anvil. But not one could make it stir.

"The man is not here that shall achieve the sword," said the archbishop, "but doubt not God will make him known. But let us provide ten knights, men of good fame, to keep guard over the sword."

So it was ordained, and a proclamation was made that everyone who wished might try to win the sword. And upon New Year's Day the barons arranged to have a great tournament, in which all knights who would joust or tourney might take a part. This was ordained to keep together the Lords and Commons, for the archbishop trusted that it would be made known who should win the sword.

On New Year's Day, after church, the barons rode to the field, some to joust, and some to tourney, and so it happened that Sir Ector, who had large estates near London, came also to the tournament; and with him rode Sir Kay, his son, with young Arthur, his foster brother.

As they rode, Sir Kay found he had lost his sword, for he had left it at his father's lodging, so he begged young Arthur to go and fetch it for him.

"That will I, gladly," said Arthur, and he rode fast away.

But when he came to the house, he found no one at home,

for everyone had gone to see the jousting, and could not find the sword. Then Arthur was angry and said to himself:

"I will ride to the churchyard and take the sword with me that sticketh in the stone, for my brother, Sir Kay, shall not be without a sword this day."

When he came to the churchyard, he alighted, tied his horse, and went to the tent. But he found there no knights who should have been guarding the sword, for they were all away at the joust. Seizing the sword by the handle, he lightly and fiercely pulled it out of the stone, then took his horse and rode his way, till he came to Sir Kay, his brother, to whom he delivered the sword.

As soon as Sir Kay saw it, he knew well it was the sword of the stone, so he rode to his father, Sir Ector, and said, "Sir, lo, here is the sword of the stone, wherefore I must be king of this land."

When Sir Ector saw the sword, he turned back and came to the church, and there they all three alighted and went into the church, and he made his son swear truly how he got the sword.

"By my brother Arthur," said Sir Kay, "for he brought it to me."

"How did you get this sword?" said Sir Ector to Arthur.

And the boy told him.

"Now," said Sir Ector, "I understand you must be king of this land."

"Wherefore I?" said Arthur; "and for what cause?"

"Sir," said Ector, "because God will have it so; for never man could draw out this sword but he that shall rightly be king. Now let me see whether you can put the sword there as it was and pull it out again."

"There is no difficulty," said Arthur, and he put it back into the stone.

Then Sir Ector tried to pull out the sword, and failed; and Sir Kay also pulled with all his might, but it would not move.

"Now you shall try," said Sir Ector to Arthur.

"I will, well," said Arthur, and pulled the sword out easily.

At this Sir Ector and Sir Kay knelt down on the ground before him.

"Alas," said Arthur, "mine own dear father and brother, why do you kneel to me?"

"Nay, nay, my Lord Arthur, it is not so; I was never your father, nor of your blood; but I know well you are of higher blood than I thought you were."

Then Sir Ector told him all, how he had taken him to bring up, and by whose command; and how he had received him from Merlin. And when he understood that Ector was not his father, Arthur was deeply grieved.

"Will you be my good, gracious lord when you are king?" asked the knight.

"If not, I should be to blame," said Arthur, "for you are the man in the world to whom I am the most beholden, and my good lady and mother, your wife, who has fostered and kept me as well as her own children. And if ever it be God's will that I be king, as you say, you shall desire of me what I shall do, and I shall not fail you; God forbid I should fail you."

"Sir," said Sir Ector, "I will ask no more of you but that you will make my son, your foster brother Sir Kay, agent in charge of all your lands."

"That shall be done," said Arthur, "and by my faith, never man but he shall have that office while he and I live."

Then they went to the archbishop and told him how the sword was achieved, and by whom.

On Twelfth Day, all the barons came to the stone in the churchyard, so that any who wished might try to win the sword. But not one of them all could take it out, except Arthur. Many of them, therefore, were very angry and said it was a great shame to them and to the country to be governed by a boy not of high blood, for as yet none of them knew that he was the son of King Uther Pendragon. So they agreed to delay the decision till Candlemas, which is the second day of February.

But when Candlemas came, and Arthur once more was the only one who could pull out the sword, they put it off till Easter; and when Easter came, and Arthur again prevailed in the presence of them all, they put it off till the Feast of Pentecost.

Then, by Merlin's advice, the archbishop summoned some of the best knights that were to be got—such knights as in his own day King Uther Pendragon had best loved, and trusted most—and these were appointed to attend young Arthur and never to leave him night or day till the Feast of Pentecost.

When the great day came, all manner of men once more made the attempt, and once more not one of them could prevail but Arthur. Before all the Lords and Commons there assembled, he pulled out the sword, whereupon all the Commons cried out at once:

"We will have Arthur for our king! We will put him no more delay, for we all see that it is God's will that he shall be our king, and he who holdeth against it, we will slay him."

And therewith they knelt down all at once, both rich and poor, and besought pardon of Arthur, because they had delayed him so long; and Arthur forgave them.

After that, he was crowned at once, and there he swore to his Lords and Commons to be a true king and to govern with true justice from thenceforth all the days of his life.

"The Adventure of the Windmills"

from *Don Quixote de la Mancha*
by
MIGUEL DE CERVANTES

About the story:

Don Quixote's joust with the windmills is but a small part of the legend of this deranged, childlike creature, but it is enough for a youngster right now; the book itself does not make particularly good oral reading. But just the knowledge of this hero's quest to bring back chivalry and justice will serve your children well when they later hear the musical The Man of La Mancha *or encounter the word* quixotic *[QUICK-sah-tic].*

Approximate reading time: 10 minutes

Pronunciation and vocabulary guide:

mania [MAY-nee-ah]: excessive or unreasonable enthusiasm

knight errant [AIR-ant]: a knight who travels in search of adventures

Bucephalus [byoo-SEFF-uh-lus]

Rozinante [roe-zih-NAHN-tay]

Quixote [key-HOE-tay]

sublime: lofty, grand, exalted

de la Mancha [day-luh-MAHN-sha]: of the Mancha (province)

Dulcinea [dull-sin-AA-ah]

Briareus [bry-AIR-ee-us]

O nce upon a time there lived in a certain village in a province of Spain called la Mancha a gentleman named Quixada or Queseda—historians do not agree about the exact surname—whose house was full of old lances, battle-axes, and other types of armor and weapons. He was around the age of fifty, a man of hard features and a withered face. He was an early riser and had once been quite fond of hunting; but now, for a great portion of the year, he devoted himself to reading old books about the days of knighthood, and this with such keen delight that he forgot all about the pleasures of the hunt and neglected all his household duties as well. His mania [MAY-nee-ah] and folly grew to such a pitch that he sold many acres of his lands to buy books that related the exploits and adventures of the Knights of the Round Table, which he took to be accurate histories of happenings that occurred in these chivalrous days of old.

So eagerly did he plunge into the reading of these books that he often spent whole days and nights poring over them; and in the end, through little sleep and much reading, his brain became tired, and he fairly lost his wits. His fancy was filled with those things that he read—enchantments, quarrels, battles, challenges, wounds, wooings, loves, tempests, and other impossible follies, and those romantic tales so firmly took hold of him that he believed no history to be so certain and sincere as they were.

Finally, his wits being extinguished, he was seized with one of the strangest whims that ever a madman stumbled on in this world, for it seemed to him right and necessary that he himself should become a knight errant [AIR-ant] and ride through the world in armor to seek adventures and experience himself all that he had read about the knights of yore. Therefore, he resolved that he would make a name for himself by revenging the injuries of others and courting all manner of dangers and difficulties, until in the end he should be rewarded for his valor by the king of some mighty empire. So he dredged up the rusty armor that had belonged to his great-grandfather and had lain neglected in a forgotten corner of his house, and he scoured and polished it as best he could.

Now, a singular necessity of any true knight was a trusty and noble horse on which to ride into battle and to spirit away maidens who had been captured by dragons and such. And for this purpose he called upon his own carriage horse, which, though bare-boned and ragged, seemed to him a better steed than Bucephalus [byoo-SEFF-uh-lus], the noble animal that carried Alexander the Great when he went into battle. He spent four days inventing a name for his horse, saying to himself that it was only fitting that so famous a knight's horse, and so good a beast, should have a new and high-sounding name that was worthy of his new position in life. After having chosen and discarded any number of names, he finally hit upon Rozinante [roe-zih-NAHN-tay], which to him was sublime and well sounding.

The name being thus given to his horse, he made up his mind to give himself a name also, and in that thought he labored another eight days. Finally he determined to call himself Don Quixote [key-HOE-tay], and remembering that the great knights of olden times were not satisfied with a mere dry name, but added to it the name of their kingdom or country, he, like a good knight, added to his own name that of his province and called himself Don Quixote de la Mancha [day-luh-MAHN-sha].

His armor being scoured, his horse named, and himself now furnished with a new name as well, he now lacked nothing but a lady on whom he might bestow his service and affection. "For," he said to himself, remembering what he had read in the books of knightly adventures, "if I should encounter some giant, as knights errant ordinarily do, and if I should knock him to the ground with one blow, or cut him in two, perhaps, or finally make him yield to me, it would be only right and proper that I should have some lady to whom I might present him."

Now, you may believe that the heart of the knight danced with joy when he found out one whom he might call his lady. For, they say, there lived in the next village a hale, buxom country wench with whom he was sometimes in love, though she had never known it or taken notice of him whatsoever. She was known as Aldonca Lorenso, but he determined that she, too, should be renamed and should carry a title not too distant from her own, but one that should also tell others that she was a princess or a lady of quality. Thus it was that he called her Dulcinea [dull-sin-AA-ah], a name sufficiently strange, romantic, and musical for the lady of so brave a knight.

All that he lacked now was a squire to attend to his wishes and to accompany him and Rozinante on his search for adventure. For this purpose he chose a poor plowman he met along the way, one who had many children, and who called himself Sancho Panza.

One day, while they were journeying along, Sancho Panza said to his master, "I pray you have good care, Sir Knight, and that you remember that you have promised to make me the governor of an island, for I shall be able to govern it no matter how great it may be."

And Don Quixote replied, "Thou must understand, friend Sancho, that it was a custom very much used by ancient knights errant to make their squires governors of the islands and kingdoms they conquered, and I am resolved that so good a custom shall be kept up by me. And if thou livest and I live, it may well be that I might conquer a kingdom and crown thee king of it."

"By the same token," said Sancho Panza, "if I were a king, then should Joan, my wife, become a queen and my children princes?"

"There is no doubt of that," said Don Quixote.

"Oh, I doubt it," replied Sancho, "for I am persuaded that though it rained kingdoms down upon the earth, none of them would sit well on my wife Joan. She would just not do as a queen. She might scrape through as a countess, but I have my doubts of that, too."

As they were talking, they caught sight of some thirty or forty windmills on a plain that lay ahead of them. As soon as Don Quixote saw them he said to his squire, "Fortune is guiding our way better than we could hope. For behold, friend Sancho, how there appear thirty or forty monstrous giants with whom I mean to do battle and take all their lives. With their spoils we will begin to be rich, for this is fair reward from battle, and it is doing great service to clear away these evil fellows from off the face of the earth."

"What giants?" inquired Sancho, amazed.

"Those thou seest there," replied his master, "with the long arms."

"Take care, sir," cried Sancho, "for those we see yonder are not giants but windmills, and those things which seem to be arms are their sails, which, being whirled round by the wind, make the mill go."

"It is clear," answered Don Quixote, "that thou art not yet experienced in the matter of adventures. They *are* giants, and if thou art afraid, get thee away home, whilst I enter into cruel and unequal battle with them."

So saying, he clapped spurs to Rozinante, without heeding the cries by which Sancho Panza warned him that he was going to encounter not giants but windmills. He shouted to the windmills in a loud voice, "Fly not, cowards and vile creatures, for it is only one knight that comes against you to do battle!"

A slight breeze having sprung up at this moment, the great sail arms began to move, and on seeing this, Don Quixote shouted out again, "Although you should wield more arms than had the giant Briareus [bry-AIR-ee-us], I shall make you pay for your insolence!"

Saying this, and commending himself most devoutly to his Lady Dulcinea, and setting his lance in rest, he charged at Rozinante's best gallop and attacked the first mill before him. Thrusting his lance through the sail, the wind turned it with such violence that it broke his weapon into slivers, carrying him and his horse up and whirling around, till they finally tumbled off, rolling over the plain, the knight being sorely damaged.

Sancho Panza hastened to help him as fast as his long-eared Dapple could go, and when he came up he found the knight unable to stir, such a shock had he received in his fall.

"Bless me," said Sancho, "did I not tell you that you should look well what you did, for they were none other than windmills, nor could anyone think otherwise unless he had windmills for brains?"

"Peace, friend Sancho," said Don Quixote, "for the things of war are constantly changing, and I think this must be the work of some sorcerer who hath changed these giants into windmills to take from me the glory of the victory. But in the end his evil magic shall avail but little against the goodness of my sword."

"May it prove so," said Sancho, as he helped his master to rise and remount Rozinante, who, poor steed, was also much bruised by the fall.

And off again they rode, for there were other adventures waiting, other monsters to slay, other wrongs to make right.

from *Gulliver's Travels*

by
JONATHAN SWIFT
(as retold by Donald G. Mitchell)

About the story:

Jonathan Swift began writing Gulliver's Travels *as a satire of the popular travel literature of the day. However, he expanded the project and used the story to satirize common human vices, though making them appear to be the actions of strange peoples.*

The original tale, which was told by Gulliver himself, is written in seventeenth-century style and is quite difficult to read or tell. The version used here was an attempt by Donald G. Mitchell, more than a century ago, to recast the adventures into storytelling form. Although the language of the original is lost, the young listener will be introduced to the wonder of being a giant in a land of people only six inches tall.

Approximate reading time: 6 minutes
Pronunciation and vocabulary guide:
   Lilliput [LILL-ih-put]
   Lilliputian [lill-ih-PYOO-shun]
   Blefuscu [bleh-FUSS-kyoo]
   Blefuscan [bleh-FUSS-kan]

*T*hree hundred years ago, while George the First was King of Great Britain, there was a story about some sailing voyages that everyone in the realm read with great wonder and delight. The story dealt with a voyager named Lemuel Gulliver, a surgeon who had signed on as ship's doctor aboard the *Antelope* in 1699, which was bound for the South Seas.

The voyage was terribly hard—a good many of the men died at sea; and on the fifth of November the ship drove onto a rock and split to pieces. Seven of the men got clear, including Gulliver, and rowed until the fierce wind upset their small boat. His six companions were drowned, but Gulliver touched bottom and walked a mile through the water till he reached land. Then, exhausted, he lay down to doze.

He says he must have slept about nine hours, and when he awoke he felt stiff and couldn't turn over. He tried to lift his arm, but he couldn't. Presently he found out that there was a cord across his breast and another across the middle of his body; and then he found that his legs were tied, and his arms; and it seemed to him—though he couldn't tell for certain—that his hair was fastened to the ground. This was all strange enough, but it was stranger yet when he felt something walk up over his left leg and come on across his body, almost to his chin, so that by turning his eyes down, he could see a little fellow, about six inches high, formed just like a man, with a bow and arrows in his hand. One would have been enough, but when he felt forty more walking over his legs and arms and pulling themselves up by his hair, he roared out—as I think you and I would have done.

At this they all scampered; and some of them hurt themselves badly by tumbling off his body, though this Gulliver did not know until some time afterward. The poor voyager, who was thus lying on his back, struggled a little, and finally freed his left arm, which was very lucky for him because these little people, who were much frightened, began to shoot arrows at him and would most certainly have put out his eyes if he had not covered them with his hand.

But, by little and little, he was able to look about him, and he saw that there were thousands and thousands of these odd little people in the surrounding fields. With his free arm, he made signs that he was hungry and thirsty, and they brought him food, a wagon load at a time, which he took up between his thumb and finger; and their casks of wine—no bigger than a teacup—he emptied in a way that made them gape in amazement. But these little people had put sleeping powder in the wine, and Gulliver dozed off so soundly that he didn't know that they had brought up an immense cart, rolled him onto it, and with fifteen hundred of the king's horses, pulled him into town. There they chained him by one leg, near to the entrance of their largest temple, with a door four feet high, so that he was able to crawl under cover when he awoke.

Of course, all the little people round about came to see Gulliver, whom they called "The Man-Mountain." And the king, who had a majestic figure, owing to the fact that he was taller by half an inch than any of his subjects, appointed officers to put Gulliver on display, and the subjects paid them money to see the great spectacle.

After some time, Gulliver was able to pick up their language, though they couldn't have spoken louder than our crickets, if even that loud. He learned that the name of this strange country was Lilliput [LILL-ih-put], and he was soon introduced to all the distinguished people in the land, even the royalty, whom he greatly impressed. He helped the Lilliputians [lill-ih-PYOO-shuns] in their war with the neighboring country of Blefuscu [bleh-FUSS-kyoo] by wading across the ocean that separated the two nations (which was nothing but a small pond to him) and tying a cord to the bows of fifty of the enemy's ships that were lying in harbor. Then, although the Blefuscan [bleh-FUSS-kan] soldiers fired clouds of arrows at him from the shore, Gulliver put on his spectacles to protect his eyes and pulled the ships back to Lilliput and presented them to the king.

The King of Lilliput was, of course, delighted with this service, and he made Gulliver a prince on the spot. He also thought it would be a good thing if Gulliver should, someday, wade across again and drag over the rest of the enemy's fleet, but Gulliver did not think very well of this, a difference that created a decided coolness between him and the king. In time, many of the high officers in Lilliput grew to dislike Gulliver, especially the royal treasurer who had calculated the enormous amount it was costing to feed and clothe the giant, and he found himself out of place in their land. He decided to escape to the island of Blefuscu, taking a Lilliputian man-of-war to carry his clothes. After making his peaceful intentions known, he was warmly welcomed by the emperor and his people, even though he had drawn away so many of their ships.

There Gulliver remained for some time, until one day he spied a small English boat, bottom side up, in the sea near Blefuscu, and with the aid of hundreds of local mechanics and craftsmen, he repaired the boat so that it was seaworthy once again. He stocked the boat with provisions—the meat of a hundred midget oxen and three hundred sheep and also some live sheep and cattle—and he sailed away, hoping to find his home again.

Two days later he encountered an English merchant ship whose captain kindly took him on board and asked him how he happened to be at sea in such a small vessel. Gulliver told him his tale and described the people he had encountered, but the captain would not believe such a fantastic tale. Whereupon Gulliver pulled some of the tiny sheep and cattle from his pocket as evidence of the truth of his story, and, of course, the captain could no longer accuse him of being mad.

Gulliver finally arrived home to his wife and children, and he was able to make a great deal of money exhibiting the tiny livestock he had brought back from his voyage. But soon he yearned for the sea once again and shortly signed on another ship and embarked upon more adventures, even more fantastic than those you have just heard.

"Ulysses and the Cyclops"

from *The Odyssey*
by
HOMER

About the story:

> *Here is a famous adventure of Ulysses, a Greek king whose wisdom was responsible in large part for the Greeks' victory over the Trojans. That war is recounted in another epic attributed to Homer entitled* **The Iliad.** *Ulysses had many similar adventures and had to overcome a variety of adversaries and obstacles to return home to his wife, Penelope, who waited faithfully for him for twenty years, in spite of being almost constantly besieged by suitors who assured her that Ulysses was dead.*

Approximate reading time: 15 minutes
Pronunciation and vocabulary guide:

> **Odyssey** [ODD-ess-ee]: a long wandering or voyage
> **Ulysses** [you-LISS-eez]: also called Odysseus [oh-DISS-ee-us], from which comes the title
> **abated** [uh-BAY-tedd]: died down, moderated
> **Cyclopes** [SYE-clopps]: plural of Cyclops
> **Cyclops** [SYE-clopps]
> **Polyphemus** [poll-ee-FEE-mus]
> **Agamemnon** [agg-uh-MEM-non]: King of all the Greek chiefs
> **Zeus** [ZOOSE]: King of the Greek gods
> **Poseidon** [poe-SYE-don]: Greek god of the sea
> **Laertes** [lay-AIR-teez]

When the great city of Troy was finally taken, after ten long years of battle, all the Greek chiefs set sail for their homes. But there was wrath in heaven against them; the gods were angered by the way these mortals praised themselves for the victory instead of thanking the gods, who had actually brought it to pass. Therefore these chiefs found their homeward voyages cursed and their returns unhappy: One was shipwrecked, another was slain by his wife when he arrived home, and others found all things at home troubled and changed and were driven to seek new dwellings elsewhere. But none of these chiefs wandered farther and suffered more on his voyage home than did the wise Ulysses [you-LISS-eez].

Ulysses had brought twelve ships with him to Troy, each with a hundred valiant men aboard. And now, ten years later, he was returning with those same twelve ships, although fully half the original complement of warriors and friends lay buried under the Trojan plain.

The fierce winds and high seas caused them to change their course many times. When the winds abated [uh-BAY-tedd] they took to their oars and rowed for many days till they came to the country where the Cyclopes [SYE-clopps] dwell. Now, a mile or so from the shore there was an island, very fair and fertile, but uninhabited, and in this place they harbored their ships and the crews slept by them, waiting for the morning.

At daybreak, Ulysses, for he was ever fond of adventure and desired to know all about every land he visited, took one of the ships and its crew and rowed to the land. There was a great hill sloping to the shore, and there rose up here and there smoke from the caves where the Cyclopes dwelled alone, seldom talking with each other, for they were crude and savage folk, each ruling his own household and not caring for others. Now very close to the shore was one of these caves, huge and deep, with shrubbery around the mouth and shaded by tall oaks and pines. So Ulysses chose out of the crew the twelve bravest and told the rest to guard the ship, for he wanted to see what manner of dwelling this was, and who lived there. He had his sword by his side, and on his shoulder a mighty skin of wine, sweet-smelling and strong, with which he might win the heart of some fierce savage, should he chance to meet with such, as indeed his prudent heart forecasted that he might.

So they entered the cave and judged that it was the dwelling of some rich and skillful shepherd. For within there were pens for the young sheep and goats, divided all according to their age, and there were baskets full of cheeses, and full milkpails lined the walls. But the Cyclops [SYE-clopps] himself was away in the pastures. Then the companions of Ulysses urged him to depart and take with him, if he wished, a store of cheeses and several lambs and kid goats. But he would not, for he wished to see, as was his way, what manner of host this strange shepherd might be. And he was soon to find out!

It was evening when the Cyclops came home, a mighty giant, twenty feet in height, or more. On his shoulder he bore a vast bundle of pine logs for his fire, and threw them down outside the cave with a great crash, and drove the flocks within, and closed the entrance with a huge rock, which twenty wagons and more could not carry. Then he milked the herd, and half the milk he curdled for cheese, and half he set ready for himself to drink at supper. Next he kindled a fire with the pine logs, and the flame lighted up all the cave, showing him Ulysses and his comrades.

"Who are ye?" cried Polyphemus [poll-ee-FEE-mus], for that was the giant's name. "Are ye traders, or pirates?"

Ulysses shuddered at the dreadful voice and shape, but summoned up all his bravery and answered, "We are no pirates, mighty sir, but Greeks, sailing back from Troy, and subjects of the great King Agamemnon [agg-uh-MEM-non], whose fame is spread from one end of heaven to the other. And we are come to beg hospitality of thee in the name of Zeus [ZOOSE], who rewards or punishes hosts and guests according to how faithful they are to each other."

"Nay," said the giant, "it is but idle talk to tell me of Zeus and the other gods. We Cyclopes take no account of gods, for we hold ourselves to be much better and stronger than they. But come, tell me where have you left your ship?"

But Ulysses guessed that what the giant had in mind was to break the ship apart and make all hope of escape impossible. Therefore, he answered him craftily, "We have no ship, for King Poseidon [poe-SYE-don] broke it apart, driving it onto a jutting rock on this coast, and we whom thou seest are all that did escape from the waves."

Polyphemus answered nothing, but suddenly snatched up two of the men, as a man might snatch up two small puppies, and dashed them on the ground, and tore them limb from limb, and devoured them, taking huge swallows of milk in between, leaving not a morsel, not even the very bones. But the others, when they saw this dreadful deed, could only weep and pray to Zeus for help. And when the giant had ended his vile meal, he lay down among his sheep and slept.

Then Ulysses thought long and hard about whether he should slay the monster as he slept, for he had no doubt that his good sword would pierce to the giant's heart, mighty as he was. But, being very wise, he remembered that, should he slay him, he and his comrades would be trapped forever, for who would move away the great rock that lay against the door of the cave? So they waited till the morning. When the monster awoke, he milked his flocks, and afterward, seizing two men, devoured them for his breakfast. Then he went to the pastures, but put the great rock back on the mouth of the cave, just as a man would put a cork back in a bottle.

All that day the wise Ulysses pondered over what he might do to save himself and his companions, and the end of his thinking was this: There was a mighty pole in the cave, green wood of an olive tree, big as a ship's mast, which Polyphemus was drying by the fire to use as a walking staff. Ulysses cut off about six feet of this pole, and his comrades sharpened it and hardened it in the fire, and then hid it away. At evening the giant came back and drove his sheep into the cave, even shutting in the rams instead of leaving them outside as before. And, having done his shepherd's work, he made his cruel feast as before. Then Ulysses came forward with the wineskin in his hand, and said, "Drink, Cyclops, now that thou hast feasted. Drink, and see what precious things we had in our ship. But no one hereafter will come to thee with gifts like this, if thou treatest strangers as cruelly as thou has treated us."

Then the Cyclops drank, and was mightily pleased, and said, "Give me more to drink, and tell me thy name, stranger, and I will give thee a gift such as a host should give. In truth this is a fine liquor. We, too, have vines, but they bear not wine like this, which indeed must be such as the gods drink in heaven."

Then Ulysses gave him the cup again, and he drank. Three times he gave it to him, and three times he drank, not knowing what it was and how it would work within his brain.

Then Ulysses spoke to him. "Thou didst ask my name, Cyclops. Lo! my name is No Man. And now that thou knowest my name, thou shouldst give me thy gift."

And the giant said, "My gift shall be that I will eat thee last of all thy company."

And as he spoke he fell back in a drunken sleep. Then Ulysses told his comrades to call upon all their bravery, for now was the time for them to commence their escape. They thrust the stake of olive wood into the fire till the tip burst into flame, and they plunged the fiery point deep into the monster's eye, for he had but one eye, and that in the middle of his forehead, with the eyebrow below it. And Ulysses leaned with all his force upon the stake, the burning wood hissing in the eye just as a red-hot iron hisses in the water when a blacksmith tempers steel for a sword.

Then the giant leaped up, and tore away the stake, and cried aloud, so that all the Cyclopes who dwelled on the mountainside heard him and came to his cave, asking him, "What is wrong, Polyphemus? Why dost thou cry out in the peaceful night, scaring away the sheep? Is anyone robbing thee of thy sheep, or seeking to slay thee by trickery or force?"

And the giant answered, "No Man is slaying me by his trickery."

"Well, then," they said, "if no man is harming you, we can be of no help. The sickness you are suffering must have been sent by Zeus and, therefore, cannot be avoided. Only the god Poseidon, who is our father, can aid you in this; you must pray to him."

Then they departed, and Ulysses rejoiced at the success of his trick of telling the giant that his name was No Man.

But then the Cyclops, knowing that in spite of his pain and blindness the flocks must still be put out to pasture, rolled away the great stone from the door of the cave, and sat in the middle of the opening with his hands outstretched, to feel whether perhaps the men within the cave would attempt to slip out among the sheep, and thus foil Ulysses' plan.

All that day, Ulysses thought long and hard about how he and his friends might escape, finally lighting upon an idea for which he gave thanks to Zeus. The giant did, after all, drive the rams with the other sheep into the cave, and these, being larger and stronger, would permit the men to fasten themselves under the bellies of the beasts. The next morning, as the giant again positioned himself in the middle of the cave door, Ulysses tied each of the six men (for six were now all that remained of the twelve who had ventured with him from the ship) to the undercoat of a ram with twigs that the giant used for his bed. He then surrounded each with other rams close by. And there was one mighty ram, far larger than all the others, and to this Ulysses clung, grasping the fleece tightly with both hands.

As the rams rushed forth to pasture, the giant felt the back of each as it went by, never thinking of what might be underneath. Last of all went the great ram. And the Cyclops knew him as he passed, and said, "How is this that thou, the leader of the flock, now lags behind? Thou hast always been the first to run to the pastures and streams in the morning, and the first to come back to the fold when evening fell; and now thou art last of all. Perhaps thou art troubled about thy master's eye, which some wretch—No Man, they call him—has destroyed, having first plied me with wine. He has not escaped, I know. Oh, how I wish that thou couldst speak and tell me where he is lurking, for I would dash out his brains upon the ground and avenge myself of this No Man."

So speaking, he let him pass out of the cave. But when they were out of reach of the giant, Ulysses loosed his hold of the ram, and then unbound his comrades. And they hastened to their ship, not forgetting to drive before them a good share of the Cyclops's fat sheep. Right glad were those who remained on the ship to see them. Though they felt like weeping for those who had died, Ulysses did not permit them to do so, for he feared that the noise of their crying might let the giant know where they were. They all pulled lustily on the oars, hurrying to leave forever this accursed land. And when they had rowed a hundred yards or so, so that a man's voice could yet be heard by one who stood upon the shore, Ulysses stood up in the ship and shouted:

"He was no coward, O Cyclops, whose comrades thou didst so foully slay in thy den. And thou art justly punished, monster, for devouring thy guests in thy dwelling. May the gods make thee suffer even worse things than these!"

Then the Cyclops, in his wrath, lifted a heavy rock from the top of a large hill and hurled it down to where he had heard the voice. Right in front of the ship's bow it landed, and a great wave rose as the boulder sank, and washed the ship back to the shore. But Ulysses seized a long pole with both hands and pushed the ship from the land and urged his comrades to ply their oars, nodding with his head, for he was too wise to speak and thereby let the Cyclops know where they were.

And when they had gotten twice as far as before, Ulysses attempted to speak again, but his comrades discouraged him, saying, "Let us not anger the giant anymore. When he threw that great rock and washed us back to shore, we thought we were surely lost. If he hears you now, he may crush our ship this time, for who knows how far he can hurl those mighty bolts."

But Ulysses would not be persuaded, and he rose and called out, "Hear, Cyclops! If any man asks who blinded thee, say that it was the warrior Ulysses, son of Laertes [lay-AIR-teez], who dwells in Ithaca."

And the Cyclops answered with a groan, "Long ago, there was a prophet who foretold to me that one Ulysses would rob me of my sight. But I looked for a great, strong man who would subdue me by force, and now a weakling has done the deed, having subdued me with wine."

Then Cyclops lifted up his hands to Poseidon and prayed.

"Hear me, Poseidon, if I am indeed thy son and thou my father. May this Ulysses never reach his home! or, if the Fates have ordered that he should reach it, may he come alone, all his comrades lost, and may he find terrible trouble at his house!"

With this he hurled another mighty rock, which almost smashed into the rudder, yet missed by a hairsbreadth. So Ulysses and his comrades escaped, and they came to the island where they found the rest of their mates, who had waited in fear that they had perished. Then Ulysses divided up among them all the sheep that had been taken from Cyclops, and they sacrificed the great ram to Zeus. They feasted on the sheep and drank wine all that day, and when the night came on, they lay down upon the shore and slept.

"The Golden Touch"

adapted from *The Wonder Book*
by
NATHANIEL HAWTHORNE

About the story:

*The story of King Midas and his golden touch dates back
to the Greek myths, and no one knows who its original
author was. Nathaniel Hawthorne, an American writer
of the mid-nineteenth century (1804–1864), thought that
this story—like many other ancient legends—was ideal
for telling to children, and he included the tale in his
collection for storytellers entitled* **The Wonder Book.**
The other tales in this book and in Hawthorne's **Tangle-
wood Tales** *are equally enjoyable and suitable for oral
reading. Although the author is better known for his
more somber short stories and novels that deal with
life's struggle between good and evil—* **The Scarlet Letter**
and **The House of the Seven Gables,** *for example—he
envied children their sense of wonder, and he hoped to
ignite their imagination through the telling of tales like
"The Golden Touch."*

Approximate reading time: 28 minutes

Pronunciation and vocabulary guide:

bequeath [bee-QUEETHE]: to hand down or give in a
will

innumerable [inn-NEW-merr-uh-bull]: too many to be
counted

ruddy: reddish in color

disconsolate [dis-CAHN-soh-luht]: sad, dejected

gilded: appearing gold in color

spectacles: eyeglasses

wrought [RAWT, rhymes with THOUGHT]: caused

aghast [uh-GASST]: amazed, terrified

transmuted [tranz-MEW-tehd]: changed in form, converted

quandary [QUAHN-derr-ree]: a puzzlement, a dilemma
ravenous [RAVV-en-us]: famished, starved
perplexity: bewilderment, confusion
congealing [conn-JEE-ling]: becoming hard or stiff
insatiable [inn-SAY-shuh-bull]: unable to be satisfied
tumult [TOO-muhlt]: disturbance, agitation, an out-
    burst
blight: disease

M any years ago, there lived a very rich man, and a
king besides, who was named Midas, and who
lived in a palace with his little daughter, Marygold.
This King Midas was fonder of gold than of anything else in
the world. He valued his royal crown chiefly because it was
composed of that precious metal. If he loved anything better,
or half so well, it was the one little maiden who played so
merrily around her father's footstool. But the more Midas
loved his daughter, the more did he desire and seek for wealth.
He thought, foolish man!, that the best thing he could possibly
do for this dear child would be to bequeath [bee-QUEETHE]
her the largest pile of golden coins that had ever been heaped
together since the world was made. Thus, he gave all his
thoughts and all his time to this one purpose. If ever he happened to gaze for an instant at the gold-tinted clouds of sunset,
he wished that they were real gold and that they could be
squeezed safely into his strongbox. When little Marygold ran
to meet him, with a bunch of buttercups and dandelions, he
used to say, "Pooh, pooh, child! If these flowers were as
golden as they look they would be worth the picking!"
    And yet, in his earlier days, before he was so entirely pos-
sessed of this insane desire for riches, King Midas had shown
a great taste for flowers. He had planted a garden, in which
grew the biggest, sweetest, and most beautiful roses that any
mortal ever saw or smelled. These roses were still growing in
the garden, as large, as lovely, and as fragrant as when Midas
used to pass whole hours in gazing at them and inhaling their
perfume. But now, if he looked at them at all, it was only to
calculate how much the garden would be worth if each of the
innumerable [inn-NEW-merr-uh-bull] rose petals were a thin
plate of gold. And though he once was fond of music, the only

melody for poor Midas now was the chink of one coin against another.

Midas had gotten to be so exceedingly unreasonable that he could scarcely bear to see or touch any object that was not gold. He made it his custom, therefore, to pass a large portion of every day in a dark and dreary room, underground, in the basement of his palace. It was here that he kept his wealth. To this dismal hole—for it was little better than a dungeon— Midas went whenever he wanted to be particularly happy. Here, after carefully locking the door, he would take a bag of gold coins, or a gold cup as big as a washbowl, or a heavy golden bar, or a pound of gold dust, and bring them from the obscure corners of the room into the one bright and narrow sunbeam that fell from the dungeonlike window. He valued the sunbeam for no other reason but that his treasure would not shine without its help. And then he would count and re-count the coins in the bag; toss up the bar and catch it as it came down; sift the gold dust through his fingers; look at the funny image of his own face that was reflected in the surface of the cup; and whisper to himself, "Oh Midas, rich King Midas, what a happy man you are!"

Midas called himself a happy man, but deep inside he felt that he was not yet quite as happy as he might be. The very tiptop of enjoyment would never be reached unless the whole world were to become his treasure room and be filled with yellow metal that was his and his alone.

Midas was enjoying himself in his treasure room one day, as usual, when he perceived a shadow fall over the heaps of gold; and looking suddenly up, what should he behold but the fig- ure of a stranger, standing in the bright and narrow sunbeam! It was a young man, with a cheerful and ruddy face. Whether it was the imagination of King Midas that threw a yellow tinge over everything, or whatever the cause might be, he could not help fancying that the smile of the stranger had a kind of golden radiance in it. Certainly there was now a brighter gleam upon all the piled-up treasures than before. Even the remotest corners were lighted when the stranger smiled, as with tips of flame and sparkles of fire.

Now Midas knew that he had carefully turned the key in the lock and that no mortal strength could possibly break into his treasure room, and so, of course, he concluded that his visitor must be something more than mortal. But the stranger's appearance was so good-humored and kindly that it would have been unreasonable to suspect him of intending any mischief. It was far more probable that he came to do Midas a favor. And what could that favor be, unless to multiply his heaps of treasure?

The stranger gazed about the room, and when his lustrous smile had glistened upon all the golden objects that were there, he turned again to Midas.

"You are a wealthy man, friend Midas!" he observed. "I doubt whether any other four walls on earth contain so much gold as you have contrived to pile up in this room."

"I have done pretty well, pretty well," answered Midas in a discontented tone. "But, after all, it is only a trifle when you consider that it has taken me my whole life to get it together. If one could live a thousand years, he might have time to grow rich!"

"What!" exclaimed the stranger. "Then you are not satisfied?"

Midas shook his head.

"And tell me, what *would* satisfy you?" asked the stranger. "Merely for the curiosity of the thing, I should be glad to know."

Midas paused and meditated. He had a feeling that this stranger, with such a golden luster in his good-humored smile, had come here with both the power and the purpose of gratifying his utmost wishes. Now, therefore, was the fortunate moment when he had but to speak and obtain whatever possible, or seemingly impossible, thing, it might come into his head to request. So he thought, and thought, and thought, and heaped up one golden mountain upon another in his imagination, without being able to imagine them big enough. At last, a bright idea occurred to King Midas. It seemed really as bright as the glistening metal that he loved so much.

Raising his head, he looked the illustrious stranger in the face.

"Well, Midas," observed his visitor, "I see that you have now hit upon something that will satisfy you. Tell me your wish."

"It is only this," replied Midas. "I am weary of collecting my treasures with so much trouble and then seeing a heap so small after I have done my very best. And so I wish that everything I touch will be changed to gold!"

The stranger's smile grew so very broad that it seemed to fill the room like an outburst of the sun.

"The Golden Touch!" he exclaimed. "You certainly deserve credit, friend Midas, for striking out so brilliant a conception. But are you quite sure that this will satisfy you?"

"How could it fail?" said Midas.

"And will you never regret the possession of it?"

"What could ever make me do that?" replied Midas. "This is all I need to become perfectly happy."

"Be it as you wish, then," replied the stranger, waving his hand to say farewell. "Tomorrow, at sunrise, you will find yourself gifted with the Golden Touch."

The figure of the stranger then became exceedingly bright, and Midas had to close his eyes to shield them from the glare. On opening them again, he beheld only one yellow sunbeam in the room, and, all around him, the glistening of the precious metal which he had spent his life in hoarding up.

Whether Midas slept as usual that night, it is hard to say. Asleep or awake, however, his mind was probably in the state of a child's, to whom a beautiful new plaything has been promised in the morning. At any rate, the first glow of the sun had scarcely peeped over the hills when King Midas awoke and, stretching his arms out of bed, began to touch the objects that were within reach. He was anxious to prove whether the Golden Touch had really been given him, as the stranger had promised. So he laid his finger on a chair by the bedside, and on various other things, but was grievously disappointed to perceive that they remained constructed of exactly the same substance as before. Indeed, he felt very much afraid that he had only dreamed about the lustrous stranger, or else that the latter had been making fun of him.

He lay in a very disconsolate [dis-CONN-soh-luht] mood, regretting the downfall of his hopes, and kept growing sadder and sadder, until the earliest sunbeam shone through the window and gilded the ceiling over his head. It seemed to Midas that this bright yellow sunbeam was reflected in rather a singular way on the white covering of the bed. Looking more closely, to his astonishment and delight, he found that this linen fabric had been changed into what seemed to be a woven texture of the purest and brightest gold! The Golden Touch had come to him with the first sunbeam!

Midas bolted up, in a kind of joyful frenzy, and ran about the room, grasping at everything that happened to be in his way. He seized one of the bedposts, and it became immediately a wondrous golden pillar. He pulled aside a window curtain in order to shed more light on the wonders he was performing, and the tassel grew heavy in his hand—a mass of gold. He hurriedly put on his clothes and was enraptured to see himself in a magnificent suit of gold cloth, which retained its flexibility and softness, although it burdened him a little with its weight. He drew out his handkerchief, which little Marygold had hemmed for him. That was likewise gold, with the dear child's neat and pretty stitches running all along the border, in gold thread!

Somehow or other, this last transformation did not quite please King Midas. He would rather that his little daughter's handiwork should have remained just the same as when she climbed his knee and put it into his hand.

But it was not worthwhile to worry himself about so small a complaint as this. Midas now took his spectacles from his pocket and put them on his nose, in order that he might see more distinctly what he was doing. To his great astonishment, however, he discovered that he could not possibly see through them—the transparent lenses had turned to plates of yellow metal, and, of course, were worthless as spectacles, though valuable as gold. It struck Midas as rather inconvenient that, with all his wealth, he could never again be rich enough to own a pair of serviceable eyeglasses.

"It is no great matter, anyway," he said to himself very philosophically. "We cannot expect any great good without there being some accompanying inconvenience. The Golden Touch is worth the sacrifice of a pair of eyeglasses, at least, if not of one's very eyesight. My own eyes will serve for ordinary purposes, and little Marygold will soon be old enough to read to me."

Midas then went out into the garden and found a great number of beautiful roses in full bloom and others in all the stages of lovely bud and blossom. But Midas knew a way to make them far more precious, according to his way of thinking, than roses had ever been before. He took great pains in going from bush to bush as he exercised his magic touch, until every individual flower and bud, and even the worms at the heart of some of them, had been changed to gold. By the time this good work was completed, King Midas was summoned to breakfast; the morning air had given him an excellent appetite, and he hurried back to the palace.

Little Marygold had not yet made her appearance. Her father ordered her to be called, and, seating himself at the table, awaited the child's coming so that he could begin his own breakfast. To do Midas justice, it must be said that he really loved his daughter, and he loved her so much the more this morning on account of the good fortune that had befallen him. It was not long before he heard her coming along the passageway crying bitterly. Midas was surprised to hear this because Marygold was one of the most cheerful little people you could ever imagine and hardly shed a thimbleful of tears in a year. When Midas heard her sobs, he determined to put little Marygold into better spirits, and, leaning across the table, he touched his daughter's bowl (which was a china one with pretty figures all around it) and transformed it to gleaming gold.

Marygold slowly opened the door, still sobbing as if her heart would break.

"There now, my little lady!" cried Midas. "What in the world is the matter with you this morning?"

Marygold held out her hand, in which was one of the roses that Midas had so recently changed to gold.

"Beautiful!" exclaimed her father. "And what is there in this magnificent golden rose to make you cry?"

"Oh, dear father!" answered the child, as well as her sobs would let her, "it is the ugliest flower that ever grew! As soon as I was dressed I ran into the garden to gather some roses for you because I know you like them and like them even better when I gather them for you. But, oh dear, dear me! What do you think has happened? Such a misfortune! All the beautiful roses, that smelled so sweet and had so many lovely blushes, are spoiled and grown quite yellow, as you see this one; they no longer have any fragrance! What can be the matter with them?"

"Now, now, my dear little girl. Let's not cry about something like this," said Midas, who was ashamed to confess that he himself had wrought [RAWT, rhymes with THOUGHT] the change which so greatly afflicted her. "Sit down and eat your hot cereal. You will find it easy enough to exchange a golden rose like that, which will last hundreds of years, for an ordinary one that would wither in a day."

"But I don't care for roses like this!" cried Marygold, tossing it contemptuously away. "It has no smell, and the hard petals prick my nose!"

Midas, meanwhile, had poured out a cup of coffee, and, as a matter of course, the coffeepot, whatever metal it may have been when he took it up, was gold when he set it down. He lifted a spoonful of coffee to his lips, and, sipping it, was astonished to perceive that, the instant his lips touched the liquid, it became molten gold, and, the next moment, hardened into a lump!

"Ahh!" exclaimed Midas, rather aghast [uh-GASST].

"What is the matter, Father?" asked little Marygold, gazing at him, with tears still standing in her eyes.

"Nothing, child, nothing," said Midas. "Eat your breakfast before it gets too cold."

He took one of the little sausages on his plate, and, by way of experiment, touched it with his finger. To his horror, it was immediately transmuted [tranz-MEW-tehd] from a link of pork into a tube of golden metal, so rigid that he could not pierce it with the suddenly golden fork he held in his hand.

"I don't quite see," thought he, "how I am to get any breakfast."

Almost in despair, he helped himself to a boiled egg, which immediately underwent a change similar to those of the coffee and the sausage. The egg, indeed, might have been mistaken for one of those which the famous storybook goose was in the habit of laying, but King Midas was the only goose that had had anything to do with this matter.

"Well, this is a quandary [QUAHN-derr-ree]!" thought he, leaning back in his chair and looking quite enviously at little Marygold, who was now eating her hot cereal and milk with great satisfaction. "Such a costly breakfast before me, and I can't eat a single bite of it!"

He even tried eating very quickly, hoping he might in this

way avoid what was becoming a considerable inconvenience. He snatched a hot potato and attempted to cram it into his mouth and swallow it before it had time to change form, but the Golden Touch was too nimble for him. He found his mouth full, not of soft potato, but of solid metal, which so burned his tongue that he roared aloud, and, jumping up from the table, began to dance and stamp about the room both in pain and in fear.

"Father, dear Father!" cried little Marygold, who was a very affectionate child. "Have you burned your mouth?"

"Ah, dear child," groaned Midas dolefully, "I don't know what is to become of your poor father."

By now Midas had grown quite hungry, and when he considered how ravenous [RAVV-en-us] he would be by suppertime and the likelihood that his dinner meal would be similarly indigestible, he began to doubt whether, after all, riches are the one desirable thing in the world, or even the most desirable. But this was only a passing thought. So fascinated was Midas with the glitter of the yellow metal that he would still have refused to give up the Golden Touch for so paltry a consideration as a breakfast.

Nevertheless, so great was his hunger, and the perplexity of his situation, that he again groaned aloud, as if in serious pain. Our pretty Marygold could endure it no longer. She sat a moment, gazing at her father, and trying with all her wits to find out what was the matter with him. Then, with a sweet and sorrowful impulse to comfort him, she arose from her chair, and, running to Midas, threw her arms affectionately about his knees. He bent down and kissed her. He felt that his little daughter's love was worth a thousand times more than he had gained by the Golden Touch.

"My precious, precious Marygold!" cried he.

But Marygold made no answer.

Oh, no! What had he done? How fatal was the gift that the stranger had granted him! The moment the lips of Midas touched Marygold's forehead, a change took place. Her sweet, rosy face, so full of affection as it had been, assumed a glittery yellow color, with yellow teardrops congealing [conn-JEE-ling] on her cheeks. Her beautiful brown curls took on the same tint. Her soft and tender little form grew hard and inflexible within her father's encircling arms. Oh, terrible misfortune! The victim of his insatiable [inn-SAY-shuh-bull] desire for wealth, little Marygold was a human child no longer, but a golden statue!

Yes, there she was, with the questioning look of love, grief, and pity hardened into her face. It was the prettiest and most woeful sight that one could ever see. All the features and tokens of Marygold were there; even the beloved little dimple remained in her golden chin. But, the more perfect was the resemblance, the greater was the father's agony at beholding this golden image, which was all that was left him of a daughter. It had been a favorite phrase of Midas's, whenever he felt particularly fond of the child, to say that she was worth her weight in gold. And now the phrase had become literally true. And now, at last, when it was too late, he felt how infinitely a warm and tender heart that loved him exceeded in value all the wealth that could be piled up between the earth and sky!

While he was in this tumult [TOO-muhlt] of despair, he suddenly beheld a stranger standing near the door. Midas bent down his head, without speaking, for he recognized that same figure who had appeared to him the day before in the treasure room and had bestowed on him this disastrous power called the Golden Touch.

"Well, friend Midas," said the stranger, "tell me, how have you gotten along with the gift you asked for?"

"I am very miserable," said he.

"Very miserable, indeed!" exclaimed the stranger. "And how can that be? Have I not faithfully kept my promise to you? Have you not everything that your heart desired?"

"Gold is not everything," answered Midas. "And I have lost all that my heart really cared for."

"Ah! So you have made a discovery since yesterday?" observed the stranger. "Let us see, then. Which of these two things do you think is really of greater worth: the gift of the Golden Touch or one cup of clear cold water?"

"Oh, blessed water!" exclaimed Midas. "It will never moisten my parched throat again!"

"The Golden Touch," continued the stranger, "or a crust of bread?"

"A piece of bread," answered Midas, "is worth all the gold on earth!"

"The Golden Touch," asked the stranger, "or your own little Marygold, warm, soft, and loving as she was an hour ago?"

"Oh, my child, my dear child!" cried poor Midas, wringing his hands. "I would not have given that one small dimple in her chin for the power of changing this whole big earth into a solid lump of gold!"

"You are wiser than you were, King Midas!" said the stranger, looking seriously at him. "Your own heart, I perceive, has not been entirely changed from flesh to gold. Were it so, your case would indeed be desperate. But you appear to be still capable of understanding that the commonest things, such as lie within everybody's grasp, are more valuable than the riches which so many mortals sigh and struggle after. Tell me, now, do you sincerely desire to rid yourself of this Golden Touch?"

"It is hateful to me!" replied Midas.

A fly settled on his nose, but fell immediately to the floor, for it, too, had become gold. Midas shuddered.

"Go, then," said the stranger, "and plunge into the river that glides past the bottom of your garden. Take a vase of that river water and sprinkle it over any object that you may desire to change back again from gold into its former substance. If you do this in earnestness and sincerity, it may possibly repair the mischief that your greed has brought about."

Midas lost no time in snatching up a great earthen pitcher (but, alas, it was no longer earthen after he touched it) and hastening to the riverbank. As he scampered along, and forced his way through the shrubbery, it was positively marvelous to see how the foliage turned yellow behind him, as if the autumn had been there and nowhere else. On reaching the river, he plunged in headlong, without waiting even to pull off his clothes. "Poof! poof! poof!" snorted King Midas, as his head emerged out of the water. "Well, this is really a refreshing bath, and I think it must have quite washed away the Golden Touch. And now to fill my pitcher!"

As he dipped the pitcher into the water, it gladdened his very heart to see it change from gold into the same good, honest, earthen vessel which it had been before he touched it. Seeing a violet that grew on the bank of the river, Midas touched it with his finger and was overjoyed to find that the delicate flower retained its purple hue instead of undergoing a yellow blight. The curse of the Golden Touch had, therefore, really been removed from him.

King Midas hastened back to the palace, and one can only imagine how surprised the servants must have been to see their royal master so carefully bringing home an earthen pitcher of water. But that water, which was to undo all the mischief that his folly had brought about, was more precious to Midas than an ocean of molten gold could have been. The first thing he did, as you can well imagine, was to sprinkle it by handfuls over the golden figure of little Marygold.

As it splashed upon her, you would have laughed to see how the rosy color came back to the dear child's cheek, how she began to sneeze and sputter, and how astonished she was to find herself dripping wet, and her father still throwing more water over her!

"Please stop that, Father!" she cried. "See how you have soaked my nice frock, which I put on only this morning!"

For Marygold did not know that she had been a little golden statue; nor could she remember anything that had happened since the moment when she ran with outstretched arms to comfort poor King Midas.

Her father did not think it necessary to tell his beloved child how very foolish he had been, but contented himself with showing how much wiser he had now grown. For this purpose, he led little Marygold into the garden, where he sprinkled all the remainder of the water over the rosebushes, and in an instant, more than five thousand roses recovered their bloom. Indeed, only one effect of the Golden Touch endured, and it served as a constant reminder to Midas of his former power and foolishness: Little Marygold's hair kept a noticeable tinge of gold, a hue he had never seen in it before that fateful kiss.

When King Midas had grown quite an old man and made Marygold's children laugh by bouncing them on his knee, he was fond of telling them this marvelous story. And then he would stroke their heads and tell them that their hair, likewise, had a rich shade of gold, which they inherited from their mother.

"And to tell you the truth, my precious little folks," Midas would say, diligently bouncing the children all the while, "ever since that morning, I have hated the very sight of all other gold, except this!"

Listening Level II

(Ages 8 and up)

The tales in this section are full of adventure, and so are the listeners for whom they are intended. There is broad humor here, too, for "The Ransom of Red Chief" and "Jim Baker's Bluejay Yarn" will cause as many chuckles among adult readers as among their child listeners.

At this level the craft and the art of storytelling begin; reading aloud becomes more enjoyable to the parent, for the style of the writing is now more engrossing. Dialect begins to appear, as in The Adventures of Tom Sawyer, *and the parent must choose whether to imitate it or not, and whether to tell the tales with expressiveness and emotion or in a more subdued and relaxed manner. There is no "right" way for everyone, so do what makes you comfortable. But if you choose to try for a bit of flourish, you may find that you are a much better storyteller than you thought.*

"The Glorious Whitewasher"

from *The Adventures of Tom Sawyer*
by
MARK TWAIN

About the story:

> *Here is, perhaps, the most famous scene from* **Tom Sawyer**, *a truly American classic. Almost all of the works of Mark Twain, pen name of Samuel Langhorn Clemens, are ripe for reading aloud, and this one is no exception. Indeed, Twain was a marvelous storyteller himself, and most of his writing resembles transcripts of well-crafted oral tales. They are filled with rich dialogue in dialects that can be reproduced as the reader tells the tale.*
>
> *Reading Mark Twain aloud can be great fun, and if this passage appeals to your child, I encourage you to locate a complete copy of* **Tom Sawyer** *and tackle it chapter by chapter. Many have said that it is a boy's book, but I assure you that girls, too, will find it thoroughly entertaining.*

Approximate reading time: 15 minutes

Pronunciation and vocabulary guide:

> **reposeful** [ree-POSE-full]: causing ease and relaxation
> **mulatto** [mew-LAH-toe]: having one black and one white parent
> **white alley:** a white cat's-eye marble
> **starboard** (or stabbord): on the right
> **larboard** (or labbord): on the left
> **alacrity** [uh-LACK-rih-tee]: cheerful eagerness
> **covet** [KUV-it]: to crave
> **intrepid** [inn-TREPP-id]: fearless, courageous

Saturday morning was come, and all the summer world was bright and fresh, and brimming with life. There was a song in every heart; and if the heart was young the music issued at the lips. There was cheer in every face and a spring in every step. The locust trees were in bloom and the fragrance of the blossoms filled the air. Cardiff Hill, beyond the village and above it, was green with vegetation; and it lay just far enough away to seem a Delectable Land, dreamy, reposeful [ree-POSE-full], and inviting.

Tom appeared on the sidewalk with a bucket of whitewash and a long-handled brush. He surveyed the fence, and all gladness left him and a deep melancholy settled down upon his spirit. Thirty yards of board fence nine feet high. Life to him seemed hollow, and existence but a burden. Sighing, he dipped his brush and passed it along the topmost plank; repeated the operation; did it again; compared the insignificant whitewashed streak with the far-reaching continent of unwhitewashed fence, and sat down on a tree-box discouraged. Jim came skipping out at the gate with a tin pail, and singing "Buffalo Gals." Bringing water from the town pump had always been hateful work in Tom's eyes before, but now it did not strike him so. He remembered that there was company at the pump. White, mulatto [mew-LAH-toe], and Negro boys and girls were always there waiting their turns, resting, trading playthings, quarreling, fighting, skylarking. And he remembered that, although the pump was only a hundred and fifty yards off, Jim never got back with a bucket of water under an hour—and even then somebody generally had to go after him. Tom said, "Say, Jim, I'll fetch the water if you'll whitewash some."

Jim shook his head and said, "Can't, Marse Tom. Ole misses, she tole me I got to go an' git dis water an' not stop to fool roun' wid anybody. She say she spec' Marse Tom gwine to ax me to whitewash, an' so she tole me go 'long and 'tend to my own business—she 'lowed *she'd* tend to de whitewashin'."

"Oh, never you mind what she said, Jim. That's the way she always talks. Gimme the bucket—I won't be gone only a minute. *She* won't ever know."

"Oh, I dasn't, Marse Tom. Ole misses, she'd take an' tar de head off'n me. 'Deed she would."

"*She!* She never licks anybody—whacks 'em over the head with her thimble—and who cares for that, I'd like to know. She talks awful, but talk don't hurt—anyways it don't if she don't cry. Jim, I'll give you a marvel. I'll give you a white alley!"

Jim began to waver.

"White alley, Jim! And it's a bully taw."

"My! Dat's a mighty gay marvel, *I* tell you! But Marse Tom, I's powerful 'fraid ole misses—"

"And besides, if you will I'll show you my sore toe."

Jim was only human—this attraction was too much for him. He put down his pail, took the white alley, and bent over the toe with absorbing interest while the bandage was being unwound. In another moment he was flying down the street with his pail and a tingling rear, Tom was whitewashing with vigor, and Aunt Polly was retiring from the field with a slipper in her hand and triumph in her eye.

But Tom's energy did not last. He began to think of the fun he had planned for this day, and his sorrows multiplied. Soon the free boys would come tripping along on all sorts of delicious expeditions, and they would make a world of fun of him for having to work—the very thought of it burned him like fire. He got out his worldly wealth and examined it—bits of toys, marbles, and trash; enough to buy an exchange of *work*, maybe, but not half enough to buy so much as half an hour of pure freedom. So he returned his straitened means to his pocket and gave up the idea of trying to buy the boys. At this dark and hopeless moment an inspiration burst upon him! Nothing less than a great, magnificent inspiration.

He took up his brush and went tranquilly to work. Ben Rogers came in sight presently—the very boy, of all boys, whose ridicule he had been dreading. Ben's gait was the hop-skip-and-jump—proof enough that his heart was light and his anticipations high. He was eating an apple, and giving a long, melodious whoop, at intervals, followed by a deep-toned ding-dong-dong, ding-dong-dong, for he was personating a steamboat. As he drew near, he slackened speed, took the middle of the street, leaned far over to starboard and rounded to ponderously and with laborious pomp and circumstance—for he was personating the *Big Missouri,* and considered himself to be drawing nine feet of water. He was boat and captain and engine bells combined, so he had to imagine himself standing on his own hurricane deck giving the orders and executing them:

"Stop her, sir! Ting-a-ling-ling!" The headway ran almost out and he drew up slowly toward the sidewalk.

"Ship up to back! Ting-a-ling-ling!" His arms straightened and stiffened down his sides.

"Set her back on the stabbord! Ting-a-ling-ling! Chow! ch-chow-wow! Chow!" His right hand, meantime, describing stately circles—for it was representing a forty-foot wheel.

"Let her go back on the labbord! Ting-a-ling-ling! Chow-ch-chow-chow!" The left hand began to describe circles.

"Stop the stabbord! Ting-a-ling-ling! Stop the labbord! Come ahead on the stabbord! Stop her! Let you, outside turn over slow! Ting-a-ling-ling! Chow-ow-ow! Get out that head line! *Lively* now! Come—out with your spring line—what're you about there! Take a turn round that stump with the bight of it! Stand by that stage, now—let her go! Done with the engines, sir! Ting-a-ling-ling! *Sh't! sh't! sh't!*" (Trying the gauge cocks.)

Tom went on whitewashing—paid no attention to the steamboat. Ben stared a moment and then said, "Hi-*yi! You're* up a stump, ain't you!"

No answer. Tom surveyed his last touch with the eye of an artist, then he gave his brush another gentle sweep and surveyed the result, as before. Ben ranged up alongside of him. Tom's mouth watered for the apple, but he stuck to his work.

Ben said, "Hello, old chap, you got to work, hey?"

Tom wheeled suddenly and said, "Why, it's you, Ben! I warn't noticing."

"Say—*I'*m going in a-swimming, *I* am," said Ben. "Don't you wish you could? But of course you'd druther *work—* wouldn't you? 'Course you would!"

Tom contemplated the boy a bit, and said, "What do you call work?"

"Why, ain't *that* work?" taunted Ben.

Tom resumed his whitewashing, and answered carelessly:

"Well, maybe it is, and maybe it ain't. All I know is, it suits Tom Sawyer."

"Oh, come, now," said Ben. "You don't mean to let on that you *like* it?"

The brush continued to move.

"Like it? Well, I don't see why I oughtn't to like it," Tom

replied. "Does a boy get a chance to whitewash a fence every day?"

That put the thing in a new light. Ben stopped nibbling his apple. Tom swept his brush daintily back and forth—stepped back to note the effect—added a touch here and there—criticized the effect again—Ben watching every move and getting more and more interested, more and more absorbed. Presently he said, "Say, Tom, let *me* whitewash a little."

Tom considered, was about to consent; but he altered his mind.

"No—no—I reckon it wouldn't hardly do, Ben. You see, Aunt Polly's awful particular about this fence—right here on the street, you know—but if it was the back fence I wouldn't mind and *she* wouldn't. Yes, she's awful particular about this fence; it's got to be done very careful; I reckon there ain't one boy in a thousand, maybe two thousand, that can do it the way it's got to be done."

"No—is that so? Oh, come now—lemme just try. Only just a little—I'd let *you*, if you was me, Tom."

"Ben, I'd like to, honest Injun; but Aunt Polly—well, Jim wanted to do it, but she wouldn't let him; Sid wanted to do it, and she wouldn't let Sid. Now don't you see how I'm fixed? If you was to tackle this fence and anything was to happen to it—"

But Ben persisted. "Oh, shucks," he said, "I'll be just as careful. Now lemme try. Say—I'll give you the core of my apple."

"Well, here— No, Ben, now don't. I'm afeared—"

"I'll give you *all* of it!" interrupted Ben.

Tom gave up the brush with reluctance in his face, but alacrity [uh-LACK-rih-tee] in his heart. And while the late steamer *Big Missouri* worked and sweated in the sun, the retired artist sat on a barrel in the shade close by, dangled his legs, munched his apple, and planned the slaughter of more innocents. There was no lack of material; boys happened along every little while; they came to jeer, but remained to whitewash. By the time Ben was fagged out, Tom had traded the next chance to Billy Fisher for a kite, in good repair; and when *he* played out, Johnny Miller bought in for a dead rat and a string to swing it with— and so on, and so on, hour after hour. And when the middle of the afternoon came, from being a poor poverty-stricken boy in the morning, Tom was literally rolling in wealth. He had, besides the things before mentioned, twelve marbles, part of a jew's harp, a piece of blue bottle glass to look through, a spool cannon, a key that wouldn't unlock anything, a fragment of chalk, a glass stopper of a decanter, a tin soldier, a couple of tadpoles, six firecrackers, a kitten with only one eye, a brass doorknob, a dog collar—but no dog—the handle of a knife, four pieces of orange peel, and a dilapidated old window sash.

He had had a nice, good, idle time all the while—plenty of company—and the fence had three coats of whitewash on it! If he hadn't run out of whitewash, he would have bankrupted every boy in the village.

Tom said to himself that it was not such a hollow world, after all. He had discovered a great law of human action, without knowing it—namely, that in order to make a man or a boy covet [KUV-it] a thing, it is only necessary to make the thing difficult to attain. If he had been a great and wise philosopher, like the writer of this book, he would now have comprehended that Work consists of whatever a body is *obliged* to do and that Play consists of whatever a body is not obliged to do. And this would help him to understand why constructing artificial flowers or performing on a treadmill is work, while rolling tenpins or climbing Mont Blanc is only amusement. There are wealthy gentlemen in England who drive four-horse passenger coaches twenty or thirty miles on a daily line, in the summer, because the privilege costs them considerable money; but if they were offered wages for the service, that would turn it into work and then they would resign.

The boy mused awhile over the substantial change which had taken place in his worldly circumstances, and then wended toward headquarters to report.

Tom presented himself before Aunt Polly, who was sitting by an open window in a pleasant rearward apartment, which was bedroom, breakfast room, dining room, and library combined. The balmy summer air, the restful quiet, the odor of the flowers, and the drowsing murmur of the bees had had their effect, and she was nodding over her knitting—for she had no company but the cat, and it was asleep in her lap. Her spectacles were propped up on her gray head for safety. She had thought that of course Tom had deserted long ago, and she wondered at seeing him place himself in her power again in this intrepid [inn-TREPP-id] way. He said, "Mayn't I go and play now, Aunt?"

"What, a'ready?" she shot back. "How much have you done?"

"It's all done, Aunt."

"Tom, don't lie to me—I can't bear it."

"I ain't, Aunt; it *is* all done."

Aunt Polly placed small trust in such evidence. She went out to see for herself; and she would have been content to find twenty percent of Tom's statement true. When she found the entire fence whitewashed, and not only whitewashed but elaborately coated and recoated, and even a streak added to the ground, her astonishment was almost unspeakable. She said, "Well, I never! There's no getting round it, you *can* work when you're a mind to, Tom." And then she diluted the compliment by adding, "But it's powerful seldom you're a mind to, I'm bound to say. Well, go 'long and play; but mind you get back sometime in a week, or I'll tan you."

She was so overcome by the splendor of his achievement that she took him into the closet and selected a choice apple and delivered it to him, along with an improving lecture upon the added value and flavor a treat took to itself when it came without sin through virtuous effort. And while she closed with a happy Scriptural flourish, he "hooked" a doughnut.

"The Ransom of Red Chief"

by
O. HENRY

About the story:
> *I suppose that anyone who has a ten-year-old boy, or who has ever known a ten-year-old boy, or whoever was a ten-year-old boy, will be able to understand clearly the plight of these uninitiated kidnapers who think their greatest difficulties lie in capturing such a child. Oh, no. The maintenance is by far the harder task. It is in these stories of ordinary human sufferings that O. Henry shines his brightest, and the following tale shows him at his humorous best.*

Approximate reading time: 24 minutes
Pronunciation and vocabulary guide:
diatribe [DYE-uh-tribe]: a bitter denunciation
brake: an area of dense growth; a thicket
reconnoiter [ree-cuh-NOY-turr]: to make a preliminary inspection
scythe [sithe, long *i* sound; rhymes with WRITHE]: a long-handled, bladed tool used for reaping
sylvan [SILL-van]: like a forest
peremptory [purr-EMP-tuh-ree]: urgent
decry: to condemn or belittle
surreptitiously [sir-up-TISH-us-lee]: secretly
palatable [PAL-ih-tuh-bull]: agreeable, edible
Bedlam: formerly an insane asylum in London; now pertains to any madhouse
calliope [kuh-LYE-oh-pee]: a keyboard instrument fitted with steam whistles

*I*t looked like a good thing: but wait till I tell you. We were down South, in Alabama—Bill Driscoll and myself— when this kidnaping idea struck us. It was, as Bill afterward expressed it, "during a moment of temporary mental apparition"; but we didn't find that out till later.

There was a town down there, as flat as a flannel-cake, and called Summit, of course. It contained inhabitants of as harmless and self-satisfied a class of peasantry as ever clustered round a maypole.

Bill and me had a joint capital of about six hundred dollars, and we needed just two thousand dollars more to pull off a fraudulent real estate deal in western Illinois with. We talked it over on the front steps of the hotel. Family ties are strong in semirural communities, says we; therefore, and for other reasons, a kidnaping project ought to do better there than in the radius of newspapers that send reporters out in plain clothes to stir up talk about such things. We knew that Summit couldn't get after us with anything stronger than constables and, maybe, some lackadaisical bloodhounds and a diatribe [DYE-uh-tribe] or two in the local paper. So, it looked good.

We selected for our victim the only child of a prominent citizen named Ebenezer Dorset. The father was respectable and tight, a mortgage fancier and a stern, upright collection-plate passer and forecloser. The kid was a freckle-faced boy of ten, with bright red hair, and Bill and me figured that Ebenezer would melt down for a ransom of two thousand dollars in a flash. But wait till I tell you.

About two miles from Summit was a little mountain, covered with a dense cedar brake. On the rear elevation of this mountain was a cave. There we stored provisions.

One evening after sundown, we drove in a buggy past old Dorset's house. The kid was in the street, throwing rocks at a kitten on the opposite fence.

"Hey, little boy!" says Bill, "would you like to have a bag of candy and a nice ride?"

The boy catches Bill neatly in the eye with a piece of brick.

"That will cost the old man an extra five hundred dollars," says Bill, climbing over the wheel.

That boy put up a fight like a welterweight cinnamon bear; but, at last, we got him down in the bottom of the buggy and drove away. We took him up to the cave, and I hitched the horse in the cedar brake. After dark I drove the buggy to the little village, three miles away, where we had hired it, and walked back to the mountain.

Bill was pasting ointment over the scratches and bruises on his features. There was a fire burning behind the big rock at the entrance of the cave, and the boy was watching a pot of boiling coffee, with two buzzard tail feathers stuck in his red hair. He points a stick at me when I come up, and says, "Ha! cursed paleface, do you dare to enter the camp of Red Chief, the terror of the plains?"

"He's all right now," says Bill, rolling up his trousers and examining some bruises on his shins. "We're playing Indian. We're making Buffalo Bill's show look like magic-lantern views of Palestine in the town hall. I'm Old Hank, the Trapper, Red Chief's captive, and I'm to be scalped at daybreak. By Geronimo! that kid can kick hard."

Yes, sir, that boy seemed to be having the time of his life. The fun of camping out in a cave had made him forget that he was a captive himself. He immediately christened me Snake-eye, the Spy, and announced that, when his braves returned from the warpath, I was to be broiled at the stake at the rising of the sun.

Then we had supper; and he filled his mouth full of bacon and bread and gravy, and began to talk. He made a during-dinner speech something like this:

"I like this fine. I never camped out before; but I had a pet 'possum once, and I was nine last birthday. I hate to go to school. Rats ate up sixteen of Jimmy Talbot's aunt's speckled hen's eggs. Are there any real Indians in these woods? I want some more gravy. Does the trees moving make the wind blow? We had five puppies. What makes your nose so red, Hank? My father has lots of money. Are the stars hot? I whipped Ed Walker twice, Saturday. I don't like girls. You dassent catch toads unless with a string. Do oxen make any noise? Why are oranges round? Have you got beds to sleep on in this cave? Amos Murray has got six toes. A parrot can talk, but a monkey or a fish can't. How many does it take to make twelve?"

Every few minutes he would remember that he was a pesky redskin, and pick up his stick rifle and tiptoe to the mouth of the cave to watch for the scouts of the hated paleface. Now and then he would let out a war-whoop that made Old Hank the Trapper shiver. That boy had Bill terrorized from the start.

"Red Chief," says I to the kid, "would you like to go home?"

"Aw, what for?" says he. "I don't have any fun at home. I hate to go to school. I like to camp out. You won't take me back home again, Snake-eye, will you?"

"Not right away," says I. "We'll stay here in the cave awhile."

"All right!" says he. "That'll be fine. I never had such fun in all my life."

We went to bed about eleven o'clock. We spread down some wide blankets and quilts and put Red Chief between us. We weren't afraid he'd run away. He kept us awake for three hours, jumping up and reaching for his rifle and screeching, "Hist! pard," in mine and Bill's ears, as the fancied crackle of a twig or the rustle of a leaf revealed to his young imagination the stealthy approach of the outlaw band. At last, I fell into a troubled sleep, and dreamed that I had been kidnaped and chained to a tree by a ferocious pirate with red hair.

Just at daybreak I was awakened by a series of awful screams from Bill. They weren't yells, or howls, or shouts, or whoops, or yawps, such as you'd expect from a manly set of vocal organs—they were simply indecent, terrifying, humiliating screams, such as women emit when they see ghosts or caterpillars. It's an awful thing to hear a strong, desperate, fat man scream uncontrollably in a cave at daybreak.

I jumped up to see what the matter was. Red Chief was sitting on Bill's chest, with one hand twined in Bill's hair. In the other he had the sharp jackknife we used for slicing bacon; and he was industriously and realistically trying to take Bill's scalp, according to the sentence that had been pronounced upon him the evening before.

I got the knife away from the kid and made him lie down again. But, from that moment, Bill's spirit was broken. He lay down on his side of the bed, but he never closed an eye again in sleep as long as that boy was with us. I dozed off for a while, but along toward sunup I remembered that Red Chief had said I was to be burned at the stake at the rising of the sun. I wasn't nervous or afraid; but I sat up and lit my pipe and leaned against a rock.

"What you getting up so soon for, Sam?" asked Bill.

"Me?" says I. "Oh, I got a kind of pain in my shoulder. I thought sitting up would rest it."

"You're a liar!" says Bill. "You're afraid. You was to be burned at sunrise, and you was afraid he'd do it. And he would, too, if he could find a match. Ain't it awful, Sam? Do you think anybody will pay our money to get a little imp like that back home?"

"Sure," said I. "A rowdy kid like that is just the kind that parents dote on. Now, you and the Chief get up and cook breakfast, while I go up on the top of this mountain and reconnoiter [ree-cuh-NOY-turr]."

I went up on the peak of the little mountain and ran my eye over the vicinity. Over toward Summit I expected to see the sturdy peasants of the village armed with scythes [sithe, long *i* sound] and pitchforks beating the countryside for the dastardly kidnapers. But what I saw was a peaceful landscape dotted with one man plowing with a mule. Nobody was dragging the creek; no couriers dashed hither and yon, bringing tidings of no news to the distracted parents. There was a sylvan [SILL-van] attitude of sleepiness pervading that section of the external outward surface of Alabama that lay exposed to view. "Perhaps," says I to myself, "it has not yet been discovered that the wolves have borne away the tender lambkin from the fold. Heaven help the wolves!" says I, and I went down the mountain to breakfast.

When I got to the cave I found Bill backed up against the side of it, breathing hard, and the boy threatening to smash him with a rock half as big as a coconut.

"He put a red-hot boiled potato down my back," explained Bill, "and then mashed it with his foot; and I boxed his ears. Have you got a gun about you, Sam?"

I took the rock away from the boy and kind of patched up the argument. "I'll fix you," says the kid to Bill. "No man ever yet struck the Red Chief but he got paid for it. You better beware!"

After breakfast the kid takes a piece of leather with strings wrapped around it out of his pocket and goes outside the cave unwinding it.

"What's he up to now?" says Bill, anxiously. "You don't think he'll run away, do you, Sam?"

"No fear of it," says I. "He don't seem to be much of a homebody. But we've got to fix up some plan about the ransom. There don't seem to be much excitement around Summit on account of his disappearance; but maybe they haven't realized yet that he's gone. His folks may think he's spending the night with Aunt Jane or one of the neighbors. Anyhow, he'll be missed today. Tonight we must get a message to his father demanding the two thousand dollars for his return."

Just then we heard a kind of war-whoop, such as David might have emitted when he knocked out the champion Goliath. It was a sling that Red Chief had pulled out of his pocket, and he was whirling it around his head.

I dodged, and heard a heavy thud and a kind of a sigh from Bill, like a horse gives out when you take his saddle off. A rock the size of an egg had caught Bill just behind his left ear. He loosened himself all over and fell in the fire across the frying pan of hot water for washing the dishes. I dragged him out and poured cold water on his head for half an hour.

By and by, Bill sits up and feels behind his ear and says, "Sam, do you know who my favorite Biblical character is?"

"Take it easy," says I. "You'll come to your senses presently."

"King Herod," says he. "You won't go away and leave me here alone, will you, Sam?"

I went out and caught that boy and shook him until his freckles rattled.

"If you don't behave," says I, "I'll take you straight home. Now, are you going to be good, or not?"

"I was only funning," says he, sullenly. "I didn't mean to hurt Old Hank. But what did he hit me for? I'll behave, Snakeeye, if you won't send me home, and if you'll let me play the Black Scout today?"

"I don't know the game," says I. "That's for you and Mr. Bill to decide. He's your playmate for the day. I'm going away for a while, on business. Now, you come in and make friends with him and say you are sorry for hurting him, or home you go, at once."

I made him and Bill shake hands, and then I took Bill aside and told him I was going to Poplar Grove, a little village three miles from the cave, and find out what I could about how the kidnaping had been regarded in Summit. Also, I thought it best to send a peremptory [purr-EMP-tuh-ree] letter to old man Dorset that day, demanding the ransom and dictating how it should be paid.

"You know, Sam," says Bill, "I've stood by you without batting an eye in earthquakes, fire, and flood—in poker games, dynamite outrages, police raids, train robberies, and cyclones. I never lost my nerve yet till we kidnaped that two-legged skyrocket of a kid. He's got me going. You won't leave me long with him, will you, Sam?"

"I'll be back sometime this afternoon," says I. "You must keep the boy amused and quiet till I return. And now we'll write the letter to old Dorset."

Bill and I got paper and pencil and worked on the letter while Red Chief, with a blanket wrapped around him, strutted up and down, guarding the mouth of the cave. Bill begged me tearfully to make the ransom fifteen hundred dollars instead of two thousand. "I ain't attempting," says he, "to decry the celebrated moral aspect of parental affection, but we're dealing with humans, and it ain't human for anybody to give up two thousand dollars for that forty-pound chunk of freckled wild-cat. I'm willing to take a chance at fifteen hundred dollars. You can charge the difference to me."

So, to relieve Bill, I acceded, and we collaborated a letter that ran this way:

EBENEZER DORSET, ESQ.:

We have your boy concealed in a place far from Summit. It is useless for you or the most skillful detectives to attempt to find him. Absolutely, the only terms on which you can have him restored to you are these: We demand fifteen hundred dollars in large bills for his return; the money to be left at midnight tonight at the same spot and in the same box as your reply—hereinafter described. If you agree to these terms, send your answer in writing by a solitary messenger tonight at half-past eight o'clock. After crossing Owl Creek on the road to Poplar Grove, there are three large trees about a hundred yards apart, close to the fence of the wheat field on the right-hand side. At the bottom of the fencepost, opposite the third tree, will be found a small pasteboard box.

The messenger will place the answer in this box and return immediately to Summit.

If you attempt any treachery or fail to comply with our demand as stated, you will never see your boy again.

If you pay the money as demanded, he will be returned to you safe and well within three hours. These terms are final, and if you do not accede to them, no further communication will be attempted.

TWO DESPERATE MEN

I addressed this letter to Dorset, and put it in my pocket. As I was about to start, the kid comes up to me and says:

"Aw, Snake-eye, you said I could play the Black Scout while you was gone."

"Play it, of course," says I. "Mr. Bill will play with you. What kind of a game is it?"

"I'm the Black Scout," says Red Chief, "and I have to ride to the stockade to warn the settlers that the Indians are coming. I'm tired of playing Indian myself. I want to be the Black Scout."

"All right," says I. "It sounds harmless to me. I guess Mr. Bill will help you foil the pesky savages."

"What am I to do?" asks Bill, looking at the kid suspiciously.

"You are the hoss," says Black Scout. "Get down on your hands and knees. How can I ride to the stockade without a hoss?"

"You'd better keep him interested," said I, "till we get the scheme going. Loosen up."

Bill gets down on his all fours, and a look comes in his eye like a rabbit's when you catch it in a trap.

"How far is it to the stockade, kid?" he asks, in a husky manner of voice.

"Ninety miles," says the Black Scout. "And you have to hump yourself to get there on time. Whoa, now!"

The Black Scout jumps on Bill's back and digs his heels in his side.

"For heaven's sake," says Bill, "hurry back, Sam, as soon as you can. I wish we hadn't made the ransom more than a thousand. Say, you quit kicking me or I'll get up and warm you good."

I walked over to Poplar Grove and sat around the post office and store, talking with the chaw-bacons that came in to trade. One whiskerando says that he hears Summit is all upset on account of Elder Ebenezer Dorset's boy having been lost or stolen. That was all I wanted to know. I bought some smoking tobacco, referred casually to the price of black-eyed peas, posted my letter surreptitiously [sir-up-TISH-us-lee], and came away. The postmaster said the mail carrier would come by in an hour to take the mail to Summit.

When I got back to the cave, Bill and the boy were not to be found. I explored the vicinity of the cave, and risked a yodel or two, but there was no response.

So I lighted my pipe and sat down on a mossy bank to await developments.

In about half an hour I heard the bushes rustle, and Bill wobbled out into the little glade in front of the cave. Behind him was the kid, stepping softly like a scout, with a broad grin on his face. Bill stopped, took off his hat, and wiped his face with a red handkerchief. The kid stopped about eight feet behind him.

"Sam," says Bill, "I suppose you'll think I'm a renegade, but I couldn't help it. I'm a grown person with masculine habits of self-defense, but there is a time when all systems of egotism fail. The boy is gone. I sent him home. All is off. There was martyrs in old times," goes on Bill, "that suffered death rather than give up the particular graft they enjoyed. None of 'em ever was subjugated to such supernatural tortures as I have been. I tried to be faithful to our plan, but there came a limit."

"What's the trouble, Bill?" I asks him.

"I was rode," says Bill, "the ninety miles to the stockade, not barring an inch. Then, when the settlers was rescued, I was given oats. Sand ain't a palatable [PAL-ih-tuh-bull] substitute. And then, for an hour I had to try to explain to him why there was nothin' in holes, how a road can run both ways, and what makes the grass green. I tell you, Sam, a human can only stand so much. I takes him by the neck of his clothes and drags him down the mountain. On the way he kicks my legs black and blue from the knees down; and I've got to have two or three bites on my thumb and hand cauterized.

"But he's gone"—continues Bill—"gone home. I showed him the road to Summit and kicked him about eight feet nearer there at one kick. I'm sorry we lose the ransom; but it was either that or Bill Driscoll to the madhouse."

Bill is puffing and blowing, but there is a look of indescribable peace and growing content on his rose-pink features.

"Bill," says I, "there isn't any heart disease in your family, is there?"

"No," says Bill, "nothing chronic except malaria and accidents. Why?"

"Then you might turn around," says I, "and have a look behind you."

Bill turns and sees the boy, and loses his complexion and sits down plump on the ground and begins to pluck aimlessly at grass and little sticks. For an hour I was afraid of his mind. And then I told him that my scheme was to put the whole job through immediately and that we would get the ransom and be off with it by midnight if old Dorset fell in with our proposition. So Bill braced up enough to give the kid a weak sort of a smile and a promise to play the Russian in a Japanese war with him as soon as he felt a little better.

I had a scheme for collecting that ransom without danger of being caught by counterplots that ought to commend itself to professional kidnapers. The tree under which the answer was to be left—and the money later on—was close to the road fence with big, bare fields on all sides. If a gang of constables should be watching for anyone to come for the note, they could see him a long way off crossing the fields or in the road. But no, sirree! At half-past eight I was up in that tree as well hidden as a tree toad, waiting for the messenger to arrive.

Exactly on time, a half-grown boy rides up the road on a bicycle, locates the pasteboard box at the foot of the fencepost, slips a folded piece of paper into it, and pedals away again back toward Summit.

I waited an hour and then concluded the thing was square. I slid down the tree, got the note, slipped along the fence till I struck the woods, and was back at the cave in another half an hour. I opened the note, got near the lantern, and read it to Bill. It was written with a pen in a crabbed hand, and the sum and substance of it was this:

TWO DESPERATE MEN:

Gentlemen: I received your letter today by post, in regard to the ransom you ask for the return of my son. I think you are a little high in your demands, and I hereby make you a counter-proposition, which I am inclined to believe you will accept. You bring Johnny home and pay me two hundred and fifty dollars in cash, and I agree to take him off your hands. You had better come at night, for the neighbors believe he is lost, and I couldn't be responsible for what they would do to anybody they saw bringing him back. Very respectfully,

EBENEZER DORSET

"Great Pirates of Penzance," says I, "of all the impudent—"

But I glanced at Bill, and hesitated. He had the most appealing look in his eyes I ever saw on the face of a dumb or a talking brute.

"Sam," says he, "what's two hundred and fifty dollars, after all? We've got the money. One more night of this kid will send me to a bed in Bedlam. Besides being a thorough gentleman, I think Mr. Dorset is a spendthrift for making us such a liberal offer. You ain't going to let the chance go, are you?"

"Tell you the truth, Bill," says I, "this little lamb has somewhat got on my nerves, too. We'll take him home, pay the ransom, and make our getaway."

We took him home that night. We got him to go by telling him that his father had bought a silver-mounted rifle and a pair of moccasins for him, and we were to hunt bears the next day.

It was just twelve o'clock when we knocked at Ebenezer's front door. Just at the moment when I should have been abstracting the fifteen hundred dollars from the box under the tree, according to the original proposition, Bill was counting out two hundred and fifty dollars into Dorset's hand.

When the kid found out we were going to leave him at home he started up a howl like a calliope [kuh-LYE-oh-pee] and fastened himself as tight as a leech to Bill's leg. His father peeled him away gradually, like a mustard plaster.

"How long can you hold him?" asks Bill.

"I'm not as strong as I used to be," says old Dorset, "but I think I can promise you ten minutes."

"Enough," says Bill. "In ten minutes I shall cross the Central, Southern, and Middle Western states, and be legging it trippingly for the Canadian border."

And, as dark as it was, and as fat as Bill was, and as good a runner as I am, he was a good mile and a half out of Summit before I could catch up with him.

Romeo and Juliet

adapted from the play
by
WILLIAM SHAKESPEARE

About the story:
*William Shakespeare lived in England approximately
400 years ago (1564–1616) during the reign of Queen Eliz-
abeth—a time of high excitement and progress in the
country. It was an age that showed a great deal of interest in the writing and acting of plays; in fact, the first
real theater in England was built during this time. The
poorest and the most common people of the day, as well
as the richest and most noble, enjoyed the two hours
they regularly spent watching a production of a new or
favorite play. Shakespeare helped fill this craving for
plays both by acting in and, more importantly, by writing a total of 37 comedies and tragedies. His plays are
still performed frequently today, and* Julius Caesar,
Hamlet, *and* Romeo and Juliet *have been favorites
throughout the world for centuries.*

The theme of Romeo and Juliet, *a boy and a girl who
love each other in spite of the hatred between their families, was not originated by Shakespeare; this theme was
the basis for many older works as well as, more recently,
the musical* West Side Story. *But Shakespeare told the
story in language so moving that his version easily
stands above all the others as a timeless masterpiece.
There have been several movies made of this play; the
most recent (and perhaps the best) is the 1967 production
by Franco Zeffirelli, which can be a profitable and enjoyable follow-up, for parents and children alike, to the
story presented here.*

Approximate reading time: 22 minutes
Pronunciation and vocabulary guide:
   Verona [verr-ROH-nah]
   Capulet [CAPP-yoo-lett]

Montague [MAHN-tug-yoo]
enmity [ENN-mih-tee]: hatred, hostility
move'd [MOO-vedd]
Benvolio [benn-VOH-lee-oh]
premonition [pree-muh-NISH-un]: a warning of the future
Mercutio [merr-CUE-shee-oh]
Tybalt [TIBB-uhlt]
perverse: stubborn, peevish, contrary
inconstancy [inn-CONN-stan-see]: fickleness, capriciousness
banished: expelled, forced to leave the country or territory
Mantua [MAN-chew-ah]
reconcile [RECK-uhn-sile]: to settle or resolve a dispute
charnel-house: a vault where bones of the dead are stored
chapless: jawless
vial [VIE-uhl]: a small, glass container
crypt [rhymes with SCRIPT]: a burial chamber

Two households, both alike in dignity,
   In fair Verona, where we lay our scene,
From ancient grudge break to new mutiny,
   Where civil blood makes civil hands unclean.
From forth the fatal loins of these two foes
   A pair of star-cross'd lovers take their life;
Whose misadventured piteous overthrows
   Doth with their death bury their parents' strife.

L ong ago, in the town of Verona [verr-ROH-nah], there were two wealthy families: the Capulets [CAPP-yoo-lets] and the Montagues [MAHN-tug-yooz]. There had been an old quarrel between these families; no one could remember the original point at issue, but their hatred for each other continued to grow just the same, until now, so deadly was the enmity [ENN-mih-tee] between them that it extended to their remotest kin. Indeed, even a servant of the house of

Montague could not, by sheer chance, encounter a servant of the house of Capulet on the street without there being fierce words exchanged, and sometimes even bloodshed. Needless to say, the frequent brawling between these two families had brought an end to the happy quiet of Verona's streets, for the townspeople knew that a violent disturbance could, and often did, break out suddenly at any time or place.

One of these family street brawls was interrupted by the appearance of the prince and his soldiers on horseback. The prince had, for many years, tried to encourage the families toward a peaceful coexistence, but to no avail. Now he would endure their quarrel no longer.

> "Rebellious subjects, enemies to peace,
> On pain of torture, from those bloody hands
> Throw your mistemper'd weapons to the ground,
> And hear the sentences of your move'd [MOO-vedd]
>   prince.
> Three civil brawls, bred of an airy word,
> By thee, old Capulet, and Montague,
> Have thrice disturb'd the quiet of our streets.
> If ever you disturb our streets again,
> Your lives shall pay the forfeit of the peace."

From then on all knew that the next man to take part in this feud would be put to death.

It so happened that old Lord Capulet decided to throw a great dinner party and to invite all the fairest ladies and noblest gentlemen of Verona to attend. In fact, anyone at all would be welcome provided only that he or she was not a member of the family called Montague. To this feast came the lady Rosaline, who was loved by young Romeo, the son of old Lord Montague. Of course Romeo, being a Montague, could not accompany his love to the party, and this disappointed him greatly. However, his friend Benvolio [benn-VOH-lee-oh] pointed out that Romeo could wear a mask to the party and, behind this disguise, there he could see Rosaline and compare her with the most beautiful women of Verona. Benvolio believed that such a comparison would reveal to Romeo that his love for Rosaline was misplaced; she, after all, had never returned his love or shown him the slightest courtesy or affection, yet Romeo continued to love her and to dream that someday she would love him, too.

Romeo agreed to go, but he felt a strange premonition [pree-muh-NISH-un] that somehow his fate would be changed by what happened at the party:

> ". . . for my mind misgives
> Some consequence yet hanging in the stars
> Shall bitterly begin his fearful date
> With this night's revels . . ."

Benvolio's plan seemed reasonable, and so, to this feast in the very house of the Capulets came young Romeo and his friends Benvolio and Mercutio [merr-CUE-shee-oh], all wearing masks to conceal their well-known affiliation with the family of Montague. They were welcomed at the door by Lord Capulet himself, who recalled his own youthful, amorous adventures and the fact that he had occasionally found it beneficial to hide his identity behind a mask. The three lads began dancing and chatting with any lady who met their eye, until Romeo was suddenly taken aback by a beauty so radiant that she seemed to teach the torches to burn bright—"like a snowy dove trooping with crows," he said, so richly did her beauty and perfections shine above all the other ladies present. But no sooner did Romeo utter these exclamations than they were overheard by Tybalt [TIBB-uhlt], a nephew of Lord Capulet, who recognized the sound of Romeo's voice. And Tybalt, having a fiery and passionate temper, could not tolerate a Montague sneaking in to sneer at his family's friends behind the cover of a mask. He stormed and raged and would have slain Romeo right there had not Lord Capulet intervened on Romeo's behalf, saying that Romeo had, after all, behaved quite like a gentleman so far, and that he was often described as a virtuous and well-behaved youth, even though he was a Montague. So Tybalt grudgingly put up his sword, but he swore that sooner or later he would make Romeo pay dearly for his intrusion.

The commotion having subsided for the present and the party having resumed, Romeo sought out the angel who had so bedazzled him with her beauty. He took her hand in the gentlest manner, calling it a shrine, and saying that he was merely a blushing pilgrim who wanted only to worship at this shrine. If he had dishonored her hand in any way by touching it, he would kiss it as a means of atonement. "Good pilgrim," answered the lady, "you do wrong your hand too much. For saints have hands that pilgrim's hands do touch." She reminded him that it is altogether proper and respectable for a worshiping pilgrim to touch palm to palm even with a saint. "Have not saints lips, too?" Romeo asked. "Ay, pilgrim, lips that they must use in prayer," she replied. "Oh, then, dear saint," he exclaimed, "let lips do what hands do."

But, just as the two were enjoying these first sparks of romance, the lady was called away to her mother. It was then Romeo learned the identity of the peerless beauty who had so suddenly and completely captured his heart. She was none other than Juliet, the daughter of Lord and Lady Capulet! He had unknowingly fallen deeply in love with someone his family considered their foe. And Juliet, likewise, discovered that the masked pilgrim with whom she had been in such passionate conversation was Romeo, the only son of the hated family called Montague!

At midnight, Romeo and his friends departed. But instead of returning home, Romeo left the others and leaped the orchard wall at the rear of the Capulet estate, hoping to catch one last glimpse of Juliet. And soon, being concealed both by the orchard and the dark of night, he saw Juliet lean out her bedroom window. Romeo was spellbound by her beauty, which to him was far greater than that even of the moon:

> "But, soft! what light through yonder window breaks?
> It is the east, and Juliet is the sun.
> Arise, fair sun, and kill the envious moon,
> Who is already sick and pale with grief,
> That thou her maid art far more fair than she . . ."

Then he heard her sigh, "O Romeo, Romeo! wherefore art thou Romeo?" (which was that age's way of saying "Why must you be called Romeo?"). She, still thinking that no one could possibly hear what she was saying, mused that if Romeo would reject his family name, he need only swear his love for her and she would no longer be a Capulet:

> " 'Tis but thy name that is my enemy;
> Thou art thyself though, not a Montague.
> What's Montague? it is not hand, nor foot,
> Nor arm, nor face, nor any other part
> Belonging to a man. O, be some other name!
> What's in a name? that which we call a rose
> By any other name would smell as sweet;
> So Romeo would, were he not Romeo call'd,
> Retain that dear perfection which he owes
> Without that title. Romeo, doff thy name,
> And for that name which is no part of thee
> Take all myself."

Upon hearing this, Romeo could no longer stay silent. He sprang from his hiding place and cried out that she could name him whatever she wished; he would no longer be known as Romeo if that name displeased her. Juliet, alarmed to find that someone had overheard her private thoughts, demanded to know the name of the intruder. And when Romeo spoke again, she immediately recognized the sound of his voice, and she warned him of the danger he would be in if any of her family found him there. "Better my life should be ended by their hate," Romeo replied, "than prolonged without your love."

Juliet knew that she could not be perverse or coy in the way that was customary for discreet ladies to treat their suitors, for Romeo had heard from her own lips a confession of her love for him. And so she spoke frankly to him about her feelings, but she begged him not to conclude that her easy yielding indicated an inconstancy [inn-CONN-stan-see] of heart, for although her behavior toward him would not be considered prudent by the other ladies of her day, her love for Romeo would prove more true and lasting than affairs that began in a more conventional and artificial manner.

As they exchanged their vows of love, Juliet was, several times, called by her governess to bed, and when it seemed that her excuses would no longer be accepted, Juliet bid Romeo good night, saying that if his love was indeed honorable and if his purpose was to marry her, she would send a messenger to him early the next day, who would report back to her the time and place that Romeo had arranged for their wedding. She left him then, saying "Good night, good night! Parting is such sweet sorrow, that I shall say good night till it be morrow."

The day was breaking when they parted, and Romeo was far too excited from his meeting with Juliet to sleep. So, instead of going home, he went to the monastery to find his friend and confessor, Friar Laurence. The good friar, seeing Romeo up and about so early, conjectured that his sleeplessness must be due to yet another rejection of his love by Rosaline. But when Romeo revealed to him his new passion for Juliet and asked him to marry them that day, the friar saw a chance for patching up the feud between the Capulets and the Montagues through this matrimonial alliance between the families. He assured Romeo that he would help him in his quest:

"But come, young waverer, come, go with me,
In one respect I'll thy assistant be;
For this alliance may so happy prove,
To turn your household's rancor to pure love."

Juliet learned from her messenger that Friar Laurence would perform the ceremony that very day, and she hurried to meet Romeo at the monastery. There they were joined in holy marriage, the friar praying that heaven would smile upon their union and bury the strife between their families. When the ceremony was over, Juliet returned home and waited in lonely ecstasy for her new husband, who had promised to come to her in the orchard that night.

Later that afternoon, however, fate began to show its hand, for Romeo and his friends Benvolio and Mercutio encountered a group of Capulets while walking through the streets of Verona. Leading the group was Tybalt, who was still seething from his near-fight with Romeo at the feast. Tybalt cursed Romeo and anyone who would be low enough to associate with this villain Montague, but Romeo ignored his taunts saying that he apologized for any wrong he may have done Tybalt in the past, and that he now had reason to feel toward Tybalt as he would toward one of his own kin. Mercutio, who was still unaware of Romeo's marriage to Juliet, could not understand why Romeo would not accept Tybalt's challenge to his family's honor, and feeling offended himself, he drew his sword and fought a vicious battle with Tybalt. During the fight, Mercutio suffered a deep wound and within a few minutes lay dead on the street. Romeo could hold his temper no longer. He lashed out at Tybalt with his sword and avenged Mercutio's death by killing the man who had slain his friend. A crowd of citizens quickly gathered at the scene, and soon the prince himself arrived and sentenced Romeo to be banished: "Let Romeo hence in haste, else, when he's found, that hour will be his last."

When the news of what happened reached Juliet, she was at first outraged at Romeo, for Tybalt, after all, had been her cousin. But then her rage turned to relief at the thought that it might just as easily have been Romeo who was slain; still, his banishment would mean that they might always have to live apart. Romeo, however, was at this time being encouraged by Friar Laurence, who advised him to leave immediately for Mantua [MAN-chew-ah] and wait for the friar to make a general announcement of Romeo's marriage; the families would then reconcile [RECK-uhn-sile] their differences, the friar predicted, and the prince would pardon Romeo so that he could return to Verona. The plan seemed convincing enough, and so Romeo decided to make his way secretly to Juliet's and there to spend the night with her before leaving for Mantua.

When it was dark, he again climbed the orchard wall and then the wall of the house itself, up to Juliet's bedroom balcony. They passed the remainder of the night in unbridled joy and rapture, being together, secretly husband and wife, for the first time. The song of the lark heralded the unwelcome morning, and Romeo reluctantly left, knowing that it would mean death if he were found in Verona after daybreak.

Indeed, Friar Laurence's plan might have worked had not fate intervened once again to thwart our lovers' hopes. Lord Capulet—not knowing, of course, that his daughter had already secretly married Romeo—arranged a marriage for her to a young nobleman named Count Paris. Juliet begged her father to cancel the match with every reason she could imagine, but he was deaf to all her excuses. She was to prepare herself to become the wife of Count Paris on the following Thursday.

Not knowing what to do or where to turn, Juliet appealed to

Friar Laurence for help. He asked whether she would consider anything, no matter how desperate the remedy may be, in order to avoid this marriage, and she answered:

> "O, bid me leap, rather than marry Paris,
> From off the battlements of yonder tower,
> Or walk in thievish ways; or bid me lurk
> Where serpents are; chain me with roaring bears;
> Or shut me nightly in a charnel-house,
> O'er-covered quite with dead men's rattling bones,
> With reeky shanks and yellow chapless skulls;
> Or bid me go into a new-made grave
> And hide me with a dead man in his shroud;
> Things that, to hear them told, have made me tremble;
> And I will do it, without fear or doubt,
> To live an unstain'd wife to my sweet love."

The good friar then explained his scheme. She was to return home and be merry, pretending to assent to her father's wishes. On the night before the wedding, though, she was to drink the contents of a vial [VIE-uhl] that the friar would give her, which would make her soon appear cold and lifeless and would give everyone to think that she was, in fact, dead. But the drug would not actually end her life; it would just give her the appearance of being dead for forty-two hours. She would be taken to the monastery by her grieving family for burial; meanwhile Friar Laurence would send for Romeo so that he would be at her side when she awoke. The two could then go together to Mantua and live in happiness forever after.

Juliet did just as the friar had instructed, and on the morning of her proposed marriage, her seemingly lifeless corpse was discovered by the young count; the uncontrollable joy that was Lord and Lady Capulet's only the day before now became unimaginable grief, and Juliet's body was borne to the monastery, there to be buried in the family vault.

Bad news, which always travels faster than good, now brought the dismal story of Juliet's death to Romeo before Friar Laurence's messenger could apprise him of what had actually taken place. In shock and grief, Romeo saw no value in his own life now that it could never be spent with Juliet, and so he bought a bottle of strong poison and carried it with him to Verona, there to be at the side of his love and join her in death.

He reached the monastery at midnight and found Count Paris mourning at the gate of the crypt [rhymes with SCRIPT] where Juliet lay. A fight ensued between the two, one Juliet's secret husband and the other Juliet's acknowledged husband-to-be, and Paris fell, mortally wounded. Romeo entered the tomb and saw his love; it appeared that even death had no power to change her matchless beauty, so fresh and blooming did she appear—almost as if she were asleep:

> "O my love! my wife!
> Death, that hath suck'd the honey of thy breath,
> Hath had no power yet upon thy beauty:
> Thou art not conquer'd; beauty's ensign yet
> Is crimson in thy lips and in thy cheeks,
> And death's pale flag is not advanced there."

Here Romeo kissed her lips one last time and then swallowed the poison he had brought.

Shortly thereafter, Juliet stirred, for the forty-two hours had now elapsed, and the effects of the potion she had swallowed were beginning to wear away. Just at this time, Friar Laurence entered the crypt, too, in order to aid Juliet in her recovery. He saw Romeo and Paris lying dead in the tomb, swords drawn, blood on the floor, and he could not imagine what had taken place. He begged Juliet to leave this fateful place, saying that there had been a power far greater than theirs that had spoiled their plans. But she, seeing the cup clutched in Romeo's hands, guessed that he had swallowed poison; she tried to drink from the cup herself so that she might die with him, but no poison remained. She kissed his still-warm lips in hope that a drop or two might have lingered there, but again there was none. So, taking up Romeo's dagger, she plunged it violently into her chest and fell dead at his side.

The commotion of the fight between Romeo and Paris had alerted the townspeople, and soon a crowd was gathered at the monastery, including Lord Capulet, Lord Montague, and the prince. Friar Laurence explained what had taken place as best he could, how he had married Romeo and Juliet and how he had devised a plan for them to be together. A letter written by Romeo to his father when he first learned of Juliet's death explained the rest, and now everyone understood the tragedy that had befallen these two star-crossed lovers. And, although their deaths led Lord Capulet to offer his hand to Lord Montague, and both to swear eternal friendship and an end to their quarrels forever, oh, what a price they had paid for this peace. "For," as the prince said, "never was a story of more woe than this of Juliet and her Romeo."

"Rip Van Winkle"

by
WASHINGTON IRVING

About the story:

Washington Irving began writing as a hobby, although he enjoyed the pursuit infinitely more than the practice of law or his work in the family's struggling import business. In 1817, while he was in his early thirties, he decided to devote his entire efforts to writing, and he created several truly American stories that could be sold together as a book, **The Sketch Book.** *These stories were set in America and were based on American legends and happenings, which gave them the flavor of the new land and which made them appealing to readers both here and in Europe.*

Among the characters that Irving carved forever into American legend were the unfortunate Ichabod Crane, in "The Legend of Sleepy Hollow," and the lazy but kindly Rip Van Winkle, who is given the opportunity to carry an untainted knowledge of the past into the future, but who chooses simply to exist, as he had before. What would your children do with such a gift? What would their reaction be to someone who had slept for twenty years?

Approximate reading time: 40 minutes

Pronunciation and vocabulary guide:

Stuyvesant [STY-vess-ant]

obsequious [obb-SEE-quee-us]: fawning, complying

conciliating: gaining favor by pleasing acts, appeasing

pliant [PLY-ant]: easily influenced, yielding

malleable [MAL-ee-uh-bull]: capable of being shaped or influenced

vehemently [VEE-eh-ment-lee]: forcefully, violently

grizzled: gray

crevasse [creh-VASS]: a deep fissure, as in a glacier

ninepins: an early form of bowling

flagons [FLAG-uns]: large, bulging, short-necked bottles

impenetrable [imm-PEN-ih-tra-bull]: unable to be pierced

addled [ADD-uld]: confused, muddled

phlegm [FLEMM]: apathetic coldness or indifference

haranguing [harr-ANG-ing]: pompous, expressive speech

akimbo [uh-KIM-bo]: having the hand on the hip and the elbow turned outward

corroborated [cuh-RAH-buh-ray-ted]: to confirm or support with evidence

impunity [imm-PYOON-in-tee]: immunity from punishment

despotism [DESS-puh-tizz-um]: a government in which the ruler has unlimited power

Anyone who has made a voyage up the Hudson River must remember the Catskill Mountains. They are a dismembered branch of the great Appalachian family, and are seen away to the west of the river, swelling up to a noble height, and lording it over the surrounding country. Every change of season, every change of weather, indeed every hour of the day produces some change in the magical hues and shapes of these mountains; and they are regarded by all the good wives, far and near, as perfect barometers. When the weather is fair and settled, they are clothed in blue and purple, and print their bold outlines on the clear evening sky; but sometimes, when the rest of the landscape is cloudless, they will gather a hood of gray vapors about their summits, which, in the last rays of the setting sun, will glow and light up like a crown of glory.

At the foot of these fairy mountains, the voyager may have seen the light smoke curling up from a village, whose shingle roofs gleam among the trees just where the blue tints of the upland melt away into the fresh green of the nearer landscape. It is a little village of great antiquity, having been founded by some of the Dutch colonists, in the early times of the province, just about the beginning of the government of the good Peter Stuyvesant [STY-vess-ant] (may he rest in peace!), and there were some of the houses of the original settlers, built of small yellow bricks brought from Holland, having latticed windows and gable fronts, topped by weathervanes.

In this village, and in one of these very houses (which, to tell the precise truth, was sadly time-worn and weather-beaten), there lived many years ago (during the time that the country was still a province of Great Britain) a simple, good-natured fellow, of the name of Rip Van Winkle. He was a descendant of the Van Winkles who figured so gallantly in the chivalrous days of Peter Stuyvesant, and accompanied him to the siege of Fort Christina. He inherited, however, very little of the warlike character of his ancestors. I have observed that he was a simple, good-natured man; he was moreover a kind neighbor, and an obedient, henpecked husband. Indeed, this last condition might explain that meekness of spirit which gained him such universal popularity; for those men are most apt to be obsequious [obb-SEE-quee-us] and conciliating to neighbors, who are under the discipline of shrews at home. Their tempers, doubtless, are rendered pliant [PLY-ant] and malleable [MAL-ee-uh-bull] in the fiery furnace of domestic tribulation, and a stern lecture at home is worth all the church sermons in the world for teaching the virtues of patience and long-suffering. A scolding wife may, therefore, in some respects, be considered a tolerable blessing; and if so, Rip Van Winkle was blessed in abundance.

Certain it is that he was a great favorite among all the good wives of the village, who, as usual with the amiable sex, took his part in all family squabbles, and never failed, whenever they talked those matters over in their evening gossipings, to lay all the blame on Dame Van Winkle. The children of the village, too, would shout with joy whenever he approached. He took part in their games, made their playthings, taught them to fly kites and shoot marbles, and told them long stories of ghosts, witches, and Indians. Whenever he went strolling about the village, he was surrounded by a troop of them hanging on his shirt, clambering on his back, and playing a thousand tricks on him, knowing he would take it all in fun; and not a dog would bark at him throughout the neighborhood.

The one great flaw in Rip's makeup was an overpowering dislike for all kinds of profitable labor. It could not be from the want of diligence or perseverance; for he would sit on a wet rock, with a fishing rod as long and heavy as a lance, and fish all day without a murmur, even though he would not be encouraged by a single nibble. He would carry a hunting rifle on his shoulder for hours on end, trudging through woods and swamps, and up hill and down dale, to shoot a few squirrels or wild pigeons. He would never refuse to assist a neighbor even in the roughest toil, and he always pitched in when the townsfolk gathered to husk corn or build stone fences. The women of the village, too, used to employ him to run their errands, and to do such little odd jobs as their less obliging husbands would not do for them—in a word, Rip was ready to attend to anybody's business but his own; but as to doing family duty, and keeping his farm in order, he found it impossible.

In fact, he declared it was of no use to work on his farm; it was the most pestilent little piece of ground in the whole country; everything about it went wrong, and would go wrong in spite of him. His fences were continually falling to pieces; his cow would either go astray, or get among the cabbages; weeds were sure to grow quicker in his fields than anywhere else; the rain always made a point of setting in just as he had some outdoor work to do; so that though his estate had dwindled away under his management, acre by acre, until there was little more left than a mere patch of corn and potatoes, yet it was the worst conditioned farm in the neighborhood.

His children, too, were as ragged and wild as if they belonged to nobody. His son Rip, an urchin born in his father's likeness, seemed certain to inherit the habits as well as the clothes of his father. He was generally seen trooping like a colt at his mother's heels, dressed in a pair of his father's cast-off buckskins, which he had struggled to hold up with one hand, as a fine lady does with her train in bad weather.

Rip Van Winkle, however, was one of those happy mortals, of foolish, well-oiled dispositions, who take the world easy, eat white bread or brown, whichever can be got with least thought or trouble, and would rather starve on a penny than work for a pound. If left to himself, he would have whistled life away, in perfect contentment; but his wife kept continually harping at him about his idleness, his carelessness, and the ruin he was bringing on his family.

Morning, noon, and night, her tongue was incessantly going, and everything he said or did was sure to produce a torrent of criticism. Rip had but one way of replying to all lectures of the kind, and that, by frequent use, had grown into a habit. He shrugged his shoulders, shook his head, cast up his eyes, but said nothing. This, however, always provoked a fresh volley from his wife, so that he was forced to take to the outside of the house—the only side which, in truth, belongs to a henpecked husband.

Rip's sole friend at home was his dog Wolf, who was as much henpecked as his master; for Dame Van Winkle regarded them as companions in idleness, and even looked upon Wolf with an evil eye, as the cause of his master's going so often astray. True it is, in all points of spirit befitting an honorable dog, he was as courageous an animal as ever scoured the woods, but his courage could not withstand the terror of her constant scorn. The moment Wolf entered the house, his crest fell, his tail drooped to the ground, or curled between his legs, he sneaked about with a gallows air, casting many a sidelong glance at Dame Van Winkle, and at the least flourish of a broomstick or ladle, he would fly to the door in yelping anticipation of the forthcoming assault.

Time grew worse and worse with Rip Van Winkle, as years of matrimony rolled on: a sharp temper never mellows with age, and a sharp tongue is the only edge tool that grows keener with constant use. For a long while he used to console himself, when driven from home, by frequenting a kind of club of the sages, philosophers, and other idle men of the village, which met on a bench outside a small inn whose sign bore a rosy picture of His Majesty George the Third. Here they used to sit in the shade of a long lazy summer's day, talking listlessly over village gossip, or telling endless sleepy stories about nothing. But it would have been worth any statesman's money to have heard the profound discussions which sometimes took place, when by chance an old newspaper fell into their hands, from some passing traveler. How solemnly they would listen to the contents, as drawled out by Derrick Van Bummel, the schoolmaster, a dapper, learned little man, who was not stumped by even the most gigantic word in the dictionary; and how sagely they would deliberate upon public events some months after they had taken place.

The opinions of the group were completely controlled by Nicholas Vedder, a village leader and the owner of the inn, at the door of which he took his seat from morning till night, just moving sufficiently to avoid the sun, and keep in the shade of a large tree; so that the neighbors could tell the hour by his movements as accurately as by a sundial. It is true, he was rarely heard to speak, but smoked his pipe incessantly. His followers, however (for every great man has his followers), perfectly understood him, and knew how to learn his opinions. When anything that was read or said displeased him, he was observed to smoke his pipe vehemently [VEE-eh-ment-lee], and to send forth short, frequent, and angry puffs; but when pleased, he would inhale the smoke slowly and tranquilly, and send it out in light and peaceful clouds, and sometimes taking the pipe from his mouth, and letting the fragrant vapor curl about his nose, would gravely nod his head in token of perfect approval.

From even this stronghold the unlucky Rip was before long routed by his angry wife, who would suddenly break in upon the tranquillity of the meeting, and rail at all the members of the group; not even the eminent Nicholas Vedder himself was sacred from her wrath, for she charged him outright with encouraging her husband in habits of idleness.

Poor Rip was at last reduced almost to despair, and his only alternative to escape from the labor of the farm and the clamor of his wife was to take gun in hand, and stroll away into the woods. Here he would sometimes seat himself at the foot of a tree, and share what food he had brought with Wolf, with whom he sympathized as a fellow-sufferer in persecution. "Poor Wolf," he would say, "thy mistress leads thee a dog's life of it; but never mind, my lad, whilst I live thou shalt never lack a friend to stand by thee!" Wolf would wag his tail, look wistfully in his master's face, and if dogs can feel pity, I verily believe he reciprocated the sentiment with all his heart.

During one of these long rambles, on a fine autumn day, Rip had unconsciously scrambled to one of the highest parts of the

Catskill Mountains. He was on one of his favorite sports, squirrel hunting, and the still solitudes had echoed and reechoed with the blasts of his gun. Panting and fatigued, he threw himself, late in the afternoon, on a green knoll covered with mountain greenery that crowned the brow of a cliff. From an opening between the trees, he could overlook all the lower country for many a mile of rich woodland. He saw at a distance the lordly Hudson, far, far below him, moving on its silent but majestic course, with the reflection of a purple cloud, or the sail of a lagging bark, here and there sleeping on its glassy bosom, and at last losing itself in the blue highlands.

On the other side he looked down into a deep mountain glen, wild, lonely, and shagged, the bottom filled with fragments from the impending cliffs, and scarcely lighted by the reflected rays of the setting sun. For some time Rip lay musing on this scene; evening was gradually advancing; the mountains began to throw their long blue shadows over the valleys; he saw that it would be dark long before he could reach the village; and he heaved a heavy sigh when he thought of encountering the terrors of Dame Van Winkle.

As he was about to descend he heard a voice from a distance hollering, "Rip Van Winkle! Rip Van Winkle!" He looked around, but could see nothing but a crow winging its solitary flight across the mountain. He thought his ears must have deceived him, and turned again to descend, when he heard the same cry ring through the still evening air, "Rip Van Winkle! Rip Van Winkle"—at the same time Wolf bristled up his back, and giving a low growl, skulked to his master's side, looking fearfully down into the glen. Rip now felt a vague apprehension coming over him; he looked anxiously in the same direction, and perceived a strange figure slowly toiling up the rocks, and bending under the weight of something he carried on his back. He was surprised to see any human being in this lonely and unfrequented place, but supposing it to be some one of the neighborhood in need of his assistance, he hastened down to lend a hand.

On nearer approach, he was still more surprised at the uniqueness of the stranger's appearance. He was a short, square-built old fellow, with thick bushy hair, and a grizzled beard. He was dressed in antique Dutch fashion—a light cloth jacket strapped round the waist—several pairs of knee-length trousers, the outer one quite large, decorated with rows of buttons down the sides, and bunches at the knees. He bore on his shoulders a stout keg, that seemed full of liquor, and made signs for Rip to approach and assist him with the load. Though rather shy and distrustful of this new acquaintance, Rip complied with his usual cheery eagerness, and taking turns carrying the keg, they clambered up a narrow gully, apparently the dry bed of a mountain torrent. As they ascended, Rip every now and then heard long rolling peals, like distant thunder, that seemed to come out of a deep ravine, or rather a crevasse [creh-VASS] between lofty rocks, toward which their rugged path led. He paused for an instant, but supposing it to be the muttering of one of those brief thunder showers which often take place in the mountain heights, he proceeded. Passing through the ravine, they came to a hollow, like a small amphitheater, surrounded by cliff walls rising straight up and topped by trees that shot their branches over the brink so that you only caught glimpses of the azure sky, and the bright evening cloud. During the whole time, Rip and his companion had labored on in silence; for though Rip puzzled about what could be the object of carrying a keg of liquor up this wild mountain, yet there was something strange and incomprehensible about the unknown, that inspired awe and pricked his curiosity.

On entering the amphitheater, new objects of wonder presented themselves. On a level spot in the center was a company of odd-looking characters playing ninepins. They were dressed in quaint outlandish fashion: They wore jackets of varying styles, some had long knives in their belts, and most of them had enormous trousers, of similar style with that of the guide's. Their physical makeups, too, were peculiar: One had a large head, broad face, and small piggish eyes; the face of another seemed to consist entirely of nose, and was topped by a sugarloaf hat, set off with a little red cock's tail. They all had beards, of various shapes and colors. There was one who seemed to be the commander. He was a stout old gentleman, with a weather-beaten look; he wore a laced overshirt, broad belt and hanger, high-crowned hat and feather, red stockings, and high-heeled shoes, with roses in them. The whole group reminded Rip of the figures in an old Flemish painting that hung in the parlor of the village parson, and which had been brought over from Holland at the time of the settlement.

What seemed particularly odd to Rip was, that though these folks were evidently amusing themselves, yet they maintained the gravest faces, the most mysterious silence, and were, all in all, the most melancholy party of pleasure he had ever witnessed. Nothing interrupted the stillness of the scene but the noise of the balls, which, whenever they were rolled, echoed along the mountains like rumbling peals of thunder.

As Rip and his companion approached them, they suddenly halted their play, and stared at him with such a fixed statuelike gaze, and such strange, uncouth, lackluster appearances, that his heart turned within him, and his knees knocked together. His companion now emptied the contents of the keg into large flagons [FLAG-uns], and made signs to him to wait upon the company. He obeyed with fear and trembling; they quaffed the liquor in profound silence, and then returned to their game.

Little by little, Rip's awe and apprehension eased. He even ventured, when no eye was fixed upon him, to taste the beverage, which he found had much of the flavor of the best Holland ales. He was naturally a thirsty soul, and was soon tempted to take another drink. One taste provoked another, and he reiterated his visits to the flagon so often that at length his senses were overpowered, his eyes swam in his head, his head gradually declined, and he fell into a deep sleep.

On waking, he found himself on the green knoll from which he had first seen the old man of the glen. He rubbed his eyes —it was a bright sunny morning. The birds were hopping and twittering among the bushes, and the eagle was wheeling aloft, and breasting the pure mountain breeze. "Surely," thought Rip, "I have not slept here all night." He recalled the occurrences before he fell asleep. The strange man with the keg of liquor—the mountain ravine—the wild retreat among the rocks—the woebegone party at ninepins—the flagon—"Oh! that wicked flagon!" thought Rip; "what excuse shall I make to Dame Van Winkle?"

He looked round for his gun, but in place of the clean, well-oiled rifle, he found an old hunting piece lying by him, the barrel encrusted with rust, the hammer falling off, and the stock worm-eaten. He now suspected that the stern roisterers of the mountain had played a trick on him, and having plied him with liquor, had robbed him of his gun. Wolf, too, had disappeared, but he might have strayed away after a squirrel or partridge. He whistled after him and shouted his name, but all in vain; the echoes repeated his whistle and shout, but no dog was to be seen.

He determined to revisit the scene of the last evening's revelry, and if he met with any of the party, to demand his dog and gun. As he rose to walk, he found himself stiff in the joints, and wanting in his usual activity. "These mountain beds do not agree with me," thought Rip, "and if this frolic should lay me up with a fit of the rheumatism, I shall have a blessed time with Dame Van Winkle." With some difficulty he got down into the glen; he found the gully up which he and his companion had ascended the preceding evening; but to his astonishment a mountain stream was now foaming down it, leaping from rock to rock, and filling the glen with babbling murmurs. He, however, scrambled up its sides, working his toilsome way through thickets of birch, sassafras, and witch hazel; and sometimes tripped up or entangled by the wild grapevines that twisted their coils and tendrils from tree to tree and spread a kind of network in his path.

At length he reached to where the ravine had opened through the cliffs to the amphitheater; but no traces of such opening remained. The rocks presented a high, impenetrable [imm-PEN-ih-tra-bull] wall, over which the torrent came tumbling in a sheet of feathery foam, and fell into a broad deep basin, black from the shadows of the surrounding forest. Here, then, poor Rip was brought to a standstill. He again called and whistled after his dog; he was only answered by the cawing of a flock of idle crows, sporting high in the air about a dry tree that overhung a sunny gorge; and who, secure in their elevation, seemed to look down and scoff at the poor man's puzzlements. What was to be done? The morning was passing away, and Rip felt famished for want of his breakfast. He grieved to give up his dog and gun; he dreaded to meet his wife; but it would not do to starve among the mountains. He shook his head, shouldered the rusty rifle, and, with a heart full of trouble and anxiety, turned his steps homeward.

As he approached the village, he met a number of people,

but none whom he knew, which somewhat surprised him, for he had thought himself acquainted with everyone in the country round. Their dress, too, was a different fashion from that to which he was accustomed. They all stared at him with equal marks of surprise, and whenever they cast eyes upon him, invariably stroked their chins. The constant recurrence of this gesture induced Rip, involuntarily, to do the same, when, to his astonishment, he found his beard had grown a foot long.

He had now entered the skirts of the village. A troop of strange children ran at his heels, hooting after him, and pointing at his gray beard. The dogs, too, not one of which he recognized for an old acquaintance, barked at him as he passed. The very village was altered: It was larger and more populous. There were rows of houses which he had never seen before, and those which had been his familiar haunts had disappeared. Strange names were over the doors—strange faces at the windows—everything was strange. His mind now misgave him; he began to doubt whether both he and the world around him were not bewitched. Surely this was his native village, which he had left but a day before. There stood the Catskill Mountains—there ran the silver Hudson at a distance —there was every hill and dale precisely as it had always been —Rip was sorely perplexed—"That flagon last night," thought he, "has addled [ADD-uld] my poor head sadly!"

It was with some difficulty that he found the way to his own house, which he approached with silent awe, expecting every moment to hear the shrill voice of Dame Van Winkle. He found the house gone to decay—the roof fallen in, the windows shattered, and the doors off the hinges. A half-starved dog, that looked like Wolf, was skulking about it. Rip called him by name, but the cur snarled, showed his teeth, and passed on. This was an unkind cut indeed. "My very dog," sighed poor Rip, "has forgotten me!"

He entered the house, which, to tell the truth, Dame Van Winkle had always kept in neat order. It was empty, forlorn, and apparently abandoned. This desolateness overcame all his fears of Dame Van Winkle—he called loudly for his wife and children—the lonely chambers rang for a moment with his voice, and then all again was silence.

He now hurried forth, and hastened to his old resort, the

village inn—but it, too, was gone. A large rickety wooden building stood in its place, with great gaping windows, some of them broken, and mended with old hats and petticoats, and over the door was painted "The Union Hotel, by Jonathan Doolittle." Instead of the great tree that used to shelter the quiet little Dutch inn of yore, there now was reared a tall naked pole, with something on the top that looked like a red night-cap, and from it was fluttering a flag, on which was an unusual arrangement of stars and stripes—all this was strange and incomprehensible. He recognized on the sign, however, the ruby face of King George, under which he had smoked so many a peaceful pipe, but even this was oddly changed. The red coat was changed for one of blue and buff, a sword was held in the hand instead of a scepter, the head was decorated with a cocked hat, and underneath was painted in large characters, GENERAL WASHINGTON.

There was, as usual, a crowd of folk about the door, but none that Rip recollected. The very character of the people seemed changed. There was a busy, bustling, provocative tone about it, instead of the accustomed phlegm [FLEMM] and drowsy tranquillity. He looked in vain for the sage Nicholas Vedder, with his broad face, double chin, and fair long pipe, uttering clouds of tobacco smoke, instead of idle speeches; or Van Brummel, the schoolmaster, doling forth the contents of an ancient newspaper. In place of these, a lean and gaunt fellow, with his pockets full of handbills, was haranguing [harr-ANG-ing] vehemently about the right of citizens—election—members of Congress—liberty—Bunker's Hill—heroes of seventy-six—and other words that were incomprehensible jargon to the bewildered Van Winkle.

The appearance of Rip, with his long, grizzled beard, his rusty hunting rifle, his uncouth dress, and the army of women and children that had gathered at his heels, soon attracted the attention of the tavern politicians. They crowded round him, eyeing him from head to foot, with great curiosity. The orator bustled up to him, and drawing him partly aside, inquired "On which side he voted?" Rip stared in vacant stupidity. Another short but busy little fellow pulled him by the arm, and rising on tiptoe, inquired in his ear "Whether he was Federal or Democrat." Rip was equally at a loss to comprehend the question, when a knowing, self-important old gentleman, in a sharp cocked hat, made his way through the crowd, putting them to the right and left with his elbows as he passed, and planting himself before Van Winkle, with one arm akimbo [uh-KIM-bo], the other resting on his cane, his keen eyes and sharp hat penetrating, as it were, into his very soul, demanded in an austere tone, "What brought him to the election with a gun on his shoulder, and a mob at his heels, and whether he meant to breed a riot in the village?"

"Alas! gentlemen," cried Rip, somewhat dismayed, "I am a poor, quiet man, a native of the place, and a loyal subject of the king, God bless him!"

Here a general shout burst from the bystanders—"a Tory! a Tory! a spy! a refugee! hustle him! away with him!"

It was with great difficulty that the self-important man in the cocked hat restored order and, increasing the austerity of his brow tenfold, demanded again of the unknown culprit what he came there for and whom he was seeking. The poor man humbly assured him that he meant no harm, but merely came there in search of some of his neighbors, who used to spend time about the tavern.

"Well—who are they?—name them."

Rip thought to himself a moment, and inquired, "Where's Nicholas Vedder?"

There was a silence for a little while, when an old man replied, in a thin, piping voice, "Nicholas Vedder? Why, he is dead and gone these eighteen years! There was a wooden tombstone in the churchyard that used to tell all about him, but that's rotten and gone, too."

"Where's Brom Dutcher?" asked Rip.

"Oh, he went off to the army in the beginning of the war; some say he was killed at the storming of Stony Point—others say he was drowned in the squall, at the foot of Antony's Nose. I don't know—he never came back again."

Rip thought again and asked, "Where's Van Brummel, the schoolmaster?"

A voice in the crowd replied, "He went off to the wars, too; was a great militia general, and is now in Congress."

Rip's heart died away at hearing of these sad changes in his home and friends and finding himself thus alone in the world.

Every answer puzzled him, too, by treating of such enormous lapses of time, and of matters which he could not understand: war—Congress—Stony Point!—he had no courage to ask after any more friends, but cried out in despair, "Does nobody here know Rip Van Winkle?"

"Oh, Rip Van Winkle!" exclaimed two or three. "Oh, to be sure! that's Rip Van Winkle yonder, leaning against the tree."

Rip looked, and beheld a precise counterpart of himself as he went up the mountain; apparently as lazy, and certainly as ragged. The poor fellow was now completely confounded. He doubted his own identity, and whether he was himself or another man. In the midst of his bewilderment, the man in the cocked hat demanded who he was, and what was his name.

"God knows," exclaimed he at his wit's end. "I'm not myself —I'm somebody else—that's me yonder—no—that's somebody else, got into my shoes—I was myself last night, but I fell asleep on the mountain, and they've changed my gun, and everything's changed, and I'm changed, and I can't tell what's my name, or who I am!"

The bystanders began now to look at each other, nod, wink significantly, and tap their fingers against their foreheads. There was a whisper, also, about securing the gun, and keeping the old fellow from doing mischief; at the very suggestion of which, the self-important man with the cocked hat retired with some haste. At this critical moment a fresh comely woman passed through the throng to get a peep at the gray-bearded man. She had a chubby child in her arms, which, frightened at his looks, began to cry. "Hush, Rip," cried she, "hush, you little fool; the old man won't hurt you." The name of the child, the air of the mother, the tone of her voice, all awakened a train of recollections in his mind.

"What is your name, my good woman?" asked he.

"Judith Gardener," she replied.

"And your father's name?" continued Rip.

"Ah, poor man, his name was Rip Van Winkle; it's twenty years since he went away from home with his gun, and never has been heard of since—his dog came home without him; but whether he shot himself, or was carried away by the Indians, nobody can tell. I was then but a little girl."

Rip had but one more question to ask; but he put it with a faltering voice:

"Where's your mother?"

Oh, she, too, had died but a short time since: She broke a blood vessel in a fit of passion at a New England peddler.

There was a drop of comfort, at least, in this intelligence. The honest man could contain himself no longer. He caught his daughter and her child in his arms. "I am your father!" cried he—"Young Rip Van Winkle once—old Rip Van Winkle now—Does nobody know poor Rip Van Winkle!"

All stood amazed, until an old woman, tottering out from among the crowd, put her hand to her brow, and peering under it in his face for a moment, exclaimed, "Sure enough! it is Rip Van Winkle—it is himself. Welcome home again, old neighbor—Why, where have you been these twenty long years?"

Rip's story was soon told, for the whole twenty years had been to him but as one night. The neighbors stared when they heard it; some were seen to wink at each other and put their tongues in their cheeks; and the self-important man in the cocked hat, who, when the alarm was over, had returned to the field, screwed down the corners of his mouth and shook his head—upon which there was a general shaking of the head throughout the gathering.

It was decided, however, to get the opinion of old Peter Vanderdonk, who was seen slowly advancing up the road. He was a descendant of the historian of that name, who wrote one of the earliest accounts of the province. Peter was the most ancient inhabitant of the village and well versed in all the wonderful events and traditions of the neighborhood. He recollected Rip at once and corroborated [cuh-RAH-buh-ray-ted] his story in the most satisfactory manner. He assured the company that it was a fact, handed down from his ancestor the historian, that the Catskill Mountains had always been haunted by strange beings. That it was affirmed that the great Hendrick Hudson, the first discoverer of the river and country, kept a kind of vigil there every twenty years, with his crew of the *Half-Moon*, being permitted in this way to revisit the scenes of his enterprise, and keep a guardian eye upon the river and the great city called by his name. That his father had once seen them in their old Dutch dresses playing at ninepins in the hollow of the mountain; and that he himself had heard, one summer afternoon, the sound of their balls, like distant peals of thunder.

To make a long story short, the company broke up, and returned to the more important concerns of the election. Rip's daughter took him home to live with her; she had a snug, well-furnished house and a stout cheery farmer for a husband, whom Rip recollected for one of the urchins that used to climb upon his back. As to Rip's son and heir, who was the ditto of himself, seen leaning against the tree, he was employed to work on the farm, but showed a hereditary disposition to attend to anything else but his business.

Rip now resumed his old walks and habits; he soon found many of his former cronies, though all rather the worse for the wear and tear of time, and preferred making friends among the rising generation, with whom he soon grew into great favor.

Having nothing to do at home, and being arrived at that happy age when a man can do nothing with impunity [imm-PYOON-ih-tee], he took his place once more on the bench, at the inn door, and was treated with reverence as one of the sages of the village and a chronicle of the old times "before the war." It was some time before he could get into the regular track of gossip, or could be made to comprehend the strange events that had taken place during his sleep. How that there had been a revolutionary war—that the country had thrown off the yoke of old England—and that, instead of being a subject of His Majesty George the Third, he was now a free citizen of the United States. Rip, in fact, was no politician; the changes of states and empires made but little impression on him; but there was one species of despotism [DESS-puh-tizz-um] under which he had long groaned, and that was—petticoat government. Happily, that was at an end; he had got his neck out of the yoke of marriage and could go in and out whenever he pleased, without dreading the tyranny of Dame Van Winkle. Whenever her name was mentioned, however, he shook his head, shrugged his shoulders, and cast up his eyes; which might pass either for an expression of resignation to his fate, or joy at his deliverance.

He used to tell his story to every stranger that arrived at Mr.

Doolittle's hotel. He was observed, at first, to vary on some points every time he told it, which was doubtless owing to his having so recently awakened. It at last settled down precisely to the tale I have related, and not a man, woman, or child in the neighborhood but knew it by heart. Some always pretended to doubt the reality of it, and insisted that Rip had been out of his head, and that this was one point on which he always remained flighty. The old Dutch inhabitants, however, almost universally gave it full credit. Even to this day, they never hear a thunderstorm of a summer afternoon about the Catskills but they say Hendrick Hudson and his crew are at their game of ninepins; and it is a common wish of all henpecked husbands in the neighborhood when life hangs heavy on their hands that they might have a quieting drink out of Rip Van Winkle's flagon.

"Jim Baker's Bluejay Yarn"

from *A Tramp Abroad*
by
MARK TWAIN

About the story:

> *There are three selections by Mark Twain in this volume because his writings are so appropriate to oral reading. Twain had an ear for language and dialect, and many of his stories come most alive when told aloud, for it is then that one can appreciate the consummate storyteller plying his craft. If you and your children enjoy your sessions with Twain, and especially if you enjoy repro-ducing the dialect in which stories like the following one are written, you may be encouraged to try your hand at "The Notorious Jumping Frog of Calaveras County" and, perhaps, some other tales from his* **Sketches New and Old.**

Approximate reading time: 12 minutes
Pronunciation and vocabulary guide:

metaphor [MET-ah-for]: a figure of speech in which one idea is used to represent another

countenance: appearance

Yosemite [yo-SEMM-ih-tee]: a national park in Califor-nia

*A*nimals talk to each other, of course. There can be no question about that, but I suppose there are very few people who can understand them. I never knew but one man who could. I knew he could, however, because he told me so himself. He was a middle-aged, simple-hearted miner who had lived in a lonely corner of California among the woods and mountains a good many years, and had studied the ways of his only neighbors, the beasts and birds, until he be-lieved he could accurately translate any remark which they made. This was Jim Baker. According to Jim Baker, some animals have only a limited education and use only very simple words, and scarcely ever a comparison or flowery figure; whereas certain other animals have a large vocabulary, a fine command of language and a ready and fluent delivery; consequently these latter talk a great deal; they like it, they are conscious of their talent, and they enjoy "showing off." Baker said that after long and careful observation, he had come to the conclusion that the bluejays were the best talkers he had found among birds and beasts. Said he:

"There's more *to* a bluejay than any other creature. He has got more moods and more different kinds of feelings than other creatures; and, mind you, whatever a bluejay feels, he can put into language. And no mere commonplace language, either, but rattling, out-and-out book talk—and bristling with metaphor [MET-ah-for] too—just bristling! And as for command of language—why, you never see a bluejay get stuck for a word. No man ever did. They just boil out of him! And another thing: I've noticed a good deal and there's no bird, or cow, or anything that uses as good grammar as a bluejay. You may say a cat uses good grammar. Well, a cat does—but you let a cat get excited once; you let a cat get to pulling fur with another cat on a shed, nights, and you'll hear grammar that will give you the lockjaw. Ignorant people think it's the *noise* which fighting cats make that is so aggravating but it ain't so; it's the sickening grammar they use. Now I've never heard a jay use bad grammar but very seldom, and when they do, they are as ashamed as a human, they shut right down and leave.

"You may call a jay a bird. Well, so he is, in a measure—because he's got feathers on him, and don't belong to no church, perhaps, but otherwise he is just as much a human as you be. And I'll tell you for why. A jay's gifts and instincts and feelings and interests cover the whole ground. A jay hasn't got any more principle than a Congressman. A jay will lie, a jay will steal, a jay will deceive, a jay will betray; and four times out of five, a jay will go back on his solemnest promise. The sacredness of an obligation is a thing which you can't cram into no bluejay's head. Now on top of all this there's another thing, a jay can outswear any gentleman in the mines. You think a cat can swear. Well, a cat can, but you give a bluejay a subject that calls for his reserve-powers and where is your cat? Don't talk to *me*—I know too much about this thing. And there's yet another thing, in the one little particular of scolding—just good, clean, out-and-out scolding—a bluejay can lay over anything, human or divine. Yes, sir, a jay is everything that a man is. A jay can cry, a jay can laugh, a jay can feel shame, a jay can reason and plan and discuss, a jay likes gossip and scandal, a jay has got a sense of humor, a jay knows when he is an ass just as well as you do—maybe better. If a jay ain't human, he better take in his sign, that's all. Now I'm going to tell you a perfectly true fact about some bluejays.

"When I first begun to understand jay language correctly, there was a little incident happened here. Seven years ago, the last man in this region but me moved away. There stands his house—been empty ever since, a log house with a plank roof —just one big room and no more, no ceiling, nothing between the rafters and the floor. Well, one Sunday morning I was sitting out here in front of my cabin with my cat, taking the sun and looking at the blue hills and listening to the leaves rustling so lonely in the trees, and thinking of the home away yonder in the states that I hadn't heard from in thirteen years, when a bluejay lit on that house, with an acorn in his mouth, and says, 'Hello, I reckon I've struck something.' When he spoke the acorn dropped out of his mouth and rolled down the roof, of course, but he didn't care; his mind was all on the thing he had struck. It was a knothole in the roof. He cocked his head to one side, shut one eye and put the other one to the hole, like a possum looking down a jug, then he glanced up with his bright eyes, gave a wink or two with his wings— which signifies gratification, you understand—and says, 'It looks like a hole, it's located like a hole—blamed if I don't believe it *is* a hole!'

"Then he cocked his head down and took another look; he glances up perfectly joyful this time, winks his wings and his tail both, and says, 'Oh, no, this ain't no fat thing, I reckon! If I ain't in luck!—why, it's a perfectly elegant hole!' So he flew down and got that acorn and fetched it up and dropped it in, and was just tilting his head back with the heavenliest smile on his face, when all of a sudden he was paralyzed into a listening attitude and that smile faded gradually out of his countenance like breath off'n a razor, and the queerest look of surprise took its place. Then he says, 'Why, I didn't hear it fall!' He cocked his eye at the hole again and took a long look; raised up and shook his head; stepped around to the other side of the hole and took another look from that side; shook his head again. He studied awhile, then he just went into the *de*tails—walked round and round the hole and spied into it from every point of the compass. No use. Now he took a thinking attitude on the comb of the roof and scratched the back of his head with his right foot a minute, and finally says, 'Well, it's too many for *me*, that's certain; must be a mighty long hole; however, I ain't got no time to fool around here. I got to 'tend to business; I reckon it's all right—chance it anyway.'

"So he flew off and fetched another acorn and dropped it in, and tried to flirt his eye to the hole quick enough to see what become of it but he was too late. He held his eye there as much as a minute; then he raised up and sighed, and says, 'Confound it, I don't seem to understand this thing, no way; however, I'll tackle her again.' He fetched another acorn and done his level best to see what become of it, but he couldn't. He says, 'Well, *I* never struck no such a hole as this before; I'm of the opinion it's a totally new kind of a hole.' Then he begun to get mad. He held in for a spell, walking up and down the comb of the roof and shaking his head and muttering to himself; but his feelings got the upper hand of him presently and he broke loose and cussed himself black in the face. I never see a bird take on so about a little thing. When he got through he walks to the hole and looks in again for half a minute; then he says, 'Well, you're a long hole, and a deep hole, and a mighty singular hole altogether—but I've started in to fill you and I'm d——d if I *don't* fill you, if it takes a hundred years!'

"And with that, away he went. You never see a bird work so since you was born. He laid into his work like a slave and the way he hove acorns into that hole for about two hours and a half was one of the most exciting and astonishing spectacles I ever struck. He never stopped to take a look anymore—he just hove 'em in and went for more. Well, at last he could hardly flop his wings, he was so tuckered out. He comes a-drooping down, once more, sweating like an ice-pitcher, drops his acorn in and says, '*Now* I guess I've got the bulge on you by this time!' So he bent down for a look. If you'll believe me, when his head come up again he was just pale with rage. He says, 'I've shoveled acorns enough in there to keep the family thirty years, and if I can see a sign of one of 'em I wish I may land in a museum with a belly full of sawdust in two minutes.'

"He just had strength enough to crawl up onto the comb and lean his back agin the chimbly, and then he collected his impressions and begun to free his mind. I see in a second that what I had mistook for profanity in the mines was only just the rudiments, as you may say.

"Another jay was going by and heard him doing his devotions and stops to inquire what was up. The sufferer told him the whole circumstance, and says, 'Now yonder's the hole, and if you don't believe me, go an' look for yourself.' So this fellow went and looked and comes back and says, 'How many did you say you put in there?' 'Not any less than two tons,' says the sufferer. The other jay went and looked again. He couldn't seem to make it out, so he raised a yell and three more jays come. They all examined the hole, they all made the sufferer tell it over again, then they all discussed it and got off as many leather-headed opinions about it as an average crowd of humans could have done.

"They called in more jays; then more and more, till pretty soon this whole region 'peared to have a blue flush about it. There must have been five thousand of them, and such another jawing and disputing and ripping and cussing, you never heard. Every jay in the whole lot put his eye to the hole and delivered a more chuckle-headed opinion about the mystery than the jay that went there before him. They examined the house all over, too. The door was standing half open and at last one old jay happened to go and light on it and look in. Of course, that knocked the mystery galley-west in a second. There lay the acorns, scattered all over the floor. He flopped his wings and raised a whoop. 'Come here!' he says. 'Come here, everybody; hang'd if this fool hasn't been trying to fill up a house with acorns!' They all came a-swooping down like a blue cloud, and as each fellow lit on the door and took a glance, the whole absurdity of the contract that that first jay had tackled hit him home and he fell over backward suffocating with laughter, and the next jay took his place and done the same.

"Well, sir, they roosted around here on the housetop and the trees for an hour and guffawed over that thing like human beings. It ain't any use to tell me a bluejay hasn't got a sense of humor, because I know better. And memory, too. They brought jays here from all over the United States to look down that hole, every summer for three years. Other birds, too. And they could all see the point, except an owl that come from Nova Scotia to visit the Yosemite [yo-SEMM-ih-tee], and he took this thing in on his way back. He said he couldn't see anything funny in it. But then he was a good deal disappointed about Yosemite, too."

Listening Level III

(Ages 11 and up)

Here the suggested age range begins to break down with a crash, for what eleven-to-thirteen-year-old (or any teenager, for that matter) would not be entertained by the stories in the earlier section, and how many younger children would fail to marvel at the escapades of Sherlock Holmes? Few indeed. But the age range is a useful indicator of a story's length and intensity, for although children (and adults) who are significantly above the range will find the tales rewarding, those significantly below may see them as terrifying or boring—outcomes not to be wished for in either event.

If your older children are still enchanted with oral readings, you might try other classic novels, where the chapters provide a built-in continuity. They also may provide you the opportunity of experiencing firsthand some works you have only heard about up till now.

from *The Red Badge of Courage*

by
STEPHEN CRANE

About the story:

Stephen Crane wrote The Red Badge of Courage *when he was only twenty-two years old (he died at the age of thirty); he had never been in combat, or ever witnessed combat of any kind. Yet he produced a tale of war that vividly describes not only the battles on the field but the psychological battles that warriors face as well. In this excerpt, the hero, Henry Fleming—a recruit who is little more than a boy himself—is referred to only as "the youth"; he is facing his first test in battle, and he doesn't know whether he has the courage to stay and fight.*

Although the horrors of war are vividly pictured in The Red Badge of Courage, *the entire book makes for superb oral reading. Its rich imagery is conveyed in a vocabulary which, although instructive, frequently forces schoolchildren to scurry for the dictionary several times on each page, thereby denying them much of the beauty and the impact of the tale. Such stumblings are lessened when the child hears, rather than reads, the story, and the power and the terror of the tale are allowed to come through. Still, this is no work for youngsters, so if you intend to try your hand at the whole novel, do so with discretion.*

Approximate reading time: 16 minutes
Pronunciation and vocabulary guide:
   sober: plain, subdued
   primer [PRIMM-er]: a basic or elementary textbook
   discomfited: defeated in battle
   subtle [SUH-tull]: difficult to detect, not obvious
   careering: plunging headlong
   respite [RESS-pit]: a delay or postponement
   imprecations [imm-preh-KAY-shunz]: curses

monologue [MAH-no-log]: a long speech made by one
   person
incessant [inn-SESS-ant]: unceasing
prodigal [PRAHD-ih-gull]: wasteful, lavish
ruefully: inspiring pity or compassion
vindictive [vinn-DICK-tihv]: revengeful
debris [deh-BREE]: ruins, rubble
batteries: sets of guns or heavy artillery
oratorical [or-ah-TORR-ih-kul]: like a speech

*T*here were moments of waiting. The youth thought of
the village street at home before the arrival of the circus
parade on a day in the spring. He remembered how he
had stood, a small, thrillful boy, prepared to follow the dingy
lady upon the white horse, or the band in its faded chariot. He
saw the yellow road, the lines of expectant people, and the
sober houses. He particularly remembered an old fellow who
used to sit upon a cracker box in front of the store and feign to
despise such exhibitions. A thousand details of color and form
surged in his mind. The old fellow upon the cracker box appeared in middle prominence.

Someone cried, "Here they come!"

There was rustling and muttering among the men. They displayed a feverish desire to have every possible cartridge ready
to their hands. The boxes were pulled around into various
positions and adjusted with great care. It was as if seven
hundred new bonnets were being tried on.

The tall soldier, having prepared his rifle, produced a red
handkerchief of some kind. He was engaged in knitting it
about his throat with exquisite attention to its position, when
the cry was repeated up and down the line in a muffled roar of
sound.

"Here they come! Here they come!" Gunlocks clicked.

Across the smoke-infested fields came a brown swarm of
running men who were giving shrill yells. They came on,
stooping and swinging their rifles at all angles. A flag, tilted
forward, sped near the front.

As he caught sight of them the youth was momentarily startled by a thought that perhaps his gun was not loaded. He

stood trying to rally his faltering intellect so that he might recollect the moment when he had loaded, but he could not.

A hatless general pulled his dripping horse to a stand near the colonel of the 304th. He shook his fist in the other's face. "You've got to hold 'em back!" he shouted savagely; "you've got to hold 'em back!"

In his agitation the colonel began to stammer. "A-all r-right, General, all right, by Gawd! We-we'll do our—we-we'll d-d-do —do our best, General." The general made a passionate gesture and galloped away. The colonel, perchance to relieve his feelings, began to scold like a wet parrot. The youth, turning swiftly to make sure that the rear was unmolested, saw the commander regarding his men in a highly resentful manner, as if he regretted above everything his association with them.

The man at the youth's elbow was mumbling, as if to himself: "Oh, we're in for it now! oh, we're in for it now!"

The captain of the company had been pacing excitedly to and fro in the rear. He coaxed in schoolmistress fashion, as to a congregation of boys with primers [PRIMM-erz]. His talk was an endless repetition. "Reserve your fire, boys—don't shoot till I tell you—save your fire—wait till they get close up—don't be damned fools—"

Perspiration streamed down the youth's face, which was soiled like that of a weeping urchin. He frequently, with a nervous movement, wiped his eyes with his coat sleeve. His mouth was still a little way open.

He got the one glance at the foe-swarming field in front of him and instantly ceased to debate the question of his piece being loaded. Before he was ready to begin—before he had announced to himself that he was about to fight—he threw the obedient, well-balanced rifle into position and fired a first wild shot. Directly he was working at his weapon like an automatic affair.

He suddenly lost concern for himself and forgot to look at a menacing fate. He became not a man but a member. He felt that something of which he was a part—a regiment, an army, a cause, or a country—was in a crisis. He was welded into a common personality which was dominated by a single desire. For some moments he could not flee, no more than a little finger can commit a revolution from a hand.

If he had thought the regiment was about to be annihilated,

perhaps he could have amputated himself from it. But its noise gave him assurance. The regiment was like a firework that, once ignited, proceeds superior to circumstances until its blazing vitality fades. It wheezed and banged with a mighty power. He pictured the ground before it as strewn with the discomfited.

There was a consciousness always of the presence of his comrades about him. He felt the subtle [SUH-tull] battle brotherhood more potent even than the cause for which they were fighting. It was a mysterious fraternity born of the smoke and danger of death.

He was at a task. He was like a carpenter who has made many boxes, making still another box, only there was furious haste in his movements. He, in his thought, was careering off in other places, even as the carpenter who, as he works, whistles and thinks of his friend or enemy, his home, or a saloon. And these jolted dreams were never perfect to him afterward, but remained a mass of blurred shapes.

Presently he began to feel the effects of the war atmosphere —a blistering sweat, a sensation that his eyeballs were about to crack like hot stones. A burning roar filled his ears.

Following this came a red rage. He developed the acute exasperation of a pestered animal, a well-meaning cow worried by dogs. He had a mad feeling against his rifle, which could only be used against one life at a time. He wished to rush forward and strangle with his fingers. He craved a power that would enable him to have a world-sweeping gesture and brush all back. His impotency appeared to him and made his rage into that of a driven beast.

Buried in the smoke of many rifles his anger was directed not so much against the men whom he knew were rushing toward him as against the swirling battle phantoms which were choking him, stuffing their smoke robes down his parched throat. He fought frantically for respite [RESS-pit] for his senses, for air, as a babe being smothered attacks the deadly blankets.

There was a blare of heated rage mingled with a certain expression of intentness on all faces. Many of the men were making low-toned noises with their mouths, and these subdued cheers, snarls, imprecations [imm-preh-KAY-shunz], prayers, made a wild, barbaric song that went as an undercurrent of sound, strange and chantlike, with the resounding chords of the war march. The man at the youth's elbow was babbling. In it there was something soft and tender like the monologue [MAH-no-log] of a babe. The tall soldier was swearing in a loud voice. From his lips came a black procession of curious oaths. Suddenly another broke out in a complaining way, like a man who has mislaid his hat. "Well, why don't they support us? Why don't they send supports? Do they think—"

The youth in his battle sleep heard this as one who dozes hears.

There was a singular absence of heroic poses. The men bending and surging in their haste and rage were in every impossible attitude. The steel ramrods clanked and clanged with incessant [inn-SESS-ant] din as the men pounded them furiously into the hot rifle barrels. The flaps of the cartridge boxes were all unfastened and bobbed idiotically with each movement. The rifles, once loaded, were jerked to the shoulder and fired without apparent aim into the smoke or at one of the blurred and shifting forms which upon the field before the regiment had been growing larger and larger like puppets under a magician's hands.

The officers, at their intervals, rearward, neglected to stand in picturesque attitudes. They were bobbing to and fro roaring directions and encouragements. The dimensions of their howls were extraordinary. They expended their lungs with prodigal [PRAHD-ih-gull] wills. And often they nearly stood upon their heads in their anxiety to observe the enemy on the other side of the tumbling smoke.

The lieutenant of the youth's company had encountered a soldier who had fled screaming at the first volley of his comrades. Behind the lines these two were acting a little isolated scene. The man was blubbering and staring with sheeplike eyes at the lieutenant, who had seized him by the collar and was pounding him. He drove him back into the ranks with many blows. The soldier went mechanically, dully, with his animallike eyes upon the officer. Perhaps there was to him a divinity expressed in the voice of the other—stern, hard, with no reflection of fear in it. He tried to reload his gun, but his shaking hands prevented. The lieutenant was obliged to assist him.

The men dropped here and there like bundles.

The captain of the youth's company had been killed in an early part of the action. His body lay stretched out in the position of a tired man resting, but upon his face there was an astonished and sorrowful look, as if he thought some friend had done him an ill turn. The babbling man was grazed by a shot that made the blood stream widely down his face. He clasped both hands to his head. "Oh!" he said, and ran. Another grunted suddenly as if he had been struck by a club in the stomach. He sat down and gazed ruefully. In his eyes there was mute, indefinite reproach. Further up the line a man, standing behind a tree, had had his knee joint splintered by a ball. Immediately he had dropped his rifle and gripped the tree with both arms. And there he remained, clinging desperately and crying for assistance, that he might withdraw his hold upon the tree.

At last an exultant yell went along the quivering line. The firing dwindled from an uproar to a last vindictive [vinn-DICK-tihv] popping. As the smoke slowly eddied away, the youth saw that the charge had been repulsed. The enemy were scattered into reluctant groups. He saw a man climb to the top of the fence, straddle the rail, and fire a parting shot. The waves had receded, leaving bits of dark debris [deh-BREE] upon the ground.

Some in the regiment began to whoop frenziedly. Many were silent. Apparently they were trying to contemplate themselves.

After the fever had left his veins, the youth thought that at last he was going to suffocate. He became aware of the foul atmosphere in which he had been struggling. He was grimy and dripping like a laborer in a foundry. He grasped his canteen and took a long swallow of the warmed water.

A sentence with variations went up and down the line. "Well, we've helt 'em back. We've helt 'em back; derned if we haven't." The men said it blissfully, leering at each other with dirty smiles.

The youth turned to look behind him and off to the right and off to the left. He experienced the joy of a man who at last finds leisure in which to look about him.

Underfoot there were a few ghastly forms motionless. They lay twisted in fantastic contortions. Arms were bent and heads were turned in incredible ways. It seemed that the dead men must have fallen from some great height to get into such positions. They looked to be dumped out upon the ground from the sky.

From a position in the rear of the grove, a battery was throwing shells over it. The flash of the guns startled the youth at first. He thought they were aimed directly at him. Through the trees he watched the black figures of the gunners as they worked swiftly and intently. Their labor seemed a complicated thing. He wondered how they could remember its formula in the midst of confusion.

The guns squatted in a row like savage chiefs. They argued with abrupt violence. It was a grim powwow. Their busy servants ran hither and thither.

A small procession of wounded men were going drearily toward the rear. It was a flow of blood from the torn body of the brigade.

To the right and to the left were the dark lines of other troops. Far in front he thought he could see lighter masses protruding in points from the forest. They were suggestive of unnumbered thousands.

Once he saw a tiny battery go dashing along the line of the horizon. The tiny riders were beating the tiny horses.

From a sloping hill came the sounds of cheerings and clashes. Smoke welled slowly through the leaves.

Batteries were speaking with thunderous oratorical [or-ah-TORR-ih-kal] effort. Here and there were flags, the red in the stripes dominating. They splashed bits of warm color upon the dark lines of troops.

The youth felt the old thrill at the sight of the emblem. They were like beautiful birds strangely undaunted in a storm.

As he listened to the din from the hillside, to a deep pulsating thunder that came from afar to the left, and to the lesser clamors which came from many directions, it occurred to him that they were fighting, too, over there, and over there, and over there. Heretofore he had supposed that all the battle was directly under his nose.

As he gazed around him, the youth felt a flash of astonishment at the blue, pure sky and the sun gleaming on the trees and fields. It was surprising that Nature had gone tranquilly on with her golden process in the midst of so much devilment.

The youth awakened slowly. He came gradually back to a position from which he could regard himself. For moments he had been scrutinizing his person in a dazed way as if he had never before seen himself. Then he picked up his cap from the ground. He wriggled in his jacket to make a more comfortable fit, and kneeling, relaced his shoe. He thoughtfully mopped his reeking features.

So it was all over at last! The supreme trial had been passed. The red, formidable difficulties of war had been vanquished.

He went into an ecstasy of self-satisfaction. He had the most delightful sensations of his life. Standing as if apart from himself, he viewed that last scene. He perceived that the man who had fought thus was magnificent.

He felt that he was a fine fellow. He saw himself even with those ideals which he had considered as far beyond him. He smiled in deep gratification.

But, all of a sudden, cries of amazement broke out along the ranks of the new regiment. "Here they come ag'in! Here they come ag'in!"

"The Adventure of the Speckled Band"

by
SIR ARTHUR CONAN DOYLE

About the story:

Sir Arthur Conan Doyle was a practicing physician when he introduced Sherlock Holmes to the world in a book entitled A Study in Scarlet *in 1887. Subsequent stories about his detective hero proved so popular that when Doyle "killed" Holmes in* The Memoirs of Sherlock Holmes, *a public outcry forced him to bring him back. Doyle's next book,* The Hound of the Baskervilles, *found Sherlock Holmes alive and well.*

The figure of the tall, gaunt detective wearing a checkered deerstalker hat and smoking a large, curved pipe has become a classic, and has been brought to the movie screen by Basil Rathbone and others. In the tale that follows, your children will not only become acquainted with Mr. Holmes and his companion Dr. Watson but they will also be privy to the workings of a superior mind as it uses reason alone to defeat the forces of evil.

This tale, like most in the series, begins slowly, almost ploddingly, as the facts of the case are laid out. But when the action begins, it rushes headlong toward its eventual conclusion, and we are left in awe of Holmes's ability to ferret out the vital clues from what we thought was a mere tale of woe. So grab your magnifying glass, and let's be off!

Approximate reading time for Part One: 32 minutes
Pronunciation and vocabulary guide (for Part One):
   Surrey: a county in southern England
   dogcart: this open, horse-drawn carriage had its seat perched atop a large box, which held the hunters' dogs
   dissolute [DISS-uh-loot]: without morals

the days of the Regency: the period (1811–1820) when
King George III's insanity allowed his son to reign in
his place

morose [more-OSE]: gloomy, melancholy

a thousand pounds: a British pound used to equal five
U.S. dollars

parapet [PAIR-uh-pit]: a low wall at the edge of a roof
or bridge

fortnight: two weeks

livid [LIH-vihd]: discolored in a purplish or bluish hue

aperture [APP-er-chur]: an opening

gaiters: leggings; spats

Doctors' Commons: the offices in England where wills
are kept

O n glancing over my notes of the seventy-odd cases in
which I have during the last eight years studied the
methods of my friend Sherlock Holmes, I find many
tragic, some comic, a large number merely strange, but none
commonplace; for, working as he did rather for the love of his
art than for the acquirement of wealth, he refused to associate
himself with any investigation which did not tend toward the
unusual, and even the fantastic. Of all these varied cases, however, I cannot recall any which presented more singular features than that which was associated with the well-known
Surrey family of the Roylotts of Stoke Moran. The events in
question occurred in the early days of my association with
Holmes, when we were sharing rooms as bachelors in Baker
Street. It is possible that I might have placed them upon record
before, but a promise of secrecy was made at the time, from
which I have only been freed during the last month by the
untimely death of the lady to whom the pledge was given. It is
perhaps as well that the facts should now come to light, for I
have reasons to know that there are widespread rumors as to
the death of Dr. Grimesby Roylott which tend to make the
matter even more terrible than the truth.

It was early in April in the year 1883 that I woke one morning
to find Sherlock Holmes standing, fully dressed, by the side of

my bed. He was a late riser as a rule, and as the clock on the mantelpiece showed me that it was only a quarter past seven, I blinked up at him in some surprise, and perhaps just a little resentment, for I was myself regular in my habits.

"Very sorry to wake you up, Watson," said he, "but it's the common lot this morning. Mrs. Hudson has been awakened, she retorted upon me, and I on you."

"What is it, then—a fire?" I asked.

"No; a client. It seems that a young lady has arrived in a considerable state of excitement, who insists upon seeing me. She is waiting now in the sitting room. Now, when young ladies wander about the metropolis at this hour of the morning and wake sleepy people up out of their beds, I presume that it is something very pressing which they have to communicate. Should it prove to be an interesting case, you would, I am sure, wish to follow it from the outset. I thought, at any rate, that I should call you and give you the chance."

"My dear fellow, I would not miss it for anything."

I had no keener pleasure than in following Holmes in his professional investigations, and in admiring the rapid deductions, as swift as intuitions, and yet always founded on a logical basis, with which he unraveled the problems which were submitted to him. I rapidly threw on my clothes and was ready in a few minutes to accompany my friend down to the sitting room. A lady dressed in black and heavily veiled, who had been sitting in the window, rose as we entered.

"Good morning, madam," said Holmes, cheerily. "My name is Sherlock Holmes. This is my intimate friend and associate, Dr. Watson, before whom you can speak as freely as before myself. Ha! I am glad to see that Mrs. Hudson has had the good sense to light the fire. Pray draw up to it, and I shall order you a cup of hot coffee, for I observe that you are shivering."

"It is not cold which makes me shiver," said the woman, in a low voice, changing her seat as requested.

"What, then?" asked my companion.

"It is fear, Mr. Holmes. It is terror." She raised her veil as she spoke, and we could see that she was indeed in a pitiable state of agitation, her face all drawn and gray, with restless, frightened eyes, like those of some hunted animal. Her features and figure were those of a woman of thirty, but her hair was shot with premature gray, and her expression was weary and haggard. Sherlock Holmes ran her over with one of his quick, all-comprehensive glances.

"You must not fear," said he, soothingly, bending forward and patting her forearm. "We shall soon set matters right, I have no doubt. You have come in by train this morning, I see."

"You know me, then?" the lady asked.

"No," replied Holmes, "but I observe the second half of a return ticket in the palm of your left glove. You must have started early, and yet you had a good drive in a dogcart, along heavy roads, before you reached the station."

The lady gave a violent start and stared in bewilderment at my companion.

"There is no mystery, my dear madam," said he, smiling. "The left arm of your jacket is spattered with mud in no less than seven places. The marks are perfectly fresh. There is no vehicle but a dogcart which throws up mud in that way and then only when you sit on the lefthand side of the driver."

"Whatever your reasons may be, you are perfectly correct," said she. "I started from home before six, reached Leatherhead at twenty past, and came in by the first train to Waterloo. Sir, I can stand this strain no longer; I shall go mad if it continues. I have no one to turn to—none, save only one, who cares for me, and he, poor fellow, can be of little aid. I have heard of you, Mr. Holmes; I have heard of you from Mrs. Farintosh, whom you helped in the hour of her sore need. It was from her that I had your address. Oh, sir, do you not think that you could help me, too, and at least throw a little light through the dense darkness which surrounds me? At present it is out of my power to reward you for your services, but in a month or six weeks I shall be married, with the control of my own income, and then at least you shall not find me ungrateful."

Holmes turned to his desk and, unlocking it, drew out a small case-book, which he consulted.

"Farintosh," said he. "Ah, yes, I recall the case; it was concerned with an opal tiara. I think it was before your time, Watson. I can only say, madam, that I shall be happy to devote the same care to your case as I did to that of your friend. As to reward, my profession is its own reward; but you are at liberty to defray whatever expenses I may be put to, at the time which suits you best. And now I beg that you will lay before us everything that may help us in forming an opinion upon the matter."

"Alas!" replied our visitor, "the very horror of my situation lies in the fact that my fears are so vague, and my suspicions depend so entirely upon small points, which might seem trivial to another, that even he to whom of all others I have a right to look for help and advice looks upon all that I tell him about it as the fancies of a nervous woman. He does not say so, but I can read it from his soothing answers and averted eyes. But I have heard, Mr. Holmes, that you can see deeply into the manifold wickedness of the human heart. You may advise me how to walk amid the dangers which encompass me."

"I am all attention, madam."

"My name is Helen Stoner, and I am living with my step-father, who is the last survivor of one of the oldest Saxon families in England, the Roylotts of Stoke Moran, on the west-ern border of Surrey."

Holmes nodded his head. "The name is familiar to me," said he.

"The family was at one time among the richest in England, and the estates extended over the borders into Berkshire in the north and Hampshire in the west. In the last century, however, four successive heirs were of a dissolute [DISS-uh-loot] and wasteful disposition, and the family ruin was eventually com-pleted by a gambler in the days of the Regency. Nothing was left save a few acres of ground, and the two-hundred-year-old house, which is itself crushed under a heavy mortgage. The last squire dragged out his existence there, living the horrible life of an aristocratic pauper; but his only son, my stepfather, seeing that he must adapt himself to the new conditions, ob-tained an advance from a relative, which enabled him to take a medical degree, and went out to Calcutta, where, by his professional skill and his force of character, he established a large practice. In a fit of anger, however, caused by some rob-beries which had been perpetrated in the house, he beat his native butler to death and narrowly escaped a capital sentence. As it was, he suffered a long term of imprisonment, and after-ward returned to England a morose [more-OSE] and disap-pointed man.

"When Dr. Roylott was in India he married my mother, Mrs.

Stoner, the young widow of Major-General Stoner of the Bengal Artillery. My sister Julia and I were twins, and we were only two years old at the time of my mother's remarriage. She had a considerable sum of money—not less than a thousand pounds a year—and this she bequeathed to Dr. Roylott entirely while we resided with him, with a provision that a certain annual sum should be allowed to each of us in the event of our marriage. Shortly after our return to England my mother died —she was killed eight years ago in a railway accident near Crewe. Dr. Roylott then abandoned his attempts to establish himself in practice in London and took us to live with him in the old ancestral house at Stoke Moran. The money which my mother had left was enough for all our wants, and there seemed to be no obstacle to our happiness.

"But a terrible change came over our stepfather about this time. Instead of making friends and exchanging visits with our neighbors, who had at first been overjoyed to see a Roylott of Stoke Moran back in the old family seat, he shut himself up in his house and seldom came out save to indulge in ferocious quarrels with whoever might cross his path. Violence of temper approaching to mania has been hereditary in the men of the family, and in my stepfather's case it had, I believe, been intensified by his long residence in the tropics. A series of disgraceful brawls took place, two of which ended in the police court, until at last he became the terror of the village, and the folks would fly at his approach, for he is a man of immense strength, and absolutely uncontrollable in his anger.

"Last week he hurled the local blacksmith over a parapet [PAIR-uh-pit] into a stream, and it was only by paying over all the money which I could gather together that I was able to avert another public exposure. He had no friends at all save the wandering gypsies, and he would give these vagabonds leave to encamp upon the few acres of bramble-covered land which represent the family estate and would accept in return the hospitality of their tents, wandering away with them sometimes for weeks on end. He has a passion also for Indian animals, which are sent over to him by a correspondent, and he has at this moment a cheetah and a baboon, which wander freely over his grounds, and are feared by the villagers almost as much as their master.

"You can imagine from what I say that my poor sister Julia and I had no great pleasure in our lives. No servant would stay with us, and for a long time we did all the work of the house. She was but thirty at the time of her death, and yet her hair had already begun to whiten, even as mine has."

"Your sister is dead, then?" asked Holmes.

"She died just two years ago," replied Miss Stoner, "and it is of her death that I wish to speak to you. You can understand that, living the life which I have described, we were little likely to see anyone of our own age and position. We had, however, an aunt, my mother's maiden sister, Miss Honoria Westphail, who lives near Harrow, and we were occasionally allowed to pay short visits at this lady's house. Julia went there at Christmas two years ago and met there a half-pay major of marines, to whom she became engaged. My stepfather learned of the engagement when my sister returned and offered no objection to the marriage; but within a fortnight of the day which had been fixed for the wedding, the terrible event occurred which has deprived me of my only companion."

Sherlock Holmes had been leaning back in his chair with his eyes closed and his head sunk in a cushion, but he half opened his lids now and glanced across at his visitor.

"Pray be precise as to details," said he.

"It is easy for me to be so," she returned, "for every event of that dreadful time is seared into my memory. The manor house is, as I have already said, very old, and only one wing is now inhabited. The bedrooms in this wing are on the ground floor, the sitting rooms being in the central block of the buildings. Of these bedrooms the first is Dr. Roylott's, the second my sister's, and the third my own. There is no communication between them, but they all open out into the same corridor. Do I make myself plain?"

"Perfectly so." Holmes nodded.

She continued. "The windows of the three rooms open out upon the lawn. That fatal night Dr. Roylott had gone to his room early, though we knew that he had not retired to rest, for my sister was troubled by the smell of the strong Indian cigars which it was his custom to smoke. She left her room, therefore, and came into mine, where she sat for some time, chatting about her approaching wedding. At eleven o'clock she rose to leave me but she paused at the door and looked back.

" 'Tell me, Helen,' said she, 'have you ever heard anyone whistle in the dead of night?'

" 'Never,' said I.

" 'I suppose that you could not possibly whistle, yourself, in your sleep?'

" 'Certainly not. But why?' I asked.

" 'Because during the last few nights I have always, about three in the morning, heard a low, clear whistle. I am a light sleeper, and it has awakened me. I cannot tell where it came from—perhaps from the next room, perhaps from the lawn. I thought that I would just ask you whether you had heard it.'

" 'No, I have not,' I said. 'It must be those wretched gypsies in the plantation.'

" 'Very likely,' my sister replied. 'And yet if it were on the lawn, I wonder that you did not hear it also.'

" 'Ah, but I sleep more heavily than you,' I replied.

" 'Well, it is of no great consequence, at any rate.' She smiled back at me, closed my door, and a few moments later I heard her key turn in the lock."

"Indeed," said Holmes. "Was it your custom always to lock yourselves in at night?"

"Always," said our guest.

"And why?" asked Holmes.

"I think that I mentioned to you that the doctor kept a cheetah and a baboon," she replied. "We had no feeling of security unless our doors were locked."

"Quite so," Holmes said. "Pray proceed with your statement."

"I could not sleep that night. A vague feeling of impending misfortune impressed me. My sister and I, you will recollect, were twins, and you know how subtle are the links which bind two souls which are so closely allied. It was a wild night. The wind was howling outside, and the rain was beating and splashing against the windows. Suddenly, amid all the hubbub of the gale, there burst forth the wild scream of a terrified woman. I knew that it was my sister's voice. I sprang from my bed, wrapped a shawl round me, and rushed into the corridor. As I opened my door I seemed to hear a low whistle, such as my sister described, and a few moments later a clanging sound, as if a mass of metal had fallen. As I ran down the passage, my sister's door was unlocked and revolved slowly upon its hinges. I stared at it horror-stricken, not knowing what was about to issue from it. By the light of the corridor lamp I saw my sister appear at the opening, her face blanched with terror, her hands groping for help, her whole figure swaying to and fro like that of a drunkard. I ran to her and threw my arms round her, but at that moment her knees seemed to give way and she fell to the ground. She writhed as one who is in terrible pain, and her limbs were dreadfully convulsed. At first I thought that she had not recognized me, but as I bent over her she suddenly shrieked out in a voice which I shall never forget, 'Oh, my God! Helen! It was the band! The speckled band!' There was something else which she would fain have said, and she stabbed with her finger into the air in the direction of the doctor's room, but a fresh convulsion seized her and choked her words. I rushed out, calling loudly for my stepfather, and I met him hastening from his room in his dressing gown. When he reached my sister's side she was unconscious, and though he poured brandy down her throat and sent for medical aid from the village, all efforts were in vain, for she slowly sank and died without having recovered her consciousness. Such was the dreadful end of my beloved sister."

"One moment," said Holmes; "are you sure about this whistle and metallic sound? Could you swear to it?"

"That was what the county coroner asked me at the inquiry," said Miss Stoner. "It is my strong impression that I heard it, and yet, among the crash of the gale and the creaking of an old house, I may possibly have been deceived."

"Was your sister dressed?" Holmes inquired.

"No," the lady replied, "she was in her nightdress. In her right hand was found the charred stump of a match, and in her left a matchbox."

"Showing that she had struck a light and looked about her when the alarm took place," concluded Holmes. "That is important. And what conclusion did the coroner come to?"

"He investigated the case with great care, for Dr. Roylott's conduct had long been notorious in the county, but he was unable to find any satisfactory cause of death. My evidence showed that the door had been fastened upon the inner side, and the windows were blocked by old-fashioned shutters with broad iron bars, which were secured every night. The walls were carefully sounded and were shown to be quite solid all round, and the flooring was also thoroughly examined, with the same result. The chimney is wide, but is barred up by four large staples. It is certain, therefore, that my sister was quite alone when she met her end. Besides, there were no marks of any violence upon her."

"How about poison?" asked Sherlock Holmes.

"The doctors examined her for it, but without success," was the response.

"What do you think your unfortunate sister died of, then?"

"It is my belief," Miss Stoner replied, "that she died of pure fear and nervous shock, though what it was that frightened her I cannot imagine."

"Were there gypsies in the plantation at the time?" Holmes asked.

"Yes," she said, "there are nearly always some there."

"Ah," Holmes continued, as if on a scent, "and what did you gather from this allusion to a band—a speckled band?"

"Sometimes I have thought that it was merely the wild talk of delirium," she said, "sometimes that it may have referred to some band of people, perhaps to these very gypsies in the plantation. I do not know whether the spotted handkerchiefs which so many of them wear over their heads might have suggested the strange adjective which she used."

Holmes shook his head like a man who is far from being satisfied.

"These are very deep waters," said he; "pray go on with your narrative."

And so she did. "Two years have passed since then, and my life has been until lately lonelier than ever. A month ago, however, a dear friend, whom I have known for many years, has done me the honor to ask my hand in marriage. His name is Armitage—Percy Armitage—the second son of Mr. Armitage, of Crane Water, near Reading. My stepfather has offered no opposition to the match, and we are to be married in the course of the spring. Two days ago some repairs were started in the west wing of the building, and my bedroom wall has been pierced, so that I have had to move into the chamber in which my sister died, and to sleep in the very bed in which she slept. Imagine, then, my thrill of terror when last night, as I lay awake, thinking over her terrible fate, I suddenly heard in the silence of the night the low whistle which had been the herald of her own death. I sprang up and lit the lamp, but nothing was to be seen in the room. I was too shaken to go to bed again, however, so I dressed, and as soon as it was daylight I slipped down, got a dogcart at the Crown Inn, which is opposite, and drove to Leatherhead, whence I have come on this morning with the one object of seeing you and asking your advice."

"You have done wisely," said my friend. "But have you told me all?"

"Yes, all," she replied.

"Miss Roylott, you have not. You are screening your stepfather," said Holmes.

"Why, what do you mean?" she asked, somewhat startled.

For answer, Holmes pushed back the frill of black lace which fringed the hand that lay upon our visitor's knee. Five little livid [LIH-vihd] spots, the marks of four fingers and a thumb, were printed upon the white wrist.

"You have been cruelly used," said Holmes.

The lady colored deeply and covered over her injured wrist. "He is a hard man," she said, "and perhaps he hardly knows his own strength."

There was a long silence, during which Holmes leaned his chin upon his hands and stared into the crackling fire.

"This is a very deep business," he said, at last. "There are a thousand details which I should desire to know before I decide upon our course of action. Yet we have not a moment to lose. If we were to come to Stoke Moran today, would it be possible for us to see over these rooms without the knowledge of your stepfather?"

"As it happens," she replied, "he spoke of coming into town today upon some most important business. It is probable that he will be away all day, and that there would be nothing to disturb you. We have a housekeeper now, but she is old and foolish, and I could easily get her out of the way."

"Excellent. You are not averse to this trip, Watson?"

"By no means," I said.

"Then we shall both come. What are you going to do yourself?" Holmes asked, turning to Miss Stoner.

"I have one or two things which I would wish to do now that I am in town," she replied. "But I shall return by the twelve o'clock train, so as to be there in time for your coming."

Holmes nodded in agreement. "And you may expect us early in the afternoon. I have myself some small business matters to attend to. Will you not wait and breakfast?"

"No," she replied, "I must go. My heart is lightened already since I have confided my trouble to you. I shall look forward to seeing you again this afternoon." She dropped her thick black veil over her face and glided from the room.

"And what do you think of it all, Watson?" asked Sherlock Holmes, leaning back in his chair.

"It seems to me to be a most dark and sinister business," I said.

"Dark enough and sinister enough," replied Holmes.

"And yet," I continued, "if the lady is correct in saying that the flooring and walls are sound, and that the door, window, and chimney are impassable, then her sister must have been undoubtedly alone when she met her mysterious end."

"What do you make, then, of these nocturnal whistles, and what of the very peculiar words of the dying woman?" asked Holmes.

I had no explanation.

Holmes mused aloud over the facts that had just been related to him. "When you combine the ideas of whistles at night, the presence of a band of gypsies who are on intimate terms with this old doctor, the fact that we have every reason to believe that the doctor has an interest in preventing his stepdaughter's marriage, the dying allusion to a band, and, finally the fact that Miss Helen Stoner heard a metallic clang, which might have been caused by one of those metal bars which secured the shutters falling back into their place, I think that there is good ground to think that the mystery may be cleared along those lines."

"But what, then, did the gypsies do, Holmes?"

"I cannot imagine," he replied.

"I see many objections to any such theory," I responded.

"And so do I," Holmes agreed. "It is precisely for that reason that we are going to Stoke Moran this day. I want to see whether the objections are fatal, or if they may be explained away. But . . . what in the name of the devil!"

The exclamation had been drawn from my companion by the fact that our door had been suddenly dashed open, and that a huge man had framed himself in the aperture [APP-er-chur]. His costume was a peculiar mixture of the professional and of the agricultural, having a black top hat, a long frock coat, and a pair of high gaiters, with a hunting crop swinging in his hand. So tall was he that his hat actually brushed the crossbar of the doorway, and his breadth seemed to span it across from side to side. A large face, seared with a thousand wrinkles, burned yellow with the sun, and marked with every evil passion, was turned from one to the other of us, while his deep-set, bloodshot eyes, and his high, thin, fleshless nose, gave him somewhat the resemblance to a fierce old bird of prey.

"Which of you is Holmes?" asked this apparition.

"My name, sir; but you have the advantage of me," said my companion, quietly.

"I am Dr. Grimesby Roylott, of Stoke Moran."

"Indeed, doctor," said Holmes, blandly. "Pray take a seat."

"I will do nothing of the kind. My stepdaughter has been here. I have traced her. What has she been saying to you?"

"It is a little cold for the time of year," said Holmes.

"What has she been saying to you?" screamed the old man, furiously.

"But I have heard that the crocuses promise well," continued my companion, imperturbably.

"Ha! You put me off, do you?" said our new visitor, taking a step forward and shaking his hunting crop. "I know you, you scoundrel! I have heard of you before. You are Holmes, the meddler!"

My friend smiled.

"Holmes, the busybody!"

His smile broadened.

"Holmes, the Scotland Yard Jack-in-office!"

Holmes chuckled heartily. "Your conversation is most entertaining," said he. "When you go out close the door, for there is a decided draft."

"I will go when I have said my say. Don't you dare to meddle with my affairs. I know that Miss Stoner has been here. I traced her! I am a dangerous man to fall foul of! See here." He stepped swiftly forward, seized the poker that lay near the fireplace, and bent it into a curve with his huge brown hands.

"See that you keep yourself out of my grip," he snarled and, hurling the twisted poker to the floor, he strode out of the room.

"He seems a very amiable person," said Holmes, laughing. "I am not quite so bulky, but if he had remained I might have shown him that my grip was not much more feeble than his own." As he spoke he picked up the steel poker, and with a sudden effort straightened it out again.

"Fancy his having the insolence to confuse me with the official detective force! This incident gives zest to our investigation, however, and I only trust that our little friend will not suffer from her imprudence in allowing this brute to trace her. And now, Watson, we shall order breakfast, and afterward I shall walk down to Doctors' Commons, where I hope to get some data which may help us in this matter."

It was nearly one o'clock when Sherlock Holmes returned from his excursion. He held in his hand a sheet of blue paper, scrawled over with notes and figures.

"I have seen the will of the deceased wife," said he. "To determine its exact meaning I have been obliged to work out the present prices of the investments with which it is concerned. The total income, which at the time of the wife's death was little short of eleven hundred pounds, is now, through the fall in agricultural prices, not more than seven hundred and fifty. Each daughter can claim an income of two hundred and fifty pounds, in case of marriage. It is evident, therefore, that if both girls had married, this beauty would have had a mere pittance, while even one of them would cripple him to a very serious extent. My morning's work has not been wasted, since it has proved that he has the very strongest motives for standing in the way of anything of the sort. And now, Watson, this is too serious for dawdling, especially as the old man is aware that we are interesting ourselves in his affairs; so if you are ready, we shall call a cab and drive to Waterloo. I should be very much obliged if you would slip your revolver into your pocket. An Eley's No. 2 is an excellent argument with gentlemen who can twist steel pokers into knots. That and a tooth-brush are, I think, all that we need."

Approximate reading time for Part Two: 30 minutes
Pronunciation and vocabulary guide (for Part Two):
   queried [QUEER-eed]: asked, inquired
   tangible [TAN-jib-uhl]: capable of being touched

At Waterloo we were fortunate in catching a train for Leath-erhead, where we hired a carriage at the station inn, and drove for four or five miles through the lovely Surrey lanes. It was a perfect day, with a bright sun and a few fleecy clouds in the heavens. The trees and wayside hedges were just throwing out their first green shoots, and the air was full of the pleasant smell of the moist earth. To me at least there was a strange contrast between the sweet promise of the spring and this sin-ister quest upon which we were engaged. My companion sat in the front of the carriage, his arms folded, his hat pulled down over his eyes, and his chin sunk upon his breast, buried in the deepest thought. Suddenly, however, he started, tapped me on the shoulder, and pointed over the meadows.

"Look there!" said he.

A heavily timbered park stretched up in a gentle slope, thick-ening into a grove at the highest point. From amid the branches there jutted out the gray gables and high roof-tree of a very old mansion.

"Stoke Moran?" said he.

"Yes, sir, that be the house of Dr. Grimesby Roylott," re-marked the driver.

"There is some building going on there," said Holmes; "that is where we are going."

"There's the village," said the driver, pointing to a cluster of roofs some distance to the left, "but if you want to get to the house, you'll find it shorter to hop this fence and follow the footpath over the fields. There it is, where the lady is walking."

"And the lady, I fancy, is Miss Stoner," observed Holmes,

shading his eyes. "Yes, I think we had better do as you suggest."

We got off, paid our fare, and the carriage rattled back on its way to Leatherhead.

"I thought it as well," said Holmes, as we climbed the fence, "that this fellow should think we had come here as architects, or on some definite business. It may stop his gossip. Good afternoon, Miss Stoner. You see that we have been as good as our word."

Our client of the morning had hurried forward to meet us with a face which spoke her joy. "I have been waiting so eagerly for you," she cried, shaking hands with us warmly. "All has turned out splendidly. Dr. Roylott has gone to town, and it is unlikely that he will be back before evening."

"We have had the pleasure of making the doctor's acquaintance," said Holmes, and in a few words he sketched out what had occurred. Miss Stoner turned white to the lips as she listened.

"Good heavens!" she cried. "He has followed me, then. He is so cunning that I never know when I am safe from him. What will he say when he returns?"

"He must guard himself," said Holmes, "for he may find that there is someone more cunning than himself upon his track. You must lock yourself up from him tonight. If he is violent, we shall take you away to your aunt's at Harrow. Now, we must make the best use of our time, so kindly take us at once to the rooms which we are to examine."

The building was of gray, moss-covered stone, with a high central portion, and two curving wings, like the claws of a crab, thrown out on each side. In one of these wings the windows were broken, and blocked with wooden boards, while the roof was partly caved in, a picture of ruin. The central portion was in little better repair, but the right-hand block was comparatively modern, and the blinds in the windows, with the blue smoke curling up from the chimneys, showed that this was where the family resided. Some scaffolding had been erected against the end wall, and the stonework had been broken into, but there were no signs of any workmen at the moment of our visit. Holmes walked slowly up and down the ill-trimmed lawn, and examined with deep attention the outsides of the windows.

"This window, I take it, belongs to the room in which you used to sleep, the center one to your sister's, and the one next to the main building to Dr. Roylott's chamber?"

"Exactly so," replied Miss Stoner. "But I am now sleeping in the middle one."

"Pending the alterations, as I understand," said Holmes. "By the way, there does not seem to be any very pressing need for repairs at that end wall."

"There were none. I believe that it was an excuse to move me from my room," she replied.

Holmes brightened. "Ah! that is suggestive. Now, on the other side of this narrow wing runs the corridor from which their three rooms open. There are windows in it, of course?"

"Yes, but very small ones," she responded. "Too narrow for anyone to pass through."

"And because you both locked your doors at night, your rooms were unapproachable from that side. Now, would you have the kindness to go into your room and bar your shutters."

Miss Stoner did so, and Holmes, after a careful examination through the open window, endeavored in every way to force the shutter open, but without success. There was no slit through which a knife could be passed to raise the bar. Then with his magnifying glass he studied the hinges, but they were of solid iron, built firmly into the massive masonry. "Hmm!" said he, scratching his chin in some perplexity. "My theory certainly presents some difficulties. No one could pass these shutters if they were bolted. Well, we shall see if the inside throws any light upon the matter."

A small side door led into the whitewashed corridor from which the three bedrooms opened. Holmes refused to examine the third chamber, so we passed at once to the second, that in which Miss Stoner was now sleeping, and in which her sister had met with her fate. It was a homely little room, with a low ceiling and a gaping fireplace, after the fashion of old country houses. A brown chest of drawers stood in one corner, a narrow bed in another, and a dressing table on the left-hand side of the window. These articles, with two small wickerwork chairs, made up all the furniture in the room, save for a square of carpet in the center. The paneling and woodwork were brown, worm-eaten oak, so old and discolored that it may have dated from the original building of the house. Holmes drew one of the chairs into a corner and sat silent, taking in every detail of the apartment.

"Where does that bell communicate with?" he asked, at last, pointing to a thick bell-rope which hung down beside the bed, the tassel actually lying upon the pillow.

"It goes to the housekeeper's room," our client replied.

"It looks newer than the other things," observed Holmes.

"Yes," she confirmed, "it was only put there a couple of years ago."

"Your sister asked for it, I suppose?" Holmes queried [QUEER-eed].

"No, I never heard of her using it. We used always to get what we wanted for ourselves."

"Indeed," mused Holmes, "it seemed unnecessary to put a bellpull there. You will excuse me for a few minutes while I satisfy myself as to this floor." He threw himself down upon his face with his glass in hand, and crawled swiftly backward and forward, examining minutely the cracks between the boards. Then he did the same with the woodwork with which the chamber was paneled. Finally he walked over to the bed, and spent some time in staring at it, and in running his eye up and down the wall. Then he took the bell-rope in his hand and gave it a brisk tug.

"Why, it's a fake," said he.

"Won't it ring?" Miss Stoner asked.

"No, it is not even attached to a wire. This is very interesting. You can see now that it is fastened to a hook just above where the little opening for the ventilator is."

"How very absurd!" she said. "I never noticed that before."

"Very strange!" muttered Holmes, pulling at the rope. "There are one or two very singular points about this room. For example, what a fool a builder must be to open a ventilator into another room, when, with the same trouble, he might have drawn upon the outside air!"

"The ventilator is also a rather recent addition," said the lady.

"Done about the same time as the bell-rope?" remarked Holmes.

"Yes, there were several little changes carried out about that time," she replied.

"They seem to have been of a most interesting character— dummy bell-ropes, and ventilators which do not ventilate. With your permission, Miss Stoner, we shall now carry our researches into the inner apartment."

Dr. Grimesby Roylott's chamber was larger than that of his stepdaughter, but was as plainly furnished. A camp bed, a small wooden shelf full of books, mostly of a technical character, an armchair beside the bed, a plain wooden chair against the wall, a round table, and a large iron safe were the principal things which met the eye. Holmes walked slowly round and examined each and all of them with the keenest interest.

"What's in here?" he asked, tapping the safe.

"My stepfather's business papers," she replied.

"Oh! you have seen inside, then?"

"Only once, some years ago," she answered. "I remember that it was full of papers."

"There isn't a cat in it, for example?" Holmes inquired.

"No. What would give you such a strange idea?"

"Well, look at this." He took up a small saucer of milk which stood on the top of it.

"No; we don't keep a cat," she assured him. "But there is a cheetah and a baboon."

"Ah, yes, of course!" Holmes nodded. "Well, a cheetah is just a big cat, and yet a saucer of milk would not go very far in satisfying its wants, I dare say. There is one point which I should wish to determine." He squatted down in front of the wooden chair, and examined the seat of it with the greatest attention.

"Thank you. That is quite settled," said he, rising and putting his magnifying lens in his pocket. "Hello! Here is something interesting!"

The object that had caught his eye was a small dog leash on one corner of the bed. The leash, however, was curled upon itself, and tied so as to make a loop at one end.

"What do you make of that, Watson?"

"It's a common enough leash," I responded. "But I don't know why it should be tied."

"That is not quite so common, is it?" said Holmes. "Ah, me! it's a wicked world, and when a clever man turns his brains to crime it is the worst of all. I think that I have seen enough now, Miss Stoner, and with your permission we shall walk out upon the lawn."

I had never seen my friend's face so grim or his brow so dark as it was when we turned from the scene of his investigation. We had walked several times up and down the lawn, neither Miss Stoner nor myself liking to break in upon his thoughts before he roused himself from his reverie.

"It is very essential, Miss Stoner," said he, "that you should absolutely follow my advice in every respect."

"I shall most certainly do so," she replied.

"The matter is too serious for any hesitation. Your life may depend upon your compliance."

"I assure you, Mr. Holmes, that I am completely in your hands."

"Very well," said Holmes. "First of all, both my friend and I must spend the night in your room."

We gazed at him in astonishment.

"Yes, it must be so," he continued. "Let me explain. I believe that that is the village inn over there?"

"Yes, it is called the Crown," said Miss Stoner.

"Very good. Your windows would be visible from there?"

"Why, certainly," she replied.

"You must confine yourself to your room, on pretense of a headache, when your stepfather comes back. Then when you hear him retire for the night, you must open the shutters of your window, undo the hasp, put your lamp there as a signal to us, and then withdraw quietly with everything which you are likely to want into the room which you used to occupy. I have no doubt that, in spite of the repairs, you could manage there for one night."

"Oh, yes, I could manage easily," she said.

"The rest you will leave in our hands," Holmes insisted.

"But what will you do?" she asked.

"We shall spend the night in your room, and we shall investigate the cause of this noise which has disturbed you."

"I believe, Mr. Holmes, that you have already made up your mind," said Miss Stoner, laying her hand upon my companion's sleeve.

"Perhaps I have," he replied.

"Then for pity's sake tell me what was the cause of my sister's death."

But Holmes would not comply. "I should prefer to have clearer proofs before I speak."

Still the lady persisted. "You can at least tell me whether my own thought is correct, and if she died from some sudden fright."

"No, I do not think so," said Holmes. "I think that there was probably some more tangible [TAN-jib-uhl] cause. And now, Miss Stoner, we must leave you, for if Dr. Roylott returned and saw us, our journey would be in vain. Goodbye, and be brave, for if you will do what I have told you, you may rest assured that we shall soon drive away the dangers that threaten you."

Sherlock Holmes and I had no difficulty in engaging a bedroom and sitting room at the Crown Inn. They were on the upper floor, and from our window we could command a view of the avenue gate, and of the inhabited wing of Stoke Moran Manor House. At dusk we saw Dr. Grimesby Roylott drive past, his huge form looming up beside the little figure of the lad who drove him. The boy had some slight difficulty in undoing the heavy iron gates, and we heard the hoarse roar of the doctor's voice, and saw the fury with which he shook his clenched fists at him. The carriage drove on, and a few minutes later we saw a sudden light spring up among the trees as the lamp was lit in one of the sitting rooms.

"Do you know, Watson," said Holmes, as we sat together in the gathering darkness, "I have really some scruples as to taking you tonight. There is a distinct element of danger."

"Can I be of assistance?" I asked.

"Your presence might be invaluable," Holmes answered.

"Then I shall certainly come. You speak of danger, and so you have evidently seen more in those rooms than was visible to me."

"No," he replied, "but I fancy that I may have deduced a little more. I imagine that you saw all that I did."

"But I saw nothing remarkable except the bell-rope, and what purpose that could have I confess is more than I can imagine."

"You saw the ventilator, too?" he asked.

"Yes, but I do not think it is such a very unusual thing to

have a small opening between two rooms. It was so small that a rat could hardly pass through."

"I knew that we should find a ventilator before we even came to Stoke Moran," said my companion.

"My dear Holmes!" I exclaimed somewhat doubtingly.

"Oh, yes, I did. You remember in her statement she said that her sister could smell Dr. Roylott's cigar. Now, of course that suggested at once that there must be a passage between the two rooms. It could only be a small one, or it would have been remarked upon at the coroner's inquiry. I deduced a ventilator."

"But what harm can there be in that?" I asked.

"Well, there is at least a curious coincidence of dates. A ventilator is made, a cord is hung, and a lady who sleeps in the bed dies. Does not that strike you?"

"I cannot as yet see any connection," I replied.

"Did you observe anything very peculiar about that bed?" he asked.

"No," said I.

"It was clamped to the floor. Did you ever see a bed fastened like that before?"

"I cannot say that I have," I said, somewhat puzzled.

"The lady could not move her bed," he continued. "It must always be in the same relative position to the ventilator and to the rope—for so we may call it, since it was clearly never meant for a bellpull."

"Holmes," I cried, "I seem to see dimly what you are hinting at. We are only just in time to prevent some subtle and horrible crime."

"Subtle and horrible, to be sure," he returned. "When a doctor does go wrong, he is the best of criminals. He has nerve and he has knowledge. Yes, Watson, we shall have horrors enough before this night is over; for goodness' sake let us have a quiet pipe, and turn our minds for a few hours to something more cheerful."

About nine o'clock the light among the trees was extinguished, and all was dark in the direction of the Manor House. Two hours passed slowly away, and then, suddenly, just at the stroke of eleven, a single bright light shone out right in front of us.

"That is our signal," said Holmes, springing to his feet; "it comes from the middle window."

As we went out, he exchanged a few words with the inn-keeper, explaining that we were going on a late visit to an acquaintance, and that it was possible that we might spend the night there. A moment later we were out on the dark road, a chill wind blowing in our faces, and one yellow light twinkling in front of us to guide us on our somber errand.

Making our way among the trees, we reached the lawn, crossed it, and were about to enter through the window, when out from a clump of laurel bushes there darted what seemed to be a hideous and distorted child, who threw itself upon the grass with writhing limbs, and then ran swiftly across the lawn into the darkness.

"My God!" I whispered. "Did you see it?"

Holmes was for the moment as startled as I. His hand closed like a vise upon my wrist in his agitation. Then he broke into a low laugh, and put his lips to my ear.

"That is the baboon," he murmured.

I had forgotten the strange pets which the doctor kept. There was a cheetah, too; perhaps we might find it upon our shoulders at any moment. I confess that I felt easier in my mind when, after following Holmes's example and slipping off my shoes, I found myself inside the bedroom. My companion noiselessly closed the shutters, moved the lamp onto the table, and cast his eyes round the room. All was as we had seen it in the daytime. Then creeping up to me and making a trumpet of his hand, he whispered into my ear again so gently that it was all that I could do to distinguish the words.

"The least sound would be fatal to our plans."

I nodded to show that I had heard.

"We must sit without light," he breathed, almost inaudibly. "Dr. Roylott would see it through the ventilator."

I nodded again.

"Do not go asleep; your very life may depend upon it. Have your pistol ready in case we should need it. I will sit on the side of the bed, and you in that chair."

I took out my revolver and laid it on the corner of the table.

Holmes had brought along a long, thin cane, and this he placed upon the bed beside him. By it he laid the box of matches and the stump of a candle. Then he turned down the lamp, and we were left in darkness.

How shall I ever forget that dreadful vigil? I could not hear a sound, not even the drawing of a breath, and yet I knew that my companion sat open-eyed, within a few feet of me, in the same state of nervous tension in which I was myself. The shutters cut off the least ray of light, and we waited in absolute darkness. From outside came the occasional cry of a night bird, and once at our very window a long, drawn, catlike whine, which told us that the cheetah was indeed at liberty. Far away we could hear the deep tones of the parish clock, which boomed out every quarter of an hour. How long they seemed, those quarters! Twelve struck, and one and two and three, and still we sat waiting silently for whatever might befall.

Suddenly there was the momentary gleam of a light up in the direction of the ventilator, which vanished immediately, but was succeeded by a strong smell of burning oil and heated metal. Someone in the next room had lit a lantern. I heard a gentle sound of movement, and then all was silent once more, though the smell grew stronger. For half an hour I sat with straining ears. Then suddenly another sound became audible —a very gentle, soothing sound, like that of a small jet of steam escaping continually from a kettle. The instant that we heard it, Holmes sprang from the bed, struck a match, and lashed furiously with his cane at the bellpull.

"You see it, Watson?" he yelled. "You see it?"

But I saw nothing. At the moment when Holmes struck the light I heard a low, clear whistle, but the sudden glare flashing into my weary eyes made it impossible for me to tell what it was at which my friend lashed so savagely. I could, however, see that his face was deadly pale, and filled with horror and loathing.

He had ceased to strike, and was gazing up at the ventilator, when suddenly there broke from the silence of the night the most horrible cry to which I have ever listened. It swelled up louder and louder, a hoarse yell of pain and fear and anger all mingled in the one dreadful shriek. They say that away down in the village, and even in the distant parsonage, that cry raised the sleepers from their beds. It struck cold to our hearts, and I stood gazing at Holmes, and he at me, until the last echoes of it had died away into the silence from which it rose.

"What can it mean?" I gasped.

"It means that it is all over," Holmes answered. "And perhaps, after all, it is for the best. Take your pistol, and we will enter Dr. Roylott's room."

With a grave face he lit the lamp and led the way down the corridor. Twice he struck at the chamber door without any reply from within. Then he turned the handle and entered, I at his heels, with the cocked pistol in my hand.

It was a singular sight which met our eyes. On the table stood a lantern with the shutter half open, throwing a brilliant beam of light upon the iron safe, the door of which was ajar. Beside this table, on the wooden chair, sat Dr. Grimesby Roylott, clad in a long gray dressing gown, his bare ankles protruding beneath, and his feet thrust into red Turkish slippers. Across his lap lay the dog leash which we had noticed during the day. His chin was cocked upward and his eyes were fixed in a dreadful, rigid stare at the corner of the ceiling. Round his brow he had a peculiar yellow band, with brownish speckles, which seemed to be bound tightly round his head. As we entered he made neither sound nor motion.

"The band! The speckled band!" whispered Holmes.

I took a step forward. In an instant his strange headgear began to move, and there reared itself from among his hair the squat diamond-shaped head and puffed neck of a loathsome serpent.

"It is a swamp adder!" cried Holmes. "The deadliest snake in India. He has died within ten seconds of being bitten. Violence does, in truth, recoil upon the violent, and the schemer falls into the pit which he digs for another. Let us thrust this creature back into its den, and we can then remove Miss Stoner to some place of shelter, and let the county police know what has happened."

As he spoke he drew the dog leash swiftly from the dead man's lap, and throwing the noose round the reptile's neck, he drew it from its horrid perch, and threw it into the iron safe, which he closed upon it.

Such are the true facts of the death of Dr. Grimesby Roylott, of Stoke Moran. It is not necessary that I should prolong a narrative which has already run to too great a length, by telling how we broke the sad news to the terrified girl, how we conveyed her by the morning train to the care of her good aunt at

Harrow, of how the slow process of official inquiry came to the conclusion that the doctor met his fate while indiscreetly playing with a dangerous pet. The little which I had yet to learn of the case was told me by Sherlock Holmes as we traveled back the next day.

"I had," said he, "come to an entirely erroneous conclusion, which shows, my dear Watson, how dangerous it always is to reason from insufficient data. The presence of the gypsies, and the use of the word 'band,' which was used by the poor girl, no doubt to explain the appearance which she had caught a hurried glimpse of by the light of her match, were sufficient to put me upon an entirely wrong scent. I can only claim the merit that I instantly reconsidered my position when, however, it became clear to me that whatever danger threatened an occupant of the room could not come either from the window or the door. My attention was speedily drawn, as I have already remarked to you, to this ventilator, and to the bell-rope which hung down to the bed. The discovery that this was a dummy, and that the bed was clamped to the floor, instantly gave rise to the suspicion that the rope was there as a bridge for something passing through the hole, and coming to the bed. The idea of a snake instantly occurred to me, and when I coupled it with my knowledge that the doctor was furnished with a supply of creatures from India, I felt that I was probably on the right track. The idea of using a form of poison which could not possibly be discovered by any chemical test was just such a one as would occur to a clever and ruthless man who had had an Eastern training. The rapidity with which such a poison would take effect would also, from his point of view, be an advantage. It would be a sharp-eyed coroner, indeed, who could distinguish the two little dark punctures which would show where the poison fangs had done their work. Then I thought of the whistle. Of course he must recall the snake before the morning light revealed it to the victim. He had trained it, probably by the use of the milk which we saw, to return to him when summoned. He would put it through this ventilator at the hour that he thought best, with the certainty that it would crawl down the rope and land on the bed. It might or might not bite the occupant; perhaps she might escape every night for a week, but sooner or later she must fall victim.

"I had come to these conclusions before ever I had entered his room. An inspection of his chair showed me that he had been in the habit of standing on it, which of course would be necessary in order that he should reach the ventilator. The sight of the safe, the saucer of milk, and the loop of the leash were enough to finally dispel any doubts which may have remained. The metallic clang heard by Miss Stoner was obviously caused by her stepfather hastily closing the door of his safe upon its terrible occupant. Having once made up my mind, you know the steps which I took in order to put the matter to the proof. I heard the creature hiss, and I have no doubt that you did also, and I instantly lit the light and attacked it."

"With the result of driving it through the ventilator," I suggested.

"Correct, Watson. And also with the result of causing it to turn upon its master on the other side. Some of the blows of my cane came home, and roused its snakish temper, so that it flew upon the first person it saw. In this way I am no doubt indirectly responsible for Dr. Grimesby Roylott's death, and I cannot say that it is likely to weigh very heavily upon my conscience."

from *The Adventures of Huckleberry Finn*

by
MARK TWAIN

About the story:

>Huckleberry Finn *can be read and studied on several levels. Even if it is thought of as merely the tale of an uneducated, but crafty, Mississippi River boy who runs away and aids a black slave to do the same, it is full of rich description, colorful dialect, and exciting action.*
>
>*In this section, Huck describes a visit to a rustic river town, and a shooting that provokes the townsfolk into forming a lynch mob. High adventure for any young lad, to be sure, but Huck—and the reader—are also privileged to see one man stand up to the mob and denounce them for what they are. Here we see Twain's contempt for cowards in general and the all-too-common vigilantes of the day in particular.*
>
>*Perhaps your child has seen someone incite a group to take an action that the leader has not the courage to take alone. Or, perhaps your child may recall this tale when a similar situation happens in the future.*

Approximate reading time: 16 minutes

Pronunciation and vocabulary guide:

>**blackguarding** [BLAGG-ard-ing]: using foul and abusing language
>
>**palings** [PAY-lings]: a fence of pickets

All the streets and lanes was just mud; they warn't nothing else *but* mud—mud as black as tar and nigh about a foot deep in some places, and two or three inches deep in *all* places. The hogs loafed and grunted around everywheres. You'd see a muddy sow and a litter of pigs come lazying along the street and whollop herself right down in the way, where folks had to walk around her, and she'd stretch out and shut her eyes and wave her ears whilst the pigs was milking her and look as happy as if she was on salary. And pretty soon you'd hear a loafer sing out, "Hi! *so* boy! sick him, Tige!" and away the sow would go, squealing most horrible, with a dog or two swinging to each ear and three or four dozen more a-coming, and then you would see all the loafers get up and watch the thing out of sight and laugh at the fun and look grateful for the noise. Then they'd settle back again till there was a dogfight. There couldn't anything wake them up all over and make them happy all over, like a dogfight—unless it might be putting turpentine on a stray dog and setting fire to him, or tying a tin pan to his tail and see him run himself to death.

On the riverfront some of the houses was sticking out over the bank, and they was bowed and bent and about ready to tumble in. The people had moved out of them. The bank was caved away under one corner of some others, and that corner was hanging over. People lived in them yet but it was danger-some, because sometimes a strip of land as wide as a house caves in at a time. Sometimes a belt of land a quarter of a mile deep will start in and cave along and cave along till it all caves into the river in one summer. Such a town as that has to be always moving back, and back, and back, because the river's always gnawing at it.

The nearer it got to noon that day the thicker and thicker was the wagons and horses in the streets, and more coming all the time. Families fetched their dinners with them frcm the country and eat them in the wagons. There was considerable whisky-drinking going on and I seen three fights. By and by somebody sings out, "Here comes old Boggs!—in from the country for his little old monthly drunk; here he comes, boys!"

All the loafers look glad; I reckoned they was used to having fun out of Boggs. One of them says, "Wonder who he's a-gwyne to chaw up this time. If he'd a-chawed up all the men he's ben a-gwyne to chaw up in the last twenty year he'd have considerable ruputation now."

Another one says, "I wisht old Boggs'd threaten me, 'cuz then I'd know I warn't gwyne to die for a thousan' year."

Boggs comes a-tearing along on his horse, whooping and

yelling like an Injun and singing out, "Cler the track, thar. I'm on the waw-path and the price uv coffins is a-gwyne to raise."

He was drunk and weaving about in his saddle; he was over fifty year old and had a very red face. Everybody yelled at him and laughed at him and sassed him, and he sassed back and said he'd attend to them and lay them out in their regular turns, but he couldn't wait now because he'd come to town to kill old Colonel Sherburn and his motto was, "Meat first and spoon vittles to top off on."

He see me and rode up and says, "Whar'd you come f'm, boy? You prepared to die?"

Then he rode on. I was scared but a man says, "He don't mean nothing; he's always a-carryin' on like that when he's drunk. He's the best-naturedest old fool in Arkansaw—never hurt nobody, drunk nor sober."

Boggs rode up before the biggest store in town and bent his head down so he could see under the curtain of the awning and yells, "Come out here, Sherburn! Come out and meet the man you've swindled. You're the houn' I'm after and I'm a-gwyne to have you, too!"

And so he went on, calling Sherburn everything he could lay his tongue to, and the whole street packed with people listening and laughing and going on. By and by a proud-looking man about fifty-five—and he was a heap the best-dressed man in that town, too—steps out of the store, and the crowd drops back on each side to let him come. He says to Boggs, mighty ca'm and slow—he says, "I'm tired of this but I'll endure it till one o'clock. Till one o'clock, mind—no longer. If you open your mouth against me only once after that time you can't travel so far but I will find you."

Then he turns and goes in. The crowd looked mighty sober; nobody stirred and there warn't no more laughing. Boggs rode off blackguarding [BLAGG-ard-ing] Sherburn as loud as he could yell, all down the street; and pretty soon back he comes and stops before the store, still keeping it up. Some men crowded around him and tried to get him to shut up but he wouldn't; they told him it would be one o'clock in about fifteen minutes, and so he *must* go home—he must go right away. But it didn't do no good. He cussed away with all his might and throwed his hat down in the mud and rode over it, and pretty soon away he went a-raging down the street again with his gray hair a-flying. Everybody that could get a chance at him tried their best to coax him off of his horse so they could lock him up and get him sober; but it warn't no use—up the street he would tear again, and give Sherburn another cussing. By and by somebody says, "Go for his daughter!—quick, go for his daughter; sometimes he'll listen to her. If anybody can persuade him, she can."

So somebody started on a run. I walked down street a ways and stopped. In about five or ten minutes here comes Boggs again but not on his horse. He was a-reeling across the street toward me, bareheaded, with a friend on both sides of him a-holt of his arms and hurrying him along. He was quiet and looked uneasy and he warn't hanging back any but was doing some of the hurrying himself.

Somebody sings out, "Boggs!"

I looked over there to see who said it, and it was that Colonel Sherburn. He was standing perfectly still in the street and had a pistol raised in his right hand—not aiming it but holding it out with the barrel tilted up toward the sky. The same second I see a young girl coming on the run, and two men with her. Boggs and the men turned round to see who called him, and when they see the pistol the men jumped to one side, and the pistol barrel come down slow and steady to a level—both barrels cocked. Boggs throws up both of his hands and says, "O Lord, don't shoot!" Bang! goes the first shot and he staggers back, clawing at the air—bang! goes the second one and he tumbles backward onto the ground, heavy and solid, with his arms spread out. That young girl screamed out and comes rushing, and down she throws herself on her father, crying, and saying, "Oh, he's killed him, he's killed him!" The crowd closed up around them and shouldered and jammed one another, with their necks stretched, trying to see, and people on the inside trying to shove them back and shouting, "Back, back! give him air, give him air!"

Colonel Sherburn he tossed his pistol onto the ground, and turned around on his heels and walked off.

They took Boggs to a little drugstore, the crowd pressing around just the same and the whole town following, and I rushed and got a good place at the window, where I was close to him and could see in. They laid him on the floor and put one large Bible under his head, and opened another one and spread it on his breast; but they tore open his shirt first, and I seen where one of the bullets went in. He made about a dozen long gasps, his breast lifting the Bible up when he drawed in his breath, and letting it down again when he breathed out— and after that he laid still; he was dead. Then they pulled his daughter away from him, screaming and crying, and took her off. She was about sixteen, and very sweet and gentle-looking, but awful pale and scared.

Well, pretty soon the whole town was there, squirming and scrouging and pushing and shoving to get at the window and have a look, but people that had the places wouldn't give them up and folks behind them was saying all the time, "Say, now, you've looked enough, you fellows; 'tain't right and 'tain't fair for you to stay thar all the time, and never give nobody a chance; other folks has their rights as well as you."

There was considerable jawing back, so I slid out, thinking maybe there was going to be trouble. The streets was full, and everybody was excited. Everybody that seen the shooting was telling how it happened, and there was a big crowd packed around each one of these fellows, stretching their necks and listening. One long, lanky man, with long hair and a big white fur stovepipe hat on the back of his head, and a crooked-handled cane, marked out the places on the ground where Boggs stood and where Sherburn stood, and the people following him around from one place to t'other and watching everything he done, and bobbing their heads to show they understood and stooping a little and resting their hands on their thighs to watch him mark the places on the ground with his cane; and then he stood up straight and stiff where Sherburn had stood, frowning and having his hat brim down over his eyes, and sung out, "Boggs!" and then fetched his cane down slow to a level, and says "Bang!," staggered backward, says "Bang!" again, and fell down flat on his back. The people that had seen the thing said he done it perfect; said it was just exactly the way it all happened. Then as much as a dozen people got out their bottles and treated him.

Well, by and by somebody said Sherburn ought to be lynched. In about a minute everybody was saying it; so away they went, mad and yelling and snatching down every clothesline they come to to do the hanging with.

They swarmed up toward Sherburn's house, a-whooping and raging like Injuns, and everything had to clear the way or get run over and tromped to mush, and it was awful to see. Children was heeling it ahead of the mob, screaming and trying to get out of the way, and every window along the road was full of women's heads, and there was black boys in every tree and black men and women looking over every fence, and as soon as the mob would get nearly to them they would break and skaddle back out of reach. Lots of the women and girls was crying and taking on, scared most to death.

They swarmed up in front of Sherburn's palings [PAY-lings] as thick as they could jam together, and you couldn't hear yourself think for the noise. It was a little twenty-foot yard. Some sung out "Tear down the fence! tear down the fence!" Then there was a racket of ripping and tearing and smashing, and down she goes, and the front wall of the crowd begins to roll in like a wave.

Just then Sherburn steps out onto the roof of his little front porch with a double-barrel gun in his hand, and takes his stand perfectly ca'm and deliberate, not saying a word. The racket stopped and the wave sucked back.

Sherburn never said a word—just stood there, looking down. The stillness was awful creepy and uncomfortable. Sherburn run his eye slow along the crowd, and wherever it struck the people tried a little to outgaze him but they couldn't, they dropped their eyes and looked sneaky. Then pretty soon Sherburn sort of laughed; not the pleasant kind but the kind that makes you feel like when you are eating bread that's got sand in it.

Then he says, slow and scornful, "The idea of *you* lynching anybody! it's amusing. The idea of you thinking you had pluck enough to lynch a *man!* Because you're brave enough to tar and feather poor friendless cast-out women that come along here, did that make you think you had grit enough to lay your hands on a *man?* Why, a *man's* safe in the hands of ten thousand of your kind—as long as it's daytime and you're not behind him.

"Do I know you? I know you clear through. I was born and

raised in the South and I've lived in the North, so I know the average all around. The average man's a coward. In the North he lets anybody walk over him that wants to, and goes home and prays for a humble spirit to bear it. In the South one man, all by himself, has stopped a stage full of men in the daytime and robbed the lot. Your newspapers call you a brave people so much that you think you *are* braver than any other people —whereas you're just *as* brave and no braver. Why don't your juries hang murderers? Because they're afraid the man's friends will shoot them in the back in the dark—and it's just what they *would* do.

"So they always acquit; and then a *man* goes in the night, with a hundred masked cowards at his back, and lynches the rascal. Your mistake is that you didn't bring a man with you; that's one mistake, and the other is that you didn't come in the dark and fetch your masks. You brought *part* of a man—Buck Harkness, there—and if you hadn't had him to start you, you'd a'taken it out in blowing.

"You didn't want to come. The average man don't like trouble and danger. *You* don't like trouble and danger. But if only *half* a man—like Buck Harkness there—shouts 'Lynch him! lynch him!' you're afraid to back down—afraid you'll be found out to be what you are—*cowards*—and so you raise a yell and hang yourselves onto that half-a-man's coattail and come raging up here, swearing what big things you're going to do. The pitifulest thing out is a mob; that's what an army is—a mob; they don't fight with courage that's born in them but with courage that's borrowed from their mass and from their officers. But a mob without any *man* at the head of it is *beneath* pitifulness. Now the thing for *you* to do is to droop your tails and go home and crawl in a hole. If any real lynching's going to be done it will be done in the dark, Southern fashion; and when they come they'll bring their masks, and fetch a *man* along. Now *leave*—and take your half-a-man with you"—tossing his gun up across his left arm and cocking it when he says this.

The crowd washed back sudden and then broke all apart and went tearing off every which way, and Buck Harkness he heeled it after them, looking tolerable cheap. I could 'a' stayed if I wanted to, but I didn't want to.

from *The Call of the Wild*

by
JACK LONDON

About the story:
*The following tale consists of the first three chapters of
Jack London's masterpiece about the life of a sled dog in
the gold rush days of the Yukon. Each chapter has been
divided into two parts of similar length; the reading
times are given at the beginning of each part.*

*If you are considering using the entire book for oral
reading to your children, a caution is in order: Even older
children, and adults, too, may be stunned by the harsh-
ness and brutality that are part of the everyday existence
in the primitive world London describes, a world in
which animals and humans alike must adjust or die. In
such a setting, morals, values, and all the other characteristics of civilization vanish. Both animals and humans take on the appearance and adopt the behaviors of
their primitive ancestors.*

Chapter 1
Into the Primitive

Approximate reading time for Part One: 11 minutes
Pronunciation and vocabulary guide (for Chapter 1):
   progeny [PRAHJ-enn-ee]: offspring
   sou [SUE]: a French coin, like a penny
   wax: to increase gradually
   metamorphosed [mett-ah-MORE-fozed]: transformed
   cayuses [KY-you-sez]: native horses

soliloquize [suh-LILL-oh-kwyze]: to talk to oneself
conciliate: to gain goodwill by pleasing acts
Perrault [perr-OH]
François [FRANN-swah]

*B*uck did not read the newspapers or he would have known that trouble was brewing, not alone for himself, but for every tidewater dog, strong of muscle and with warm, long hair, from Puget Sound to San Diego. Because men, groping in the Arctic darkness, had found a yellow metal, and because steamship and transportation companies were booming the find, thousands of men were rushing into the Northland. These men wanted dogs, with strong muscles by which to toil, and furry coats to protect them from the frost.

Buck lived at a big house in the sun-kissed Santa Clara Valley. Judge Miller's place, it was called. It stood back from the road, half hidden among the trees, through which glimpses could be caught of the wide cool veranda that ran around its four sides. The house was approached by graveled driveways which wound about through widespreading lawns and under the interlacing boughs of tall poplars. At the rear things were on even a more spacious scale than at the front. There were great stables, where a dozen grooms and boys held forth, rows of vine-clad servants' cottages, an endless and orderly array of outhouses, long grape arbors, green pastures, orchards, and berry patches. Then there was the pumping plant for the artesian well and the big cement tank where Judge Miller's boys took their morning plunge and kept cool in the hot afternoon.

And over this great domain Buck ruled. Here he was born, and here he had lived the four years of his life. It was true, there were other dogs. There could not but be other dogs on so vast a place, but they did not count. They came and went, resided in the populous kennels, or lived obscurely in the recesses of the house after the fashion of Toots, the Japanese pug, or Ysabel, the Mexican hairless—strange creatures that rarely put nose out of doors or set foot to ground. On the other hand, there were the fox terriers, a score of them at least, who yelped fearful promises at Toots and Ysabel looking out of the windows at them and protected by a legion of housemaids armed with brooms and mops.

But Buck was neither house dog nor kennel dog. The whole realm was his. He plunged into the swimming tank or went hunting with the judge's sons; he escorted Mollie and Alice, the judge's daughters, on long twilight or early morning rambles; on wintry nights he lay at the judge's feet before the roaring library fire; he carried the judge's grandsons on his back, or rolled with them in the grass, and guarded their footsteps through wild adventures down to the fountain in the stableyard, and even beyond, where the paddocks were, and the berry patches. Among the terriers he stalked imperiously, and Toots and Ysabel he utterly ignored, for he was king—king over all creeping, crawling, flying things of Judge Miller's place, humans included.

His father, Elmo, a huge St. Bernard, had been the judge's inseparable companion, and Buck bid fair to follow in the way of his father. He was not so large—he weighed only one hundred and forty pounds—for his mother, Shep, had been a Scotch shepherd dog. Nevertheless, one hundred and forty pounds, to which was added the dignity that comes of good living and universal respect, enabled him to carry himself in right royal fashion. During the four years since his puppyhood he had lived the life of a sated aristocrat; he had a fine pride in himself, was ever a trifle egotistical, as country gentlemen sometimes become because of their insular situation. But he had saved himself by not becoming a mere pampered house dog. Hunting and kindred outdoor delights had kept down the fat and hardened his muscles; and to him, as to the cold-tubbing races, the love of water had been a tonic and a health preserver.

And this was the manner of dog Buck was in the fall of 1897, when the Klondike strike dragged men from all the world into the frozen North. But Buck did not read the newspapers, and he did not know that Manuel, one of the gardener's helpers, was an undesirable acquaintance. Manuel had one besetting sin. He loved to play Chinese lottery. Also, in his gambling, he had one besetting weakness—faith in a system; and this made his damnation certain. For to play a system requires money, while the wages of a gardener's helper do not lap over the needs of a wife and numerous progeny [PRAHJ-enn-ee].

The judge was at a meeting of the Raisin Growers' Association, and the boys were busy organizing an athletic club, on the memorable night of Manuel's treachery. No one saw him and Buck go off through the orchard on what Buck imagined was merely a stroll. And with the exception of a solitary man, no one saw them arrive at the little flag station known as College Park. This man talked with Manuel, and money chinked between them.

"You might wrap up the goods before you deliver 'm," the stranger said gruffly, and Manuel doubled a piece of stout rope around Buck's neck under the collar.

"Twist it, an' you'll choke 'm plentee," said Manuel, and the stranger grunted a ready affirmative.

Buck had accepted the rope with quiet dignity. To be sure, it was an unwonted performance, but he had learned to trust in men he knew, and to give them credit for a wisdom that outreached his own. But when the ends of the rope were placed in the stranger's hands, he growled menacingly. He had merely intimated his displeasure, in his pride believing that to intimate was to command. But to his surprise the rope tightened around his neck, shutting off his breath. In quick rage he sprang at the man, who met him halfway, grappled him close by the throat, and with a deft twist threw him over on his back. Then the rope tightened mercilessly, while Buck struggled in a fury, his tongue lolling out of his mouth and his great chest panting futilely. Never in all his life had he been so vilely treated, and never in all his life had he been so angry. But his strength ebbed, his eyes glazed, and he knew nothing when the train was flagged and the two men threw him into the baggage car.

The next thing he knew, he was dimly aware that his tongue was hurting and that he was being jolted along in some kind of a conveyance. The hoarse shriek of a locomotive whistling a crossing told him where he was. He had traveled too often with the judge not to know the sensation of riding in a baggage car. He opened his eyes, and into them came the unbridled anger of a kidnaped king. The man sprang for his throat, but Buck was too quick for him. His jaws closed on the hand, nor did they relax till his senses were choked out of him once more.

"Yep, has fits," the man said, hiding his mangled hand from

the baggageman, who had been attracted by the sounds of a struggle. "I'm takin' 'm up for the boss to 'Frisco. A crack dog doctor there thinks that he can cure 'm."

Concerning that night's ride, the man spoke most eloquently for himself, in a little shed back of a saloon on the San Francisco waterfront.

"All I get is fifty for it," he grumbled, "an' I wouldn't do it over for a thousand, cold cash."

His hand was wrapped in a bloody handkerchief, and the right trouser leg was ripped from knee to ankle.

"How much did the other mug get?" the saloon keeper demanded.

"A hundred," was the reply. "Wouldn't take a sou [SUE] less, so help me."

"That makes a hundred and fifty," the saloon keeper calculated, "and he's worth it, or I'm a squarehead."

The kidnaper undid the bloody wrappings and looked at his lacerated hand. "If I don't get the hydrophoby—"

"It'll be because you was born to hang," laughed the saloon keeper. "Here, lend me a hand before you pull your freight," he added.

Dazed, suffering intolerable pain from throat and tongue, with the life half throttled out of him, Buck attempted to face his tormentors. But he was thrown down and choked repeatedly, till they succeeded in filing the heavy brass collar from off his neck. Then the rope was removed, and he was flung into a cagelike crate.

There he lay for the remainder of the weary night, nursing his wrath and wounded pride. He could not understand what it all meant. What did they want with him, these strange men? Why were they keeping him pent up in this narrow crate? He did not know why, but he felt oppressed by the vague sense of impending calamity. Several times during the night he sprang to his feet when the shed door rattled open, expecting to see the judge, or the boys at least. But each time it was the bulging face of the saloon keeper that peered in at him by the sickly light of a tallow candle. And each time the joyful bark that trembled in Buck's throat was twisted into a savage growl.

But the saloon keeper left him alone, and in the morning four men entered and picked up the crate. More tormentors,

Buck decided, for they were evil-looking creatures, ragged and unkempt; and he stormed and raged at them through the bars. They only laughed and poked sticks at him, which he promptly assailed with his teeth till he realized that that was what they wanted. Whereupon he lay down sullenly and allowed the crate to be lifted into a wagon. Then he, and the crate in which he was imprisoned, began a passage through many hands. Clerks in the express office took charge of him; he was carted about in another wagon; a truck carried him, with an assortment of boxes and parcels, upon a ferry steamer; he was trucked off the steamer into a great railway depot, and finally he was deposited in an express car.

For two days and nights this express car was dragged along at the tail of shrieking locomotives; and for two days and nights Buck neither ate nor drank. In his anger he had met the first advances of the express messengers with growls, and they had retaliated by teasing him. When he flung himself against the bars, quivering and frothing, they laughed at him and taunted him. They growled and barked like detestable dogs, mewed, and flapped their arms and crowed. It was all very silly, he knew; but therefore the more outrage to his dignity, and his anger waxed and waxed. He did not mind the hunger so much, but the lack of water caused him severe suffering and fanned his wrath to fever-pitch. For that matter, high-strung and finely sensitive, the ill treatment had flung him into a fever, which was fed by the inflammation of his parched and swollen throat and tongue.

He was glad for one thing: The rope was off his neck. That had given them an unfair advantage; but now that it was off, he would show them. They would never get another rope around his neck. Upon that he was resolved.

Approximate reading time for Part Two: 11 minutes

For two days and nights he neither ate nor drank, and during those two days and nights of torment, he accumulated a fund of wrath that boded ill for whoever first fell foul of him. His eyes turned bloodshot, and he was metamorphosed [mett-ah-MORE-fozed] into a raging fiend. So changed was he that the judge himself would not have recognized him; and the express messengers breathed with relief when they bundled him off the train at Seattle.

Four men gingerly carried the crate from the wagon into a small, high-walled backyard. A stout man, with a red sweater that sagged generously at the neck, came out and signed the book for the driver. That was the man, Buck divined, the next tormentor, and he hurled himself savagely against the bars. The man smiled grimly, and brought a hatchet and a club.

"You ain't going to take him out now?" the driver asked.

"Sure," the man replied, driving the hatchet into the crate for a pry.

There was an instantaneous scattering of the four men who had carried it in, and from safe perches on top the wall they prepared to watch the performance.

Buck rushed at the splintering wood, sinking his teeth into it, surging and wrestling with it. Wherever the hatchet fell on the outside, he was there on the inside, snarling and growling, as furiously anxious to get out as the man in the red sweater was calmly intent on getting him out.

"Now, you red-eyed devil," he said, when he had made an opening sufficient for the passage of Buck's body. At the same time he dropped the hatchet and shifted the club to his right hand.

And Buck was truly a red-eyed devil, as he drew himself together for the spring, hair bristling, mouth foaming, a mad glitter in his bloodshot eyes. Straight at the man he launched his one hundred and forty pounds of fury, surcharged with the pent passion of two days and nights. In midair, just as his jaws were about to close on the man, he received a shock that checked his body and brought his teeth together with an ago-nizing clip. He whirled over, fetching the ground on his back and side. He had never been struck by a club in his life, and did not understand. With a snarl that was part bark and more scream he was again on his feet and launched into the air. And again the shock came and he was brought crushingly to the ground. This time he was aware that it was the club, but his madness knew no caution. A dozen times he charged, and as often the club broke the charge and smashed him down.

After a particularly fierce blow he crawled to his feet, too dazed to rush. He staggered limply about, the blood flowing from nose and mouth and ears, his beautiful coat sprayed and flecked with bloody slaver. Then the man advanced and deliberately dealt him a frightful blow on the nose. All the pain he had endured was as nothing compared with the exquisite agony of this. With a roar that was almost lionlike in its ferocity, he again hurled himself at the man. But the man, shifting the club from right to left, coolly caught him by the under jaw, at the same time wrenching downward and backward. Buck described a complete circle in the air, and half of another, then crashed to the ground on his head and chest.

For the last time he rushed. The man struck the shrewd blow he had purposely withheld for so long, and Buck crumpled up and went down, knocked utterly senseless.

"He's no slouch at dog-breakin', that's wot I say," one of the men on the wall cried enthusiastically.

"Druther break cayuses [KY-you-sez] any day, and twice on Sundays," was the reply of the driver, as he climbed on the wagon and started the horses.

Buck's senses came back to him, but not his strength. He lay where he had fallen, and from there he watched the man in the red sweater.

" 'Answers to the name of Buck,' " the man soliloquized [suh-LILL-oh-kwyzed], quoting from the saloon-keeper's letter which had announced the consignment of the crate and contents. "Well, Buck, my boy," he went on in a genial voice, "we've had our little ruction, and the best thing we can do is to let it go at that. You've learned your place, and I know mine. Be a good dog and all 'll go well and the goose hang high. Be a bad dog, and I'll whale the stuffin' outa you. Understand?'

As he spoke he fearlessly patted the head he had so mercilessly pounded, and though Buck's hair involuntarily bristled at touch of the hand, he endured it without protest. When the man brought him water he drank eagerly, and later bolted a generous meal of raw meat, chunk by chunk, from the man's hand.

He was beaten (he knew that); but he was not broken. He saw, once for all, that he stood no chance against a man with a club. He had learned the lesson, and in all his afterlife he never forgot it. That club was a revelation. It was his introduction to the reign of primitive law, and he met the introduction half-way. The facts of life took on a fiercer aspect; and while he faced that aspect uncowed, he faced it with all the latent cunning of his nature aroused. As the days went by, other dogs came, in crates and at the ends of ropes, some docilely, and some raging and roaring as he had come; and, one and all, he watched them pass under the dominion of the man in the red sweater. Again and again, as he looked at each brutal performance, the lesson was driven home to Buck: A man with a club was a lawgiver, a master to be obeyed, though not necessarily conciliated. Of this last Buck was never guilty, though he did see beaten dogs that fawned upon the man, and wagged their tails, and licked his hand. Also he saw one dog, that would neither conciliate nor obey, finally killed in the struggle for mastery.

Now and again men came, strangers, who talked excitedly, wheedling, and in all kinds of fashions to the man in the red sweater. And at such times that money passed between them the strangers took one or more of the dogs away with them. Buck wondered where they went, for they never came back; but the fear of the future was strong upon him, and he was glad each time when he was not selected.

Yet his time came, in the end, in the form of a little weazened man who spat broken English and many strange and uncouth exclamations which Buck could not understand.

"Sacredam!" he cried, when his eyes lit upon Buck. "Dat one dam bully dog! Eh? How much?"

"Three hundred, and a present at that," was the prompt reply of the man in the red sweater. "And seein' it's government money, you ain't got no kick coming, eh, Perrault [perr-OH]?"

Perrault grinned. Considering that the price of dogs had been boomed skyward by the unwonted demand, it was not an unfair sum for so fine an animal. The Canadian Government would be no loser, nor would its dispatches travel the slower. Perrault knew dogs, and when he looked at Buck he knew that he was one in a thousand—"One in ten t'ousand," he commented mentally.

Buck saw money pass between them, and was not surprised when Curly, a good-natured Newfoundland, and he were led away by the little weazened man. That was the last he saw of the man in the red sweater, and as Curly and he looked at receding Seattle from the deck of the *Narwhal*, it was the last he saw of the warm Southland. Curly and he were taken below by Perrault and turned over to a black-faced giant called François [FRANN-swah]. Perrault was a French-Canadian, and swarthy; but François was a French-Canadian half-breed, and twice as swarthy. They were a new kind of men to Buck (of which he was destined to see many more), and while he developed no affection for them, he nonetheless grew honestly to respect them. He speedily learned that Perrault and François were fair men, calm and impartial in administering justice, and too wise in the way of dogs to be fooled by dogs.

In the 'tween-decks of the *Narwhal*, Buck and Curly joined two other dogs. One of them was a big, snow-white fellow from Spitzbergen who had been brought away by a whaling captain, and who had later accompanied a geological survey into the Barrens.

He was friendly, in a treacherous sort of way, smiling into one's face the while he meditated some underhand trick, as, for instance, when he stole from Buck's food at the first meal. As Buck sprang to punish him, the lash of François's whip sang through the air, reaching the culprit first; and nothing remained to Buck but to recover the bone. That was fair of François, he decided, and the half-breed began his rise in Buck's estimation.

The other dog made no advances, nor received any; also, he did not attempt to steal from the newcomers. He was a gloomy, morose fellow, and he showed Curly plainly that all he desired was to be left alone, and further, that there would be trouble if he were not left alone. "Dave" he was called, and he ate and slept, or yawned between times, and took interest in nothing, not even when the *Narwhal* crossed Queen Charlotte Sound and rolled and pitched and bucked like a thing possessed. When Buck and Curly grew excited, half wild with fear, he raised his head as though annoyed, favored them with an incurious glance, yawned, and went to sleep again.

Day and night the ship throbbed to the tireless pulse of the propeller, and though one day was very like another, it was apparent to Buck that the weather was steadily growing colder.

At last, one morning, the propeller was quiet, and the *Narwhal* was pervaded with an atmosphere of excitement. He felt it, as did the other dogs, and knew that a change was at hand. François leashed them and brought them on deck. At the first step upon the cold surface, Buck's feet sank into white mushy something very like mud. He sprang back with a snort. More of this white stuff was falling through the air. He shook himself, but more of it fell upon him. He sniffed it curiously, then licked some up on his tongue. It bit like fire, and the next instant was gone. This puzzled him. He tried it again, with the same result. The onlookers laughed uproariously, and he felt ashamed, he knew not why, for it was his first snow.

Chapter 2
The Law of Club and Fang

Approximate reading time for Part One: 10 minutes
Pronunciation and vocabulary guide (for Chapter 2):
  primordial: from the earliest ages
  vicarious [vie-CARE-ee-us]: experienced by imagining the experience of another
  draught [DRAFT]: used for drawing loads
  ere [AIR]: before
  discomfiture: embarrassment
  ignominiously [igg-no-MINN-ee-us-lee]: disgracefully, shamefully
  disconsolate [dis-CAHN-so-luht]: dejected, downcast
  placatingly [PLAY-kate-ing-lee]: trying to soothe or appease
  spasmodically [spaz-MAHD-ick-uh-lee]: in sudden jerks
  geepole [JEE-pole]
  ravenous [RAV-enn-us]: extremely hungry

fastidiousness [fass-TIDD-ee-us-ness]: exacting, careful in every detail, meticulous
leeward: located away from the wind

*B*uck's first day on the Dyea beach was like a nightmare. Every hour was filled with shock and surprise. He had been suddenly jerked from the heart of civilization and flung into the heart of things primordial. No lazy, sun-kissed life was this, with nothing to do but loaf and be bored. Here was neither peace, nor rest, nor a moment's safety. All was confusion and action, and every moment life and limb were in peril. There was imperative need to be constantly alert; for these dogs and men were not town dogs and men. They were savages, all of them, who knew no law but the law of club and fang.

He had never seen dogs fight as these wolfish creatures fought, and his first experience taught him an unforgettable lesson. It is true, it was a vicarious [vie-CARE-ee-us] experience, else he would not have lived to profit by it. Curly was the victim. They were camped near the log store, where she, in her friendly way, made advances to a husky dog the size of a full-grown wolf, though not half so large as she. There was no warning, only a leap in like a flash, a metallic clip of teeth, a leap out equally swift, and Curly's face was ripped open from eye to jaw.

It was the wolf manner of fighting, to strike and leap away; but there was more to it than this. Thirty or forty huskies ran to the spot and surrounded the combatants in an intent and silent circle. Buck did not comprehend that silent intentness, nor the eager way with which they were licking their chops. Curly rushed her antagonist, who struck again and leaped aside. He met her next rush with his chest, in a peculiar fashion that tumbled her off her feet. She never regained them. This was what the onlooking huskies had waited for. They closed in upon her, snarling and yelping, and she was buried, screaming with agony, beneath the bristling mass of bodies.

So sudden was it, and so unexpected, that Buck was taken aback. He saw Spitz run out his scarlet tongue in a way he had of laughing; and he saw François, swinging an ax, spring into the mess of dogs. Three men with clubs were helping him to scatter them. It did not take long. Two minutes from the time Curly went down, the last of her assailants were clubbed off. But she lay there limp and lifeless in the bloody, trampled snow, almost literally torn to pieces, the swarthy half-breed standing over her and cursing horribly. The scene often came back to Buck to trouble him in his sleep. So that was the way. No fair play. Once down, that was the end of you. Well, he would see to it that he never went down. Spitz ran out his tongue and laughed again, and from that moment Buck hated him with a bitter and deathless hatred.

Before he had recovered from the shock caused by the tragic passing of Curly, he received another shock. François fastened upon him an arrangement of straps and buckles. It was a harness, such as he had seen the grooms put on the horses at home. And as he had seen horses work, so he was set to work, hauling François on a sled to the forest that fringed the valley, and returning with a load of firewood. Though his dignity was sorely hurt by thus being made a draught [DRAFT] animal, he was too wise to rebel. He buckled down with a will and did his best, though it was all new and strange. François was stern, demanding instant obedience, and by virtue of his whip receiving instant obedience; while Dave, who was an experienced wheeler, nipped Buck's hindquarters whenever he was in error. Spitz was the leader, likewise experienced, and while he could not always get at Buck, he growled sharp reproof now and again, or cunningly threw his weight in the traces to jerk Buck into the way he should go. Buck learned easily, and under the combined tuition of his two mates and François made remarkable progress. Ere [AIR] they returned to camp he knew enough to stop at "ho," to go ahead at "mush," to swing wide on the bends, and to keep clear of the wheeler when the loaded sled shot downhill at their heels.

"T'ree vair' good dogs," François told Perrault. "Dat Buck, heem pool lak hell. I tich heem queek as anyt'ing."

By afternoon, Perrault, who was in a hurry to be on the trail with his dispatches, returned with two more dogs. "Billee" and "Joe" he called them, two brothers, and true huskies both. Sons of the one mother though they were, they were as different as day and night. Billee's one fault was his excessive good nature, while Joe was the very opposite, sour and introspective, with a perpetual snarl and a malignant eye. Buck received them in comradely fashion, Dave ignored them, while Spitz proceeded to thrash first one and then the other. Billee wagged his tail appeasingly, turned to run when he saw that appeasement was of no avail, and cried (still appeasingly) when Spitz's sharp teeth scored his flank. But no matter how Spitz circled, Joe whirled around on his heels to face him, mane bristling, ears laid back, lips writhing and snarling, jaws clipping together as fast as he could snap, and eyes diabolically gleaming —the incarnation of belligerent fear. So terrible was his appearance that Spitz was forced to forgo disciplining him; but to cover his own discomfiture he turned upon the inoffensive and wailing Billee and drove him to the confines of the camp.

By evening Perrault secured another dog, an old husky, long and lean and gaunt, with a battle-scarred face and a single eye which flashed a warning of prowess that commanded respect. He was called Sol-leks, which means the Angry One. Like Dave, he asked nothing, gave nothing, expected nothing; and when he marched slowly and deliberately into their midst, even Spitz left him alone. He had one peculiarity which Buck was unlucky enough to discover. He did not like to be approached on his blind side. Of this offense Buck was unwittingly guilty, and the first knowledge he had of his indiscretion was when Sol-leks whirled upon him and slashed his shoulder to the bone for three inches up and down. Forever after Buck avoided his blind side, and to the last of their comradeship had no more trouble. His only apparent ambition, like Dave's, was to be left alone; though, as Buck was afterward to learn, each of them possessed one other and even more vital ambition.

That night Buck faced the great problem of sleeping. The tent, illumined by a candle, glowed warmly in the midst of the white plain; and when he, as a matter of course, entered it, both Perrault and François bombarded him with curses and cooking utensils, till he recovered from his consternation and fled ignominiously [igg-no-MINN-ee-us-lee] into the outer cold. A chill wind was blowing that nipped him sharply and bit with especial venom into his wounded shoulder. He lay down on the snow and attempted to sleep, but the frost soon drove him shivering to his feet. Miserable and disconsolate [dis-CAHN-so-luht], he wandered about among the many tents, only to find that one place was as cold as another. Here and there savage dogs rushed upon him, but he bristled his neck-hair and snarled (for he was learning fast), and they let him go his way unmolested.

Finally an idea came to him. He would return and see how his teammates were making out. To his astonishment, they had disappeared. Again he wandered about through the great camp, looking for them, and again he returned. Were they in the tent? No, that could not be, else he would not have been driven out. Then where could they possibly be? With drooping tail and shivering body, very forlorn indeed, he aimlessly circled the tent. Suddenly the snow gave way beneath his forelegs and he sank down. Something wriggled under his feet. He sprang back, bristling and snarling, fearful of the unseen and unknown. But a friendly little yelp reassured him, and he went back to investigate. A whiff of warm air ascended to his nostrils, and there, curled up under the snow in a snug ball, lay Billee. He whined placatingly [PLAY-kate-ing-lee], squirmed and wriggled to show his goodwill and intentions, and even ventured, as a bribe for peace, to lick Buck's face with his warm wet tongue.

Another lesson. So that was the way they did it, eh? Buck confidently selected a spot, and with much fuss and waste effort proceeded to dig a hole for himself. In a trice the heat from his body filled the confined space and he was asleep. The day had been long and arduous, and he slept soundly and comfortably, though he growled and barked and wrestled with bad dreams.

Approximate reading time for Part Two: 10 minutes

Nor did he open his eyes till roused by the noises of the waking camp. At first he did not know where he was. It had snowed during the night and he was completely buried. The snow walls pressed him on every side, and a great surge of fear swept through him—the fear of the wild thing for a trap. It was a token that he was harking back through his own life to the lives of his forebears; for he was a civilized dog, an unduly civilized dog, and of his own experience knew no trap and so could not of himself fear it. The muscles of his whole body contracted spasmodically [spaz-MAHD-ick-uh-lee] and, instinctively, the hair on his neck and shoulders stood on end, and with a ferocious snarl he bounded straight up into the blinding day, the snow flying about him in a flashing cloud. Ere he landed on his feet, he saw the white camp spread out before him and knew where he was and remembered all that had passed from the time he went for a stroll with Manuel to the hole he had dug for himself the night before.

A shout from François hailed his appearance. "Wot I say?" the dog driver cried to Perrault. "Dat Buck for sure learn queek as anyt'ing."

Perrault nodded gravely. As courier for the Canadian Government, bearing important dispatches, he was anxious to secure the best dogs, and he was particularly gladdened by the possession of Buck.

Three more huskies were added to the team inside an hour, making a total of nine, and before another quarter of an hour had passed they were in harness and swinging up the trail toward the Dyea Canyon. Buck was glad to be gone, and though the work was hard he found he did not particularly despise it. He was surprised at the eagerness which animated the whole team and which was communicated to him; but still more surprising was the change wrought in Dave and Sol-leks. They were new dogs, utterly transformed by the harness. All passiveness and unconcern had dropped from them. They were alert and active, anxious that the work should go well, and fiercely irritable with whatever, by delay or confusion, retarded that work. The toil of the traces seemed the supreme expression of their being, and all that they lived for and the only thing in which they took delight.

Dave was wheeler or sled dog, pulling in front of him was Buck, then came Sol-leks; the rest of the team was strung out ahead, single file, to the leader, which position was filled by Spitz.

Buck had been purposely placed between Dave and Sol-leks so that he might receive instruction. Apt scholar that he was, they were equally apt teachers, never allowing him to linger long in error, and enforcing their teaching with their sharp teeth. Dave was fair and very wise. He never nipped Buck without cause, and he never failed to nip him when he stood in need of it. As François's whip backed him up, Buck found it to be cheaper to mend his ways than to retaliate. Once, during a brief halt, when he got tangled in the traces and delayed the start, both Dave and Sol-leks flew at him and administered a sound trouncing. The resulting tangle was even worse, but Buck took good care to keep the traces clear thereafter; and ere the day was done, so well had he mastered his work, his mates about ceased nagging him. François's whip snapped less frequently, and Perrault even honored Buck by lifting up his feet and carefully examining them.

It was a hard day's run, up the canyon, through Sheep Camp, past the Scales and the timberline, across glaciers and snowdrifts hundreds of feet deep, and over the great Chilcoot Divide, which stands between the salt water and the fresh and guards forbiddingly the sad and lonely North. They made good time down the chain of lakes which fills the craters of extinct volcanoes, and late that night pulled into the huge camp at the head of Lake Bennett, where thousands of gold seekers were building boats against the breakup of the ice in the spring. Buck made his hole in the snow and slept the sleep of the exhausted just, but all too early was routed out in the cold darkness and harnessed with his mates to the sled.

That day they made forty miles, the trail being packed; but the next day, and for many days to follow, they broke their own trail, worked harder, and made poorer time. As a rule, Perrault traveled ahead of the team, packing the snow with webbed shoes to make it easier for them. François, guiding the sled at the geepole [JEE-pole], sometimes exchanged places with him, but not often. Perrault was in a hurry, and he prided himself on his knowledge of ice, which knowledge was indispensable, for the fall ice was very thin, and where there was swift water, there was no ice at all.

Day after day, for days unending, Buck toiled in the traces. Always, they broke camp in the dark, and the first gray of dawn found them hitting the trail with fresh miles reeled off behind them. And always they pitched camp after dark, eating their bit of fish, and crawling to sleep into the snow. Buck was ravenous [RAV-enn-us]. The pound and a half of sun-dried salmon, which was his ration for each day, seemed to go no-where. He never had enough, and suffered from perpetual hunger pangs. Yet the other dogs, because they weighed less and were born to the life, received a pound only of the fish and managed to keep in good condition.

He swiftly lost the fastidiousness [fass-TIDD-ee-us-ness] which had characterized his old life. A dainty eater, he found that his mates, finishing first, robbed him of his unfinished ration. There was no defending it. While he was fighting off two or three, it was disappearing down the throats of the oth-ers. To remedy this, he ate as fast as they; and, so greatly did hunger compel him, he was not above taking what did not belong to him. He watched and learned. When he saw Pike, one of the new dogs, a clever malingerer and thief, slyly steal a slice of bacon when Perrault's back was turned, he duplicated the performance the following day, getting away with the whole chunk. A great uproar was raised, but he was unsus-pected, while Dub, an awkward blunderer who was always getting caught, was punished for Buck's misdeed.

This first theft marked Buck as fit to survive in the hostile Northland environment. It marked his adaptability, his capac-ity to adjust himself to changing conditions, the lack of which would have meant swift and terrible death. It marked, further, the decay or going to pieces of his moral nature, a vain thing and a handicap in the ruthless struggle for existence. It was all well enough in the Southland, under the law of love and fel-lowship, to respect private property and personal feelings; but in the Northland, under the law of club and fang, whoso took such things into account was a fool, and insofar as he observed them he would fail to prosper.

Not that Buck reasoned it out. He was fit, that was all, and unconsciously he accommodated himself to the new mode of life. All his days, no matter what the odds, he had never run from a fight. But the club of the man in the red sweater had beaten into him a more fundamental and primitive code. Civi-lized, he could have died for a moral consideration, say the defense of Judge Miller's riding whip; but the completeness of his decivilization was now evidenced by his ability to flee from the defense of a moral consideration and so save his hide. He did not steal for joy of it, but because of the clamor of his stomach. He did not rob openly, but stole secretly and cunningly, out of respect for club and fang. In short, the things he did were done because it was easier to do them than not to do them.

His development (or retrogression) was rapid. His muscles became hard as iron and he grew callous to all ordinary pain. He achieved an internal as well as external economy. He could eat anything, no matter how loathsome or indigestible; and, once eaten, the juices of his stomach extracted the last least particle of nutriment; and his blood carried it to the farthest reaches of his body, building it into the toughest and stoutest of tissues. Sight and scent became remarkably keen, while his hearing developed such acuteness that in his sleep he heard the faintest sound and knew whether it heralded peace or peril. He learned to bite the ice out with his teeth when it collected between his toes; and when he was thirsty and there was a thick scum of ice over the waterhole, he would break it by rearing and striking it with stiff forelegs. His most conspicuous trait was an ability to scent the wind and forecast it a night in advance. No matter how breathless the air when he dug his nest by tree or bank, the wind that later blew inevitably found him to leeward, sheltered and snug.

And not only did he learn by experience, but instincts long dead became alive again. The domesticated generations fell from him. In vague ways he remembered back to the youth of the breed, to the time the wild dogs ranged in packs through the primeval forest and killed their meat as they ran it down. It was no task for him to learn to fight with cut and slash and the quick wolf snap. In this manner had fought forgotten ancestors. They quickened the old life within him, and the old tricks which they had stamped into the heredity of the breed were his tricks. They came to him without effort or discovery, as though they had been his always. And when, on the still cold nights, he pointed his nose at a star and howled long and wolflike, it was his ancestors, dead and dust, pointing nose at star and howling down through the centuries and through him. And his cadences were their cadences, the cadences which voiced their woe and what to them was the meaning of the stillness, and the cold, and dark.

Thus, as token of what a puppet thing life is, the ancient

song surged through him and he came into his own again; and he came because men had found a yellow metal in the North, and because Manuel was a gardener's helper whose wages did not lap over the needs of his wife and divers small copies of himself.

Chapter 3
The Dominant Primordial Beast

Approximate reading time for Part One: 14 minutes
Pronunciation and vocabulary guide (for Chapter 3):
> **precipitate** (adj.) [pre-SIPP-ih-tuht]: hasty, impulsive
> **malingerer** [mal-LING-er-er]: one who feigns illness to avoid work
> **preeminently** [pre-EMM-inn-ent-lee]: outstandingly
> **nocturnal:** occurring at night
> **aurora borealis** [ah-ROAR-ah borr-ee-AL-iss]: northern lights
> **insidious** [inn-SIDD-ee-us]: spreading harmfully and gradually
> **wraith** [RAYTH]: a ghost, specter
> **apex** [AA-pecks]: the highest point
> **inexorable** [inn-EGGS-orr-uh-buhl]: relentless

*T*he dominant primordial beast was strong in Buck, and under the fierce conditions of trail life it grew and grew. Yet it was a secret growth. His newborn cunning gave him poise and control. He was too busy adjusting himself to the new life to feel at ease, and not only did he not pick fights, but he avoided them whenever possible. A certain deliberateness characterized his attitude. He was not prone to rashness and precipitate [pre-SIPP-ih-tuht] action; and in the bitter hatred between him and Spitz he betrayed no impatience, shunned all offensive acts.

On the other hand, possibly because he divined in Buck a dangerous rival, Spitz never lost an opportunity of showing his teeth. He even went out of his way to bully Buck, striving constantly to start the fight which could end only in the death of one or the other.

Early in the trip this might have taken place had it not been for an unwonted accident. At the end of this day they made a bleak and miserable camp on the shore of Lake Le Barge. Driving snow, a wind that cut like a white-hot knife, and darkness, had forced them to grope for a camping place. They could hardly have fared worse. At their backs rose a perpendicular wall of rock, and Perrault and François were compelled to make their fire and spread their sleeping robes on the ice of the lake itself. The tent they had discarded at Dyea in order to travel light. A few sticks of driftwood furnished them with a fire that thawed down through the ice and left them to eat supper in the dark.

Close in under the sheltering rock Buck made his nest. So snug and warm was it, that he was loath to leave it when François distributed the fish which he had first thawed over the fire. But when Buck finished his ration and returned, he found his nest occupied. A warning snarl told him that the trespasser was Spitz. Till now Buck had avoided trouble with his enemy, but this was too much. The beast in him roared. He sprang upon Spitz with a fury which surprised them both, and Spitz particularly, for his whole experience with Buck had gone to teach him that his rival was an unusually timid dog, who managed to hold his own only because of his great weight and size.

François was surprised, too, when they shot out in a tangle from the disrupted nest and he divined the cause of the trouble. "A-a-ah!" he cried to Buck. "Gif it to heem, by Gar! Gif it to heem, the dirty t'eef!"

Spitz was equally willing. He was crying with sheer rage and eagerness as he circled back and forth for a chance to spring in. Buck was no less eager, and no less cautious, as he likewise circled back and forth for the advantage. But it was then that the unexpected happened, the thing which projected their struggle for supremacy far into the future, past many a weary mile of trail and toil.

An oath from Perrault, the resounding impact of a club upon a bony frame, and a shrill yelp of pain, heralded the breaking forth of pandemonium. The camp was suddenly discovered to be alive with skulking furry forms—starving huskies, four or five score of them, who had scented the camp from some Indian village. They had crept in while Buck and Spitz were fighting, and when the two men sprang among them with stout clubs they showed their teeth and fought back. They were crazed by the smell of the food. Perrault found one with head buried in the grub-box. His club landed heavily on the gaunt ribs, and the grub-box was capsized on the ground. On the instant a score of the famished brutes were scrambling for the bread and bacon. The clubs fell upon them unheeded. They yelped and howled under the rain of blows, but struggled nonetheless madly till the last crumb had been devoured.

In the meantime the astonished team dogs had burst out of their nests only to be set upon by the fierce invaders. Never had Buck seen such dogs. It seemed as though their bones would burst through their skins. They were mere skeletons, draped loosely in draggled hides, with blazing eyes and slavered fangs. But the hunger-madness made them terrifying, irresistible. There was no opposing them. The team dogs were swept back against the cliff at the first onset. Buck was beset by three huskies, and in a trice his head and shoulders were ripped and slashed. The din was frightful. Billee was crying as usual. Dave and Sol-leks, dripping blood from a score of wounds, were fighting bravely side by side. Joe was snapping like a demon. Once, his teeth closed on the foreleg of a husky, and he crunched down through the bone. Pike, the malingerer [mal-LING-er-er], leaped upon the crippled animal, breaking its neck with a quick flash of teeth and a jerk. Buck got a frothing adversary by the throat, and was sprayed with blood when his teeth sank through the jugular. The warm taste of it in his mouth goaded him to greater fierceness. He flung himself upon another, and at the same time felt teeth sink into his own throat. It was Spitz, treacherously attacking from the side.

Perrault and François, having cleaned out their part of the camp, hurried to save their sled dogs. The wild wave of famished beasts rolled back before them, and Buck shook himself free. But it was only for a moment. The two men were compelled to run back to save the grub, upon which the huskies returned to the attack on the team. Billee, terrified into bravery, sprang through the savage circle and fled away over the ice. Pike and Dub followed on his heels, with the rest of the team behind. As Buck drew himself together to spring after them, out of the tail of his eye he saw Spitz rush upon him, with the evident intention of overthrowing him. Once off his feet and under that mass of huskies, there was no hope for him. But he braced himself to the shock of Spitz's charge, then joined the flight out on the lake.

Later, the nine team dogs gathered together and sought shelter in the forest. Though unpursued, they were in a sorry plight. There was not one who was not wounded in four or five places, while some were wounded grievously. Dub was badly injured in a hind leg; Dolly, the last husky added to the team at Dyea, had a badly torn throat; Joe had lost an eye; while Billee, the good-natured, with an ear chewed and rent to ribbons, cried and whimpered throughout the night. At daybreak they limped warily back to camp, to find the marauders gone and the two men in bad tempers. Fully half their grub supply was gone. The huskies had chewed through the sled lashings and canvas coverings. In fact, nothing, no matter how remotely eatable, had escaped them. They had eaten a pair of Perrault's moose-hide moccasins, chunks out of the leather traces, and even two feet of lash from the end of François's whip. He broke from a mournful contemplation of it to look over his wounded dogs.

"Ah, my frien's," he said softly, "mebbe it mek you mad dog, dose many bites. Mebbe all mad dog, sacredam! Wot you t'ink, eh, Perrault?"

The courier shook his head dubiously. With four hundred miles of trail still between him and Dawson, he could ill afford to have madness break out among his dogs. Two hours of cursing and exertion got the harnesses into shape, and the wound-stiffened team was under way, struggling painfully over the hardest part of the trail they had yet encountered, and for that matter, the hardest between them and Dawson.

The Thirty Mile River was wide open. Its wild water defied

the frost, and it was in the eddies only and in quiet places that the ice held at all. Six days of exhausting toil were required to cover those thirty terrible miles. And terrible they were, for every foot of them was accomplished at the risk of life to dog and man. A dozen times, Perrault, nosing the way, broke through the ice bridges, being saved by the long pole he carried, which he so held that it fell each time across the hole made by his body. But a cold snap was on, the thermometer registering fifty below zero, and each time he broke through he was compelled for very life to build a fire and dry his garments.

Nothing daunted him. It was because nothing daunted him that he had been chosen for government courier. He took all manner of risks, resolutely thrusting his little weazened face into the frost and struggling on from dim dawn to dark. He skirted the frowning shores on rim ice that bent and crackled underfoot and upon which they dared not halt. Once, the sled broke through, with Dave and Buck, and they were half frozen and all but drowned by the time they were dragged out. The usual fire was necessary to save them. They were coated solidly with ice, and the two men kept them on the run around the fire, sweating and thawing, so close that they were singed by the flames.

At another time Spitz went through, dragging the whole team after him up to Buck, who strained backward with all his strength, his forepaws on the slippery edge and the ice quivering and snapping all around. But behind him was Dave, likewise straining backward, and behind the sled was François, pulling till his tendons cracked.

Again, the rim ice broke away before and behind, and there was no escape except up the cliff. Perrault scaled it by a miracle, while François prayed for just that miracle; and with every thong and sled lashing and the last bit of harness rove into a long rope, the dogs were hoisted, one by one, to the cliff crest. François came up last, after the sled and load. Then came the search for a place to descend, which descent was ultimately made by the aid of the rope, and night found them back on the river with a quarter of a mile to the day's credit.

By the time they made the Hootalinqua and good ice, Buck was played out. The rest of the dogs were in like condition; but

Perrault, to make up lost time, pushed them late and early. The first day they covered thirty-five miles to the Big Salmon; the next day thirty-five more to the Little Salmon; the third day forty miles, which brought them well up toward the Five Fingers.

Buck's feet were not so compact and hard as the feet of the huskies. His had softened during the many generations since the day his last wild ancestor was tamed by a cave dweller or river man. All day long he limped in agony, and camp once made, lay down like a dead dog. Hungry as he was, he would not move to receive his ration of fish, which François had to bring to him. Also, the dog driver rubbed Buck's feet for half an hour each night after supper, and sacrificed the tops of his own moccasins to make four moccasins for Buck. This was a great relief, and Buck caused even the weazened face of Perrault to twist itself into a grin one morning, when François forgot the moccasins and Buck lay on his back, his four feet waving appealingly in the air, and refused to budge without them. Later his feet grew hard to the trail, and the worn-out footgear was thrown away.

At the Pelly one morning, as they were harnessing up, Dolly, who had never been conspicuous for anything, went suddenly mad. She announced her condition by a long, heartbreaking wolf howl that sent every dog bristling with fear, then sprang straight for Buck. He had never seen a dog go mad, nor did he have any reason to fear madness; yet he knew that here was horror, and fled away from it in a panic. Straight away he raced, with Dolly, panting and frothing, one leap behind; nor could she gain on him, so great was his terror, nor could he leave her, so great was her madness. He plunged through the wooded breast of the island, fled down to the lower end, crossed a back channel filled with rough ice to another island, gained a third island, curved back to the main river, and in desperation started to cross it. And all the time, though he did not look, he could hear her snarling just one leap behind. François called to him a quarter of a mile away and he doubled back, still one leap ahead, gasping painfully for air and putting all his faith in that François would save him. The dog driver held the ax poised in his hand, and as Buck shot past him the ax crashed down upon mad Dolly's head.

Buck staggered over against the sled, exhausted, sobbing for breath, helpless. This was Spitz's opportunity. He sprang upon Buck, and twice his teeth sank into his unresisting foe and ripped and tore the flesh to the bone. Then François's lash descended, and Buck had the satisfaction of watching Spitz receive the worst whipping as yet administered to any of the team.

"One devil, dat Spitz," remarked Perrault. "Some dam day heem keel dat Buck."

"Dat Buck two devils," was François's rejoinder. "All de tam I watch dat Buck I know for sure. Lissen: Some dam fine day heem get mad lak hell an' den heem chew dat Spitz all up an' spit heem out on de snow. Sure. I know."

Approximate reading time for Part Two: 17 minutes

From then on it was war between them. Spitz, as lead dog and acknowledged master of the team, felt his supremacy threatened by this strange Southland dog. And strange Buck was to him, for of the many Southland dogs he had known, not one had shown up worthily in camp and on trail. They were all too soft, dying under the toil, the frost, and starvation. Buck was the exception. He alone endured and prospered, matching the husky in strength, savagery, and cunning. Then he was a masterful dog, and what made him dangerous was the fact that the club of the man in the red sweater had knocked all blind pluck and rashness out of his desire for mastery. He was preeminently [pre-EMM-inn-ent-lee] cunning, and could bide his time with a patience that was nothing less than primitive.

It was inevitable that the clash for leadership should come. Buck wanted it. He wanted it because it was his nature, because he had been gripped tight by that nameless, incomprehensible pride of the trail and trace—that pride which holds dogs in the toil to the last gasp, which lures them to die joyfully in the harness, and breaks their hearts if they are cut out of the harness. This was the pride of Dave as wheel dog, of Sol-leks as he pulled with all his strength; the pride that laid hold of them at break of camp, transforming them from sour and sullen brutes into straining, eager, ambitious creatures; the pride that spurred them on all day and dropped them at pitch of camp at night, letting them fall back into gloomy unrest and uncontent. This was the pride that bore up Spitz and made him thrash the sled dogs who blundered and shirked in the traces or hid away at harness-up time in the morning. Likewise it was this pride that made him fear Buck as a possible lead dog. And this was Buck's pride, too.

He openly threatened the other's leadership. He came between him and the shirks he should have punished. And he did it deliberately. One night there was a heavy snowfall, and in the morning Pike, the malingerer, did not appear. He was securely hidden in his nest under a foot of snow. François called him and sought him in vain. Spitz was wild with wrath. He raged through the camp, smelling and digging in every likely place, snarling so frightfully that Pike heard and shivered in his hiding place.

But when he was at last unearthed, and Spitz flew at him to punish him, Buck flew, with equal rage, in between. So unexpected was it, and so shrewdly managed, that Spitz was hurled backward and off his feet. Pike, who had been trembling abjectly, took heart at this open mutiny, and sprang upon his overthrown leader. Buck, to whom fair play was a forgotten code, likewise sprang upon Spitz. But François, chuckling at the incident while unswerving in the administration of justice, brought his lash down upon Buck with all his might. This failed to drive Buck from his prostrate rival, and the butt of the whip was brought into play. Half stunned by the blow, Buck was knocked backward and the lash laid upon him again and again, while Spitz soundly punished the many times offending Pike.

In the days that followed, as Dawson grew closer and closer, Buck still continued to interfere between Spitz and the culprits; but he did it craftily, when François was not around. With the covert mutiny of Buck, a general insubordination sprang up and increased. Dave and Sol-leks were unaffected, but the rest of the team went from bad to worse. Things no longer went right. There was continual bickering and jangling. Trouble was always afoot, and at the bottom of it was Buck. He kept François busy, for the dog driver was in constant apprehension of the life-and-death struggle between the two which he knew must take place sooner or later; and on more than one night the sounds of quarreling and strife among the other dogs turned him out of his sleeping robe, fearful that Buck and Spitz were at it.

But the opportunity did not present itself, and they pulled into Dawson one dreary afternoon with the great fight still to come. Here were many men, and countless dogs, and Buck found them all at work. It seemed the ordained order of things that dogs should work. All day they swung up and down the main street in long teams, and in the night their jingling bells still went by. They hauled cabin logs and firewood, freighted up to the mines, and did all manner of work that horses did in the Santa Clara Valley. Here and there Buck met Southland dogs, but in the main they were the wild wolf husky breed. Every night, regularly, at nine, at twelve, at three, they lifted a nocturnal song, a weird and eerie chant, in which it was Buck's delight to join.

With the aurora borealis [ah-ROAR-ah borr-ee-AL-iss] flaming coldly overhead, or the stars leaping in the frost dance, and the land numb and frozen under its pall of snow, this song of the huskies might have been the defiance of life, only it was pitched in minor key, with long-drawn wailings and half-sobs, and was more the pleading of life, the articulate travail of existence. It was an old song, old as the breed itself—one of the first songs of the younger world in a day when songs were sad. It was invested with the woe of unnumbered generations, this plaint by which Buck was so strangely stirred. When he moaned and sobbed, it was with the pain of living that was of old the pain of his wild fathers, and the fear and mystery of the cold and dark that was to them fear and mystery. And that he should be stirred by it marked the completeness with which he harked back through the ages of fire and roof to the raw beginnings of life in the howling ages.

Seven days from the time they pulled into Dawson, they dropped down the steep bank by the Barracks to the Yukon Trail, and pulled for Dyea and Salt Water. Perrault was carrying dispatches, if anything more urgent than those he had brought in; also, the travel pride had gripped him, and he purposed to make the record trip of the year. Several things favored him in this. The week's rest had recuperated the dogs and put them in thorough trim. The trail they had broken into the country was packed hard by later journeyers. And further, the police had arranged in two or three places deposits of grub for dog and man, and he was traveling light.

They made Sixty Mile, which is a fifty-mile run, on the first day; and the second day saw them booming up the Yukon well on their way to Pelly. But such splendid running was achieved not without great trouble and vexation on the part of François. The insidious [inn-SIDD-ee-us] revolt led by Buck had destroyed the solidarity of the team. It no longer was as one dog leaping in the traces. The encouragement Buck gave the rebels led them into all kinds of petty misdemeanors. No more was Spitz a leader greatly to be feared. The old awe departed, and they grew equal to challenging his authority. Pike robbed him of half a fish one night, and gulped it down under the protection of Buck. Another night Dub and Joe fought Spitz and made him forego the punishment they deserved. And even Billee, the good-natured, was less good-natured, and whined not half so placatingly as in former days. Buck never came near Spitz without snarling and bristling menacingly. In fact, his conduct approached that of a bully, and he was given to swaggering up and down before Spitz's very nose.

The breaking down of discipline likewise affected the dogs in their relations with one another. They quarreled and bickered more than ever among themselves, till at times the camp was a howling bedlam. Dave and Sol-leks alone were unaltered, though they were made irritable by the unending squabbling. François swore strange barbarous oaths, and stamped the snow in futile rage, and tore his hair. His lash was always singing among the dogs, but it was of small avail. Directly his back was turned they were at it again. He backed up Spitz with his whip, while Buck backed up the remainder of the team. François knew he was behind all the trouble, and Buck knew he knew; but Buck was too clever ever again to be caught redhanded. He worked faithfully in the harness, for the toil had become a delight to him; yet it was a greater delight slyly to precipitate a fight among his mates and tangle the traces.

At the mouth of the Tahkeena, one night after supper, Dub turned up a snowshoe rabbit, blundered it, and missed. In a second the whole team was in full cry. A hundred yards away was a camp of the Northwest Police, with fifty dogs, huskies all, who joined the chase. The rabbit sped down the river, turned off into a small creek, up the frozen bed of which it held steadily. It ran lightly on the surface of the snow, while the dogs plowed through by main strength. Buck led the pack, sixty strong, around bend after bend, but he could not gain. He lay down low to the race, whining eagerly, his splendid body flashing forward, leap by leap, in the wan white moonlight. And leap by leap, like some pale frost wraith [RAYTH], the snowshoe rabbit flashed on ahead.

All that stirring of old instincts which at stated periods drives men out from the sounding cities to forest and plain to kill things by chemically propelled leaden pellets, the blood lust, the joy to kill—all this was Buck's, only it was infinitely more intimate. He was ranging at the head of the pack, running the wild thing down, the living meat, to kill with his own teeth and wash his muzzle to the eyes in warm blood.

There is an ecstasy that marks the summit of life, and beyond which life cannot rise. And such is the paradox of living, this ecstasy comes when one is most alive, and it comes as a complete forgetfulness that one is alive. This ecstasy, this forgetfulness of living, comes to the artist, caught up and out of himself in a sheet of flame; it comes to the soldier, war-mad on a stricken field and refusing quarter; and it came to Buck, leading the pack, sounding the old wolf-cry, straining after the food that was alive and that fled swiftly before him through the moonlight. He was sounding the deeps of his nature, and of the parts of his nature that were deeper than he, going back into the womb of Time. He was mastered by the sheer surging of life, the tidal wave of being, the perfect joy of each separate muscle, joint, and sinew in that it was everything that was not death, that it was aglow and rampant, expressing itself in movement, flying exultantly under the stars and over the face of dead matter that did not move.

But Spitz, cold and calculating even in his supreme moods, left the pack and cut across a narrow neck of land where the creek made a long bend around. Buck did not know of this, and as he rounded the bend, the frost wraith of a rabbit still flitting before him, he saw another and larger frost wraith leap from the overhanging bank into the immediate path of the rabbit. It was Spitz. The rabbit could not turn, and as the white teeth broke its back in midair it shrieked as loudly as a stricken man may shriek. At sound of this, the cry of Life plunging down from Life's apex [AA-pecks] in the grip of Death, the full pack at Buck's heels raised a hell's chorus of delight.

Buck did not cry out. He did not check himself, but drove in upon Spitz, shoulder to shoulder, so hard that he missed the throat. They rolled over and over in the powdery snow. Spitz gained his feet almost as though he had not been overthrown, slashing Buck down the shoulder and leaping clear. Twice his teeth clipped together, like the steel jaws of a trap, as he backed away for better footing, with lean and lifting lips that writhed and snarled.

In a flash Buck knew it. The time had come. It was to the death. As they circled about, snarling, ears laid back, keenly watchful for the advantage, the scene came to Buck with a sense of familiarity. He seemed to remember it all—the white woods, the earth, and moonlight, and the thrill of battle. Over the whiteness and silence brooded a ghostly calm. There was not the faintest whisper of air—nothing moved, not a leaf quivered, the visible breaths of the dogs rising slowly and lingering in the frosty air. They had made short work of the snowshoe rabbit, these dogs that were ill-tamed wolves; and they were now drawn up in an expectant circle. They, too, were silent, their eyes only gleaming and their breaths drifting slowly upward. To Buck it was nothing new or strange, this scene of old time. It was as though it had always been, the wonted way of things.

Spitz was a practiced fighter. From Spitzbergen through the Arctic, and across Canada and the Barrens, he had held his own with all manner of dogs and achieved mastery over them. Bitter rage was his, but never blind rage. In passion to rend and destroy, he never forgot that his enemy was in like passion to rend and destroy. He never rushed till he was prepared to receive a rush; never attacked till he had first defended that attack.

In vain Buck strove to sink his teeth in the neck of the big white dog. Wherever his fangs struck for the softer flesh, they were countered by the fangs of Spitz. Fang clashed fang, and lips were cut and bleeding, but Buck could not penetrate his enemy's guard. Then he warmed up and enveloped Spitz in a whirlwind of rushes. Time and time again he tried for the snow-white throat, where life bubbled near to the surface, and each time and every time Spitz slashed him and got away. Then Buck took to rushing, as though for the throat, when, suddenly drawing back his head and curving in from the side, he would drive his shoulder at the shoulder of Spitz, as a ram by which to overthrow him. But instead, Buck's shoulder was slashed down each time as Spitz leaped lightly away.

Spitz was untouched, while Buck was streaming with blood and panting hard. The fight was growing desperate. And all the while the silent and wolfish circle waited to finish off whichever dog went down. As Buck grew winded, Spitz took to rushing, and he kept him staggering for footing. Once Buck went over, and the whole circle of sixty dogs started up; but he recovered himself, almost in midair, and the circle sank down again and waited.

But Buck possessed a quality that made for greatness—imagination. He fought by instinct, but he could fight by head as well. He rushed, as though attempting the old shoulder trick, but at the last instant swept low to the snow and in. His teeth closed on Spitz's left foreleg. There was a crunch of breaking bone, and the white dog faced him on three legs. Thrice he tried to knock him over, then repeated the trick and broke the right foreleg. Despite the pain and helplessness, Spitz struggled madly to keep up. He saw the silent circle, with gleaming eyes, lolling tongues, and silvery breaths drifting upward, closing in upon him as he had seen similar circles close in upon beaten antagonists in the past. Only this time he was the one who was beaten.

There was no hope for him. Buck was inexorable [inn-EGGS-orr-uh-buhl]. Mercy was a thing reserved for gentler climes. He maneuvered for the final rush. The circle had tightened till he could feel the breaths of the huskies on his flanks. He could see them, beyond Spitz and to either side, half crouching for the spring, their eyes fixed upon him. A pause seemed to fall. Every animal was motionless as though turned to stone. Only Spitz quivered and bristled as he staggered back and forth, snarling with horrible menace, as though to frighten off impending death. Then Buck sprang in and out; but while he was in, shoulder had at last squarely met shoulder. The dark circle became a dot on the moon-flooded snow as Spitz disappeared from view. Buck stood and looked on, the successful champion, the dominant primordial beast who had made his kill and found it good.

Poetry

Story poems have an allure to children that is uncommon in more pastoral or descriptive verses, and so they dominate here. "Casey at the Bat," "Paul Revere's Ride," "The Charge of the Light Brigade," and "The Highwayman" all tell tales that could as easily have been short stories. Yet there is an economy in poetry—a use of implication rather than explication, which demands more of the listeners' imagination while, at the same time, rewards them with phrases that continue to haunt the memory.

Poetry is not so terribly mysterious and inaccessible; it is, after all, just another form of expression. You might enjoy linking poems with some of the stories in this book; Longfellow's "The Windmill" can be an appropriate accompaniment to the telling of Don Quixote's famous joust, for example. What poems do you recall as being memorable parts of your childhood? It is a safe bet that they will also be eagerly received and rewarding offerings to your children as well.

"Casey at the Bat"

by
ERNEST LAWRENCE THAYER

Suggested listening level: I and II
Approximate reading time: 5 minutes
Pronunciation and vocabulary guide:
      pallor [PALL-er]: paleness
      visage [VIZZ-ej]: appearance

It looked extremely rocky for the Mudville nine that day;
The score stood two to four, with but an inning left to play.
So, when Cooney died at second, and Burrows did the same,
A pallor wreathed the features of the patrons of the game.

A straggling few got up to go, leaving there the rest,
With that hope which springs eternal within the human breast.
For they thought: "If only Casey could get a whack at that,"
They'd put even money now, with Casey at the bat.

But Flynn preceded Casey, and likewise so did Blake.
And the former was a pudd'n, and the latter was a fake.
So on that stricken multitude a deathlike silence sat;
For there seemed but little chance of Casey's getting to the bat.

But Flynn let drive a "single," to the wonderment of all.
And the much-despised Blakey "tore the cover off the ball."
And when the dust had lifted, and they saw what had oc-
    curred,
There was Blakey safe at second, and Flynn a-huggin' third.

Then from the gladdened multitude went up a joyous yell—
It rumbled in the mountaintops, it rattled in the dell;
It struck upon the hillside and rebounded on the flat;
For Casey, mighty Casey, was advancing to the bat.

There was ease in Casey's manner as he stepped into his place,
There was pride in Casey's bearing and a smile on Casey's face;

And when responding to the cheers he lightly doffed his hat,
No stranger in the crowd could doubt 'twas Casey at the bat.

Ten thousand eyes were on him as he rubbed his hands with
    dirt,
Five thousand tongues applauded when he wiped them on his
    shirt;
Then when the writhing pitcher ground the ball into his hip,
Defiance glanced in Casey's eye, a sneer curled Casey's lip.

And now the leather-covered sphere came hurtling through
    the air,
And Casey stood a-watching it in haughty grandeur there.
Close by the sturdy batsman the ball unheeded sped;
"That ain't my style," said Casey. "Strike one," the umpire
    said.

From the benches, black with people, there went up a muffled
    roar,
Like the beating of the storm waves on the stern and distant
    shore.
"Kill him! kill the umpire!" shouted someone on the stand;
And it's likely they'd have killed him had not Casey raised his
    hand.

With a smile of Christian charity great Casey's visage shone;
He stilled the rising tumult, he made the game go on;
He signaled to the pitcher, and once more the spheroid flew;
But Casey still ignored it, and the umpire said, "Strike two."

"Fraud!" cried the maddened thousands, and the echo an-
    swered "Fraud!"
But one scornful look from Casey and the audience was awed;
They saw his face grow stern and cold, they saw his muscles
    strain,
And they knew that Casey wouldn't let the ball go by again.

The sneer is gone from Casey's lips, his teeth are clenched in
    hate,
He pounds with cruel vengeance his bat upon the plate;

And now the pitcher holds the ball, and now he lets it go,
And now the air is shattered by the force of Casey's blow.

Oh, somewhere in this favored land the sun is shining bright,
The band is playing somewhere, and somewhere hearts are
    light;
And somewhere men are laughing, and somewhere children
    shout,
But there is no joy in Mudville: Mighty Casey has struck out.

"The Windmill"

by
HENRY WADSWORTH LONGFELLOW

Suggested listening level: I
Pronunciation and vocabulary guide:
     maize: corn
     flails: threshing sticks

Behold! a giant am I!
  Aloft here in my tower,
  With my granite jaws I devour
The maize, and the wheat, and the rye,
  And grind them into flour.

I look down over the farms;
  In the fields of grain I see
  The harvest that is to be,
And I fling to the air my arms,
  For I know it is all for me.

I hear the sound of flails
  Far off, from the threshing-floors
  In barns, with their open doors,
And the wind, the wind in my sails,
  Louder and louder roars.

I stand here in my place,
  With my foot on the rock below,
  And whichever way it may blow,
I meet it face to face
  As a brave man meets his foe.

And while we wrestle and strive,
  My master, the miller, stands
  and feeds me with his hands;
For he knows who makes him thrive,
  Who makes him lord of lands.

On Sundays I take my rest;
   Church-going bells begin
   Their low, melodious din;
I cross my arms on my breast,
   And all is peace within.

"Paul Revere's Ride"

by
HENRY WADSWORTH LONGFELLOW

Suggested listening level: I or II
Approximate reading time: 7 minutes
Pronunciation and vocabulary guide:
>   **impetuous** [imm-PET-you-us]: brash, impulsive
>   **spectral:** ghostly
>   **alders:** trees of the birch family

Listen, my children, and you shall hear
Of the midnight ride of Paul Revere,
On the eighteenth of April, in seventy-five;
Hardly a man is now alive
Who remembers that famous day and year.

He said to his friend, "If the British march
By land or sea from the town tonight,
Hang a lantern aloft in the belfry arch
Of the North Church tower as a signal light—
One, if by land, and two, if by sea;
And I on the opposite shore will be,
Ready to ride and spread the alarm
Through every Middlesex village and farm,
For the country folk to be up and to arm."

Then he said, "Good night!" and with muffled oar
Silently rowed to the Charlestown shore,
Just as the moon rose over the bar,
Where swinging wide at her moorings lay
The *Somerset*, British man-of-war;
A phantom ship, with each mast and spar
Across the moon like a prison bar,
And a huge black hulk, that was magnified
By its own reflection in the tide.

Meanwhile, his friend, through alley and street,
Wanders and watches, with eager ears,

Till in the silence around him he hears
The muster of men at the barrack door,
And the measured tread of the grenadiers,
Marching down to their boats on the shore.

Then he climbed to the tower of the Old North Church,
By the wooden stairs, with stealthy tread,
To the belfry-chamber overhead,
And startled the pigeons from their perch
On the somber rafters, that round him made
Masses and moving shapes of shade—
By the trembling ladder, steep and tall,
To the highest window in the wall,
Where he paused to listen and look down
A moment on the roofs of the town,
And the moonlight flowing over all.

Beneath in the churchyard, lay the dead,
In their night-encampment on the hill,
Wrapped in silence so deep and still
That he could hear, like a sentinel's tread,
The watchful night-wind, as it went
Creeping along from tent to tent,
And seeming to whisper, "All is well!"
A moment only he feels the spell
Of the place and the hour, and the secret dread
Of the lonely belfry and the dead;
For suddenly all his thoughts are bent
On a shadowy something far away,
Where the river widens to meet the bay—
A line of black that bends and floats
On the rising tide, like a bridge of boats.

Meanwhile, impatient to mount and ride,
Booted and spurred, with a heavy stride
On the opposite shore walked Paul Revere.
Now he patted his horse's side,
Now gazed at the landscape far and near,
Then, impetuous, stamped the earth,
And turned and tightened his saddle girth;

But mostly he watched with eager search
The belfry tower of the Old North Church,
As it rose above the graves on the hill,
Lonely and spectral and somber and still.
And lo! as he looks, on the belfry's height
A glimmer, and then a gleam of light!
He springs to the saddle, the bridle he turns,
But lingers and gazes, till full on his sight
A second lamp in the belfry burns!

A hurry of hoofs in a village street,
A shape in the moonlight, a bulk in the dark,
And beneath, from the pebbles, in passing, a spark
Struck out by a steed flying fearless and fleet:
That was all! And yet, through the gloom and the light,
The fate of a nation was riding that night;
And the spark struck out by that steed, in his flight,
Kindled the land into flame with its heat.

He has left the village and mounted the steep,
And beneath him, tranquil and broad and deep,
Is the Mystic, meeting the ocean tides;
And under the alders that skirt its edge,
Now soft on the sand, now loud on the ledge,
Is heard the tramp of his steed as he rides.

It was twelve by the village clock,
When he crossed the bridge into Medford town.
He heard the crowing of the cock,
And the barking of the farmer's dog,
And felt the damp of the river fog,
That rises after the sun goes down.

It was one by the village clock,
When he galloped into Lexington.
He saw the gilded weathercock
Swim in the moonlight as he passed,
And the meeting-house windows, blank and bare,
Gaze at him with a spectral glare,

As if they already stood aghast
At the bloody work they would look upon.

It was two by the village clock,
When he came to the bridge in Concord town.
He heard the bleating of the flock,
And the twitter of birds among the trees,
And felt the breath of the morning breeze
Blowing over the meadows brown.
And one was safe and asleep in his bed
Who at the bridge would be first to fall,
Who that day would be lying dead,
Pierced by a British musket-ball.

You know the rest. In the books you have read
How the British Regulars fired and fled—
How the farmers gave them ball for ball,
From behind each fence and farmyard wall,
Chasing the red-coats down the lane,
Then crossing the fields to emerge again
Under the trees at the turn of the road,
And only pausing to fire and load.

So through the night rode Paul Revere;
And so through the night went the cry of alarm
To every Middlesex village and farm—
A cry of defiance and not of fear,
A voice in the darkness, a knock at the door,
And a word that shall echo for evermore!
For, bourne on the night-wind of the Past,
Through all our history, to the last,
In the hour of darkness and peril and need,
The people will awaken and listen to hear
The hurrying hoof-beats of that steed,
And the midnight message of Paul Revere.

"The Highwayman"

by
ALFRED NOYES

Suggested listening level: II
Approximate reading time: 8 minutes
Pronunciation and vocabulary guide:
> **highwayman:** a robber who preys on travelers
> **claret** [KLARE-et]: dark, purplish red
> **breeches** [BRICH-ez]: knee-length trousers
> **plaiting:** braiding
> **ostler** [OAST-ler]: a stable hand at an inn
> **harry:** to harass or torment

PART I

The wind was a torrent of darkness among the gusty trees,
The moon was a ghostly galleon tossed upon cloudy seas,
The road was a ribbon of moonlight over the purple moor,
And the highwayman came riding—
 Riding—riding—
The highwayman came riding, up to the old inn-door.

He'd a French cocked-hat on his forehead, a bunch of lace at
 his chin,
A coat of the claret velvet, and breeches of brown doe-skin;
They fitted with never a wrinkle; his boots were up to the
 thigh!
And he rode with a jeweled twinkle,
 His pistol butts a-twinkle,
His rapier hilt a-twinkle, under the jeweled sky.

Over the cobbles he clattered and clashed in the dark inn-yard,
And he tapped with his whip on the shutters, but all was
 locked and barred;
He whistled a tune to the window, and who should be waiting
 there
But the landlord's black-eyed daughter,
 Bess, the landlord's daughter,
Plaiting a dark red love-knot into her long black hair.

And dark in the dark old inn-yard a stable-wicket creaked
Where Tim the ostler listened; his face was white and peaked;
His eyes were hollows of madness, his hair like moldy hay,
But he loved the landlord's daughter,
    The landlord's red-lipped daughter,
Dumb as a dog he listened, and he heard the robber say—

"One kiss, my bonny sweetheart, I'm after a prize tonight,
But I shall be back with the yellow gold before the morning
    light;
Yet, if they press me sharply, and harry me through the day,
Then look for me by moonlight,
    Watch for me by moonlight,
I'll come to thee by moonlight, though hell should bar the
    way."

He rose upright in the stirrups; he scarce could reach her hand,
But she loosened her hair i' the casement! His face burned like
    a brand
As the black cascade of perfume came tumbling over his breast;
And he kissed its waves in the moonlight,
    (Oh, sweet black waves in the moonlight!)
Then he tugged at his rein in the moonlight, and galloped
    away to the West.

PART II

He did not come in the dawning; he did not come at noon;
And out o' the tawny sunset, before the rise o' the moon,
When the road was a gypsy's ribbon, looping the purple moor,
A red-coat troop came marching—
    Marching—marching—
King George's men came marching, up to the old inn-door.

They said no word to the landlord, they drank his ale instead,
But they gagged his daughter and bound her to the foot of her
    narrow bed;
Two of them knelt at her casement, with muskets at their side!

There was death at every window;
    And hell at one dark window;
For Bess could see, through her casement, the road that *he*
    would ride.

They had tied her up to attention, with many a sniggering jest;
They had bound a musket beside her, with the barrel beneath
    her breast!
"Now keep good watch" and they kissed her. She heard the
    dead man say—
Look for me by moonlight;
    Watch for me by moonlight;
I'll come to thee by moonlight, though hell should bar the way!

She twisted her hands behind her; but all the knots held good!
She writhed her hands till her fingers were wet with sweat or
    blood!
They stretched and strained in the darkness, and the hours
    crawled by like years,
Till now, on the stroke of midnight,
    Cold, on the stroke of midnight,
The tip of one finger touched it! The trigger at least was hers!

The tip of one finger touched it; she strove no more for the
    rest!
Up, she stood up to attention, with the barrel beneath her
    breast,
She would not risk their hearing: she would not strive again;
For the road lay bare in the moonlight;
    Blank and bare in the moonlight;
And the blood of her veins in the moonlight throbbed to her
    love's refrain.

Tlot-tlot; tlot-tlot! Had they heard it? The horse-hoofs ringing
    clear,
Tlot-tlot, tlot-tlot, in the distance? Were they deaf that they did
    not hear?
Down the ribbon of moonlight, over the brow of the hill,
The highwayman came riding,

Riding, riding!
The red-coats looked to their priming! She stood up straight
and still!

Tlot-tlot, in the frosty silence! *Tlot-tlot,* in the echoing night!
Nearer he came and nearer! Her face was like a light!
Her eyes grew wide for a moment; she drew one last deep
breath,
Then her finger moved in the moonlight,
    Her musket shattered the moonlight,
Shattered her breast in the moonlight and warned him—with
her death.

He turned; he spurred to the westward; he did not know who
stood
Bowed, with her head o'er the musket, drenched with her own
red blood!
Not till the dawn he heard it, his face grew gray to hear
How Bess, the landlord's daughter,
    The landlord's black-eyed daughter,
Had watched for her love in the moonlight, and died in the
darkness there.

Back he spurred like a madman, shrieking a curse to the sky,
With the white road smoking behind him, and his rapier
brandished high!
Blood-red were his spurs in the golden moon; wine-red was
his velvet coat,
When they shot him down on the highway,
    Down like a dog on the highway,
And he lay in his blood on the highway, with a bunch of lace
at his throat.

And still of a winter's night, they say, when the wind is in the trees,
When the moon is a ghostly galleon, tossed upon cloudy seas,
When the road is a ribbon of moonlight over the purple moor,
A highwayman comes riding—
    Riding—riding—
A highwayman comes riding, up to the old inn-door.

Over the cobbles he clatters and clangs in the dark inn-yard;
And he taps with his whip on the shutters, but all is locked and barred;
He whistles a tune to the window, and who should be waiting there
But the landlord's black-eyed daughter,
    Bess, the landlord's daughter,
Plaiting a dark red love-knot into her long black hair.

"The Charge of the Light Brigade"

by
ALFRED LORD TENNYSON

Suggested listening level: II
Approximate reading time: 3 minutes
Pronunciation and vocabulary guide:
  league: approximately three miles

Half a league, half a league,
  Half a league onward,
All in the valley of Death
Rode the six hundred.
"Forward, the Light Brigade!
Charge for the guns," he said:
Into the valley of Death
  Rode the six hundred.
"Forward, the Light Brigade!"
Was there a man dismay'd?
Not tho' the soldier knew
  Someone had blunder'd.
Theirs not to make reply,
Theirs not to reason why,
Theirs but to do and die.
Into the valley of Death
  Rode the six hundred.

Cannon to right of them,
Cannon to left of them,
Cannon in front of them
  Volley'd and thunder'd;
Storm'd at with shot and shell,
Boldly they rode and well,
Into the jaws of Death,
Into the mouth of Hell
  Rode the six hundred.

Flash'd all their sabers bare,
Flash'd as they turn'd in air

Sabring the gunners there,
Charging an army, while
  All the world wonder'd.
Plung'd in the battery-smoke
Right thro' the line they broke;
Cossack and Russian
Reel'd from the saber-stroke
  Shatter'd and sunder'd.
Then they rode back, but not,
  Not the six hundred.

Cannon to right of them,
Cannon to left of them,
Cannon behind them
  Volleyed and thunder'd;
Storm'd at with shot and shell,
While horse and hero fell,
They that had fought so well
Came thro' the jaws of Death,
Back from the mouth of Hell,
All that was left of them,
  Left of six hundred.

When can their glory fade?
O the wild charge they made!
  All the world wonder'd.
Honor the charge they made!
Honor the Light Brigade,
  Noble six hundred!

"If—"

by
RUDYARD KIPLING

Suggested listening level: II and III
Approximate reading time: 2 minutes

If you can keep your head when all about you
   Are losing theirs and blaming it on you;
If you can trust yourself when all men doubt you,
   But make allowance for their doubting too;
If you can wait and not be tired by waiting,
   Or, being lied about, don't deal in lies,
Or, being hated, don't give way to hating,
   And yet don't look too good, nor talk too wise;

If you can dream—and not make dreams your master;
   If you can think—and not make thoughts your aim;
If you can meet with triumph and disaster
   And treat those two impostors just the same;
If you can bear to hear the truth you've spoken
   Twisted by knaves to make a trap of fools,
Or watch the things you gave your life to broken,
   And stoop and build 'em up with wornout tools;

If you can make one heap of all your winnings
   And risk it on one turn of pitch-and-toss,
And lose, and start again at your beginnings
   And never breathe a word about your loss;
If you can force your heart and nerve and sinew
   To serve your turn long after they are gone,
And so hold on when there is nothing in you
   Except the Will which says to them: "Hold on."

If you can talk with crowds and keep your virtue,
    Or walk with kings—nor lose the common touch;
If neither foes nor loving friends can hurt you;
    If all men count with you, but none too much;
If you can fill the unforgiving minute
    With sixty seconds' worth of distance run—
Yours is the Earth and everything that's in it,
    And—which is more—you'll be a Man, my son.

"It Couldn't Be Done"

by
EDGAR A. GUEST

Suggested listening level: All ages
Pronunciation and vocabulary guide:
   prophesy [PROFF-eh-sigh]: to make a prophecy or prediction

Somebody said that it couldn't be done,
   But he with a chuckle replied
That "maybe it couldn't," but he would be one
   Who wouldn't say so till he'd tried.
So he buckled right in with the trace of a grin
   On his face. If he worried he hid it.
He started to sing as he tackled the thing
   That couldn't be done, and he did it.

Somebody scoffed: "Oh, you'll never do that;
   At least no one ever has done it";
But he took off his coat and he took off his hat,
   And the first thing we knew he'd begun it.
With a lift of his chin and a bit of a grin,
   Without any doubting or quiddit,
He started to sing as he tackled the thing
   That couldn't be done, and he did it.

There are thousands to tell you it cannot be done,
   There are thousands to prophesy failure;
There are thousands to point out to you, one by one,
   The dangers that wait to assail you.
But just buckle in with a bit of a grin,
   Just take off your coat and go to it;
Just start to sing as you tackle the thing
   That "cannot be done," and you'll do it.

Holiday Favorites

Holidays are times when parents and children are most likely to be together, and so here are some readings to take advantage of those occasions. Of course, not all the traditional holidays are represented here; occasions like Memorial Day and Independence Day may inspire you to find additional readings that are related to these themes.

The works contained in this section need not be reserved until the holiday arrives or read only during their corresponding season. "The Gift of the Magi" and "The Legend of Sleepy Hollow," for example, will prove rewarding no matter when you choose to present them, and A Christmas Carol will stand several tellings without diminishing its value as a ritual part of Christmas Day.

"Pharaoh of the Hard Heart"

from Exodus 12:1–13:16, as retold by William Canton

About the story:

The eight-day festival of Passover celebrates the Exodus of the Jewish people from Egyptian bondage, perhaps the single most significant event in the history of the Jews. It is said that the Angel of Death "passed over" the homes of the children of Israel, but struck down the first-born child of every Egyptian family as a warning to the Pharaoh to let God's people go.

Although Jews around the world retell the story of their liberation each year at this time, it is important for children and adults of all faiths to understand the story. The historical accuracy of the plagues and miracles in the following selection is less important than exploring your children's feelings about enslavement and libera-tion. I encourage you to explore these feelings as deeply as you can.

Suggested listening level: All ages
Approximate reading time: 15 minutes
Pronunciation and vocabulary guide:
    chasm [KAZZ-um]: a deep gorge
    ibex [IH-becks]: a type of long-horned goat
    wadis [WAH-deez]: gullies that remain dry except dur-ing the rainy season
    acacia [uh-KAY-shuh]: a tropical tree
    bade [BAD]
    abate [uh-BAIT]: to reduce or lessen
    hyssop [HISS-up]: a woody plant
    lintels: the horizontal beam in the door frame

Moses dwelled in Midian forty years, and as he wandered far and wide with Jethro's flock, he came to know the secrets of the mountains, each gorge and chasm [KAZZ-um], and all their windings from sea to sea; the haunts of the ibex [IH-becks], the partridge and the quail; badger's earth and leopard's lair; the wadis [WAD-deez] where clear brooks flowed and feathery palms grew thickest and nightingales sang. For this was the wilderness, not the desert.

The mountains raised aloft their mighty buttresses and pinnacles in a wild splendor of light and color. Thyme and myrrh and other aromatic herbs grew on their savage slopes and in the clefts of the rocky walls which bounded wadi and gorge.

Moses came with his flock to the great mountain of Sinai, the mountain of God. Among the rocks he saw an acacia [uh-KAY-shuh] bush in blaze of fire. For all its burning, neither branch nor leaf was consumed, and as he approached in wonder at the sight, the Lord spoke to him out of the flames of the burning bush: "Moses, Moses, take off thy sandals; where thou standest is holy ground." And again He said, "I am the god of thy father, the God of Abraham, the God of Isaac, and the God of Jacob."

Moses covered his face, for he dared not look at God. And the Lord said, "I have seen the affliction of my people in Egypt; I have heard their cry and I know their sorrows; and I am come down to deliver them and to lead them into a good land, a land of milk and honey. Now, therefore, I send thee to Pharaoh, and thou shalt lead my people out of Egypt." But Moses answered, "Who am I, to go to Pharaoh, and to lead the children of Israel?" "I will be with thee," said the Lord. "Speak what I have told thee to the elders of Israel. They will listen to thee, they will go with thee to the King of Egypt, and thou shalt say to him, 'The Lord God of the Hebrews has appeared to us. Give us leave then to make a three-days' journey into the wilderness, to sacrifice to the Lord our God.' He will not let you go—no, not unless by the strong hand; but I will smite Egypt terribly, and then he will let you go."

Moses answered, "The elders will not believe, they will not listen. They will say, 'No Lord appeared to thee.' " God said, "What art thou holding in thy hand?" Moses replied, "A staff." "Throw it on the ground." Moses threw it down, and at once it was no staff but a serpent, and Moses fled from it. The Lord said, "Put out thy hand and take it by the tail"; and when Moses did so, it was a staff again. "That shall be a token that I have appeared to thee."

Still Moses was unwilling, and he said, "O my Lord, I am not eloquent, but am slow of speech." The Lord answered, "Who made man's mouth? Go, and I will teach thee what to say." Then Moses cried out in hopelessness, "O my Lord, send someone else, I beseech Thee." The Lord was angry then with Moses, and He said, "Is not Aaron thy brother? He is now on his way to meet thee. Thou shalt put the words into his mouth, and he shall speak them to the people for thee. I will be with thy mouth and with his mouth. Go, and take this staff with thee; with it thou shalt work wonders."

Moses set out with the staff of God in his hand into the mountain paths toward Egypt. And Aaron met him in the mount of God, and kissed him, and was glad at heart. For they were brothers; Moses now eighty years old and Aaron eighty-three.

They delivered the message of the Lord to the elders of Israel, and showed the tokens of their truth before all the people. These believed that God had heard their cry, and they bowed down and worshiped Him. But when Moses and Aaron appeared before Pharaoh, saying, "Give the children of Israel leave to go into the wilderness and sacrifice to the Lord, lest He strike all Egypt with pestilence or the sword," Pharaoh answered, "Who is the Lord that I should obey Him? I know not the Lord, and I will not let Israel go. And why do you keep the people from their labors? Get them back to work." And Pharaoh ordered his overseers to lay even heavier toil upon them; "and see you give them no more straw for brick-making, they must find straw themselves." And so the people scattered in the fields, gathering stubble for straw; and when their tally of bricks fell short of what was required, the Hebrew foremen were beaten severely; and when they complained to Pharaoh, he scorned them and accused them of idleness. Then bitterly the foremen reproached Moses and Aaron saying, "Some good service you have done us with Pharaoh and his overseers— you have put a sword into their hands to destroy us!"

Then Moses turned to the Lord God and said, "Lord, why

hast Thou dealt evilly with the children of Israel? Why hast Thou sent me? Since I spoke to Pharaoh in Thy name, he has oppressed Thy people, and Thou has not delivered them at all." The Lord bade [BAD] Moses give the people reassurance of His promises, but they would not listen because of the cruelty of their bondage.

Then said the Lord to Moses, "Go to Pharaoh, and bid him let my people go. He will not hear thee. But I will lay my hand upon Egypt, and the Egyptians shall know that I am the Lord." Moses and Aaron went in to the king's presence, but Pharaoh said in derision, "Work me a wonder as a token of the Lord." Aaron cast the staff of God upon the ground, and it was changed into an angry serpent. Then Pharaoh summoned his seers and magicians; they, too, cast down their staffs which, by illusion, became serpents, but the staff of the Lord sprang upon them and swallowed them up. Pharaoh's heart was hardened, and he would not let the people go.

At sunrise on the morrow, the King of Egypt went forth to worship at the sacred river. On the riverbank, Moses and Aaron awaited him, as God had commanded them, and they said to Pharaoh, "This is the word of the Lord, 'Let my people go that they may serve me. Hitherto thou hast not listened. Now I will show thee that I am the Lord.' " Aaron lifted up the staff and struck the river, and the waters were turned to blood. The fish died, and the waters emitted a stench most foul. For seven days the water was blood in their pots and tanks, in jars of stone and vessels of wood throughout the land of Egypt. But the magicians performed a similar feat for Pharaoh; his heart was hardened, and he would not let the children of Israel go.

Again Moses delivered the word of the Lord to Pharaoh, "Let my people go"; and again Pharaoh refused. Aaron stretched out the staff, and from the streams and pools a plague of frogs came upon the land. They swarmed into the houses; they fouled the food; they croaked in Pharaoh's bedchamber; they squatted on his bed. This wonder also the sorcerers imitated by their magic, but the plague they could not abate [uh-BAIT], and Pharaoh sought Moses and said, "Ask the Lord to take the frogs away, and I will let the people go." On the morrow the frogs died in all the houses, villages, and fields, and they were swept up in heaps. But as soon as this work was done, Pharaoh hardened his heart, and would not keep his word.

Yet again, four times, God laid His hand on Egypt. Aaron smote the dust of the ground and the dust turned to lice and ticks, plaguing man and beast. The cunning of the magicians failed them, and they said, "This is the work of God."

The Lord sent a plague of flies—black clouds of gnats, mosquitoes, dog-flies, stinging pests from the marshes, and except in the land of Goshen where the children of Israel dwelled, all Egypt was wasted with them. The third time, the Lord slew the cattle in the field, the horses and asses, the camels and sheep; but in Goshen no harm befell the beasts of Israel. The fourth time Moses took handfuls of ashes from the furnace, and flung them into the air. They drifted in small dust over the land and spread boils and sores among men and beasts.

Still, Pharaoh's heart was hardened, and he would not let the people go.

Then the Lord sent His word to the King of Egypt, "Let my people go, or this time I will send all my plagues into thy heart. Had I stricken thee with pestilence thou wouldst have vanished out of the world; but I have spared thee to show thee my power and to declare my name to all the earth"; and the Lord warned him of what would befall him on the morrow. At sunrise, Moses reached out his staff toward heaven, and the Lord sent thunder, and hail mingled with fireballs, and lightning running along the ground. All over Egypt, except in the land of Goshen, men and beasts were stricken in the open, and hail broke the trees, and flattened the crops. Pharaoh confessed his sin: "The Lord is righteous; I and my people are wicked. Beseech the Lord that there be no more mighty thunderings and driving hail. I will let you go, and withhold you no longer." Moses went out of the city and stretched up his hands to the Lord, but when the King of Egypt saw that the fire and the hail and the thunderings ceased, his heart became hard as flint.

Once more Moses spoke to Pharaoh, "Thus saith the Lord, 'How long wilt thou refuse to humble thyself to me? Let my people go, that they may serve me,'" and once again he warned him. Moses again stretched his staff against Egypt, and the Lord let a wind out of the east all that day and all night. In the morning it brought legions of locust. Such had they never been seen before, and such have they never since been seen. They covered the ground, they darkened the day, they ate up every herb of the land and all the fruit of the trees the hail had left; no green thing remained on earth or tree in the land of Egypt. Yet once again Pharaoh refused to let the people go.

Moses now stretched forth his hand toward the heavens, and for three days Egypt was clothed with darkness as though a garment had been thrown over it. They sat in the darkness, and saw not each other; for three days none rose from his place; but among the children of Israel there was light.

Moses now went unto Pharaoh and said, "This is the word of the Lord, 'Upon a midnight I will pass through the land of Egypt; and all the first-born in the land shall die—from the first-born of Pharaoh, seated on his throne, to the first-born of the servant who turns the upper stone of the mill, even to the first-born of the beasts. In all the land of Egypt there shall be such wailing as there hath never yet been, and the like shall never be again.' Then your counselors will beseech me, 'Get thee gone, thou and thy people.' Thereafter I shall go forth from Egypt."

The children of Israel made themselves ready for their pilgrimage, for "when Pharaoh does yield," said the Lord, "he will drive you hence suddenly and in haste."

On the tenth day of the month, the Hebrews took for each household an unblemished lamb or kid from the folds; on the fourteenth day, between evening and the sunset, they killed it, and roasted it whole with fire, and broke not a bone of it. In its blood they dipped a bunch of hyssop [HISS-up] and sprinkled the lintels and doorposts of their houses. When the sun had gone down and it was a new day, they feasted, each in his own house. There they remained like travelers ready to depart, their sandals on their feet and the staff of wayfaring in their hand; they ate the lamb with unleavened bread and with bitter herbs to symbolize their long sufferings.

That night no one went out of doors.

Upon the midnight the Lord God passed through Egypt, and smote all the first-born in the land, from the first-born of Pharaoh to the first-born of the captive in the dungeon and the first-born of the beasts of the field. Pharaoh rose up in the night, for the son of his delight was dead—his first-born, who had sat with him on his throne. His counselors and all the Egyptians rose up; there was a hurrying of lights, and a great cry went up in Egypt, a terrible wailing and beating of hands, for there was not a house in which there was not one dead. But the Lord saw the blood on the lintels and doorposts in the clear moonlight; He passed over the houses of the children of Israel, and harmed no one therein.

With confused sounds of voices and flying footsteps, messengers sought out Moses and Aaron. Pharaoh had instructed them to say, "Depart from among my people, you and the children of Israel. Go and serve the Lord, as you have said. Take your flocks and your herds, and get you gone. And bless me also!" The Egyptians crowded about them, and urged them to get upon their way, saying, "Hasten! or we are but dead men."

This was the night of the Lord's passover, which was observed by the children of Israel in all their generations. On that night the bondage of Israel in Egypt was four hundred and thirty years, and that same night was the end of their bondage. The month of their departure was made for them the beginning of months, the first month of the first year of a new time, for the calendar of Egypt they used no more. From that night the first-born in Israel, the first-born of man and the first-born of beast, was set apart for the Lord; it was His; and the first-born of man was redeemed at a price. The observance of these things kept forever green the tale of their deliverance; the tale was told from father to son; it was always in the mind, like a writing bound upon the arm or worn between the eyes.

"The Risen Lord"

From the Gospels of Mark, Luke, and John, as retold by William Canton

About the story:

Easter, too, is a celebration of deliverance: Christians see in the crucifixion, resurrection, and ascension of Jesus Christ a confirmation that, through Christ, they may realize life eternal. The sunrise services held by many churches symbolize the end of darkness and the dawn of hope among Christians.

The following selection relates the story of a time that many children know only by its association with colorful eggs, flowers, rabbits, and chicks. Their knowledge of the Easter story, however, may help them see these symbols as signifying new life, a celebration in which Nature joins each spring.

Suggested listening level: All ages
Approximate reading time: 11 minutes
Pronunciation and vocabulary guide:
Pharisees [FAIR-ih-seez]
sepulcher [SEPP-uhl-kerr]: a burial vault

The darkness had passed away; the three crosses on the hill of the skull stood out ghastly over against the westering sun; the Sabbath was approaching.

It was the feast of the Passover. The wine cup was blessed, and passed from hand to hand. In the holy city and all round the circuit of the hills there rose the sound of singing. The bitter herbs were eaten. Tens of thousands of children asked the same question, and in reply tens of thousands of voices were telling at the same moment the story of the bondage and the deliverance out of Egypt. And in the moonlit garden Jesus lay cold in his tomb.

When morning came, the priests and Pharisees [FAIR-ih-seez] remembered the words of Jesus that he would arise, and warned Pilate to have a guard set over the tomb till the third day, "lest," they said, "his disciples, coming by night, should steal him away and say to the people, 'He is arisen from the dead.' " "You have a guard," said Pilate, "do as you wish." So they sealed the great stone rolled against the entrance, and set a watch over the tomb.

When the Sabbath was over, and the dawn was reddening, there came forth from the open tombs in the gardens and the ravines and on the rocky terraces of the hills many bodies of the holy ones who slept; for Jesus, mindful of his dead of old time, had descended into hell, and these went up into the holy city, and they appeared to many people.

And while it was still very early, Mary Magdalene, Mary the mother of James, and Salome and Joanna came with spices and perfumes to the sepulcher [SEPP-uhl-kerr]. "Who," they said, "will roll us away the stone?"—for it was very large. As they spoke the earth shook, and an angel of the Lord, descending from heaven, rolled back the stone, and sat upon it. His face was like lightning; his garments white as snow. In their fear of him the guards were as dead men. "Be not afraid," he said to the women. "You seek Jesus, who was crucified. He is not here; he is arisen. See where they laid him. Hasten now, and tell his disciples that he goes before you into Galilee, as he said." They ran, trembling with fear and with a great joy.

Into the city fled the guards. They told the chief priests all they had seen; but the priests bribed them with great sums of money to say "His disciples came by night and stole his body, for we had fallen asleep."

And coming to Simon Peter and to John, the disciple whom Jesus loved, Mary Magdalene said, "They have taken away the Lord, and we do not know where they have laid him." Then these two disciples hastened to the place; they ran, but John arrived first and saw the grave-clothes lying therein, though he did not enter. But Simon Peter went in, breathing hard. There on the stone lay the garments of fine linen, and a little way apart from these, the head-cloth folded like a turban. They lay in the shape in which Jesus had lain the moment before he arose from them; his rising had been as the rising of light through darkness. Then John, too, entered, and he saw, and believed.

The disciples went back into the city, but Mary Magdalene, who had followed them, sat at the sepulcher weeping. Bending down, she looked and saw in the tomb two angels clothed in white, who sat, one at the head and one at the feet, where Jesus had lain. They said to her, "Why art thou weeping?" "They have taken away my Lord," she answered, "and I know not where they have laid him." With that she turned round, and saw Jesus near her, but she knew not that it was he. "Why art thou weeping?" he said to her. "Whom dost thou seek?" "Sir," she answered, thinking him to be the gardener, "if it be thou who has removed him, tell me where he lies and I will take him away." Jesus said to her, "Mary!" She sprang toward him with a glad cry. "Master!" "Do not touch me," he said, "for I am not yet ascended to my Father. But go to my brethren and tell them that I am ascending to my Father and their Father, to my God and their God."

But to the other disciples all that the woman said seemed tales of illusion.

That day two of the disciples set out for a village that lay seven miles from Jerusalem. As they journeyed over the spring-flushed hills, conversing about all these things that had happened, Jesus overtook them and walked by their side; but their eyes were withheld from knowing him. "Of what are you speaking as you go," he asked them, "that you look so sad?" One of them replied, "Art thou a stranger, all alone in Jerusalem, that thou dost not know the things that have happened these last days?" "What things?" he said. And they told him how Jesus the mighty prophet had been put to death.

"We were in hope," said they, "that it was he who should deliver Israel; but for all that, this is the third day since these things were done. And yet there have been happenings which leave us amazed. For certain women of our company, going early to the sepulcher and not finding him, returned telling us they had seen a vision of angels who say he is alive. And some of our men went and saw that these things were so; but him they did not see." Jesus said to them, "O foolish men, slow of heart to believe all that the prophets have said. Was there not need that the Christ should suffer thus and enter into his glory?" And he explained to them all that had been written concerning himself.

As they came near the village of their destination, he seemed to be going on farther, but they constrained him to abide with them, for the day was far spent. When they sat down to eat, he took bread, and asking a blessing on it, he broke it. Their eyes were opened. They knew him as he vanished from their sight.

When they could speak, they said one to the other, "Were not our hearts burning while he talked with us on the way?" Instantly they hastened back over the moonlit hills to Jerusalem. They found the disciples sitting together, with the doors barred for fear of capture, and they told them all that had happened.

They were still speaking, when lo! Jesus himself was there in the midst of them, saying, "Peace be with you!" They stood trembling with fear, thinking they saw a spirit; but he said, "Why are you perturbed, and why do such thoughts arise in you? See my hands and my feet; touch me and see. A spirit has not flesh and bone, as you see me have." And as still, despite their joy, they could not believe, he asked them, "Have you here any meat?" They gave him a portion of broiled fish and honeycomb, and he ate before their eyes.

But Thomas was not with them, and when the disciples told him they had seen the Lord, he answered, "If I do not see in his hands the print of the nails, and put my finger in the print of the nails, and put my hand into the wound in his side, I will not believe." Eight days afterward, when Thomas was with them and the doors were locked tight, Jesus stood in the midst of them. He said to Thomas, "Reach thy finger hither and see my hands; reach out thy hand, too, and put it into my side, and be not unbelieving but believing." Thomas answered, "My Lord and my God!" Then Jesus said to him, "Because thou didst see me thou hast believed, but greater are they who did not see and yet did believe."

It was now morning on the sea of Galilee. The bright mists drifted away, and on the sparkling water a fishing boat could be seen. Simon Peter was in it, and with him were several other disciples who had cast their net all night but without success. Jesus stood on the shore, but they did not know that it was he. He called to them, "Lads, have you anything to eat?" They answered, "No." "Then cast your net to starboard," he said, "and you will find what you seek." They did so, and the net was filled with such a catch of fish that they could not draw it in. Then Simon cried, "It is the Lord!" and plunged into the sea. The others came in the boat, dragging the net with its bulging catch. Lo! on the white sand there was a fire of charcoal, and fish broiling on it, and bread. Jesus said to them, "Bring the fish you have caught"; and Simon Peter ran and drew in the net full of great fishes. Then Jesus said, "Come and eat," and he took the bread and the fish, and shared it among them. But no one dared ask him any questions.

When they had finished, he said to Peter, "Simon son of John, dost thou love me more than these?" "Ay, Lord," he answered, "thou knowest I love thee"; and Jesus said, "Feed my sheep." Again he asked him, "Dost thou love me?" and again Peter answered, "Thou knowest I love thee"; and Jesus said, "Feed my sheep." Yet a third time he asked him; and Peter, remembering how he had thrice denied him, was pained at heart and said, "Lord, thou knowest all things; thou knowest that I love thee." Jesus replied, "Feed my sheep"; and gazing at him he said, "In truth, in truth I tell thee, when thou wast younger thou didst go thine own way; but when thou art come to be old, thou shalt lift up thy hands, and another shall lead thee whither thou would'st not"—foreshadowing thus by what death Peter should glorify God. "Follow me."

After these things the disciples went up into a mountain in Galilee, as he told them. And Jesus came to them and said, "Go you into all the world, teach all nations, and preach the gospel to every creature, baptizing them in the name of the Father, and of the Son, and of the Holy Spirit. I am with you all the days until the end of the world."

"The Legend of Sleepy Hollow"

by
WASHINGTON IRVING

About the story:

Halloween is the time for ghosts and goblins and apparitions of all kinds to make their annual appearance. Washington Irving brought into legend one of the most famous specters of all—the Headless Horseman of Sleepy Hollow—and it is on Halloween night that the reading of this wonderful tale can make its most vivid impression. The story presented here has been shortened somewhat so that it may be told in a single reading, but the purging of Irving's detailed descriptions of early Dutch country life has not altered the charm of his style or the fright that his tale can instill in a listener. The image of the terrified Ichabod Crane, clinging to the neck of his equally terrified steed as they race toward the deserted church, is one that will live forever in American lore and in the minds of your children.

Suggested listening level: II and III
Approximate reading time: 50 minutes
Pronunciation and vocabulary guide:
    sequestered [see-QUEST-erd]: set apart, secluded
    reverie [REV-er-ee]: daydream
    apparition [app-uh-RISH-on]: a ghost or specter
    Hessian [HESH-on]: German mercenaries who served
      with the British during the Revolutionary War
    imbibed [imm-BYBD]: absorbed or taken in by drinking
    Ichabod [ICK-uh-bod]
    maxim [MAX-imm]: a general truth or rule of conduct
    dilating [DYE-lay-ting]: expanding, swelling

anaconda: a large snake that crushes its prey, then swallows it whole
pedagogue [PEDD-uh-gahg]: teacher
swains: peasants
itinerant [eye-TINN-er-ant]: one who travels from place to place.
erudition [air-you-DIH-shun]: extensive knowledge gained chiefly from books
credulity [kredd-YOU-luh-tee]: eagerness to believe, gullibility
capacious [ca-PAY-shus]: able to contain great amounts
knight-errant [AIR-ant]: a knight who travels in search of adventures
coquette [ko-KETT]: a woman who flirts
Herculean [her-kyoo-LEE-an]: resembling Hercules in size
pliability [ply-uh-BILL-ih-tee]: flexibility; yielding
Mynheer [mine-HAIR]: a title of respect, similar to *Sir*
precipices [PRESS-ih-pih-sez]: steep cliffs
breeches [BRICH-ez]
queued [KYOOD]: braided behind the head
tractable [TRACK-tuh-bull]: yielding; docile
tête-à-tête [tay-tah-TAY]: a private chat
gnarled [NARR-uld]: bent, twisted
cranium [CRAY-nee-um]: head

*I*n one of the spacious coves of the Hudson River, at that broad expanse named by the ancient Dutch navigators the Tappaan Zee, and where they always prudently shortened sail, there lies a small market town or rural port, which by some is called Greensburgh, but which is more generally and properly known by the name of Tarry Town. This name was given, we are told, in former days, by the good housewives of the adjacent country, from the inclination of their husbands to linger about the village tavern on market days. Not far from this village, perhaps about three miles, there is a little valley, or rather lap of land among high hills, which is one of the quietest places in the whole world. A small brook

glides through it, with just murmur enough to lull one to repose; and the occasional whistle of a quail, or tapping of a
woodpecker, is almost the only sound that ever breaks in upon
the uniform tranquillity.

From the listless repose of the place, and the peculiar character of its inhabitants, who are descendants from the original
Dutch settlers, this sequestered [see-QUEST-erd] glen has long
been known by the name of SLEEPY HOLLOW, and its rustic
lads are called the Sleepy Hollow Boys throughout all the
neighboring country. A drowsy, dreamy influence seems to
hang over the land, and to pervade the very atmosphere. Some
say that the place was bewitched by a German doctor, during
the early days of the settlement; others, that an old Indian
chief, the prophet or wizard of his tribe, held his powwows
there before the country was discovered by Master Hendrick
Hudson. Certain it is, the place still continues under the sway
of some witching power, that holds a spell over the minds of
the good people, causing them to walk in a continual reverie
[REV-er-ee]. They are given to all kinds of marvelous belief; are
subject to trances and visions; and frequently see strange
sights, and hear music and voices in the air. The whole neighborhood abounds with local tales, haunted spots, and twilight
superstitions; stars shoot and meteors glare more often across
the valley than in any other part of the country.

The dominant spirit, however, that haunts this enchanted
region, and seems to be commander in chief of all the powers
of the air, is the apparition [app-uh-RISH-on] of a figure on
horseback without a head. It is said by some to be the ghost of
a Hessian [HESH-on] trooper, whose head had been carried
away by a cannonball in some nameless battle during the Revolutionary War, and who is now and again seen by the country
folk, hurrying along in the gloom of night, as if on the wings
of the wind. His haunts are not confined to the valley, but
extend at times to the adjacent roads, and especially to the
vicinity of a church that is at no great distance. Indeed, certain
of the most authentic historians of those parts, who have been
careful in collecting and collating the floating facts concerning
the specter, allege that, the body of the trooper having been
buried in the churchyard, the ghost rides forth to the scene of
battle in nightly quest of his head; and that the rushing speed

with which he sometimes passes along the hollow, like a midnight blast, is owing to his being in a hurry to get back to the churchyard before daybreak.

Such, at least, is the gist of this legendary superstition, which has furnished materials for many a wild story in that region of shadows; and the specter is known, at all the country firesides, by the name of the Headless Horseman of Sleepy Hollow.

It should be noted that this tendency toward fantasy is not confined to the native inhabitants of the valley, but is unconsciously imbibed [imm-BYBD] by everyone who resides there for a time. However wide-awake they may have been before they entered that sleepy region, they are sure, in a little time, to inhale the witching influence of the air, and begin to grow imaginative—to dream dreams, and see apparitions.

In this by-place of nature there abode, some years ago, a worthy creature of the name of Ichabod [ICK-uh-bod] Crane; who, as he expressed it, "tarried," in Sleepy Hollow, for the purpose of instructing the children of the vicinity. He was a native of Connecticut; a state which supplies the Union with pioneers for the mind as well as for the forest, and sends forth yearly its legions of frontier woodmen and country schoolmasters. The surname of Crane was not inapplicable to his person. He was tall but exceedingly lank, with narrow shoulders, long arms and legs, hands that dangled a mile out of his sleeves, feet that might have served for shovels, and his whole frame most loosely hung together. His head was small, and flat at the top, with huge ears, large green glassy eyes, and a long snipe nose, so that it looked like a weathercock, perched upon his spindle neck, to tell which way the wind blew. To see him striding along the profile of a hill on a windy day, with his clothes bagging and fluttering about him, one might have mistaken him for the spirit of famine descending upon the earth, or some scarecrow eloped from a cornfield.

His schoolhouse was a low building of one large room, crudely constructed of logs; the windows partly glazed, and partly patched with pages from old notebooks. It was most ingeniously secured at vacant hours, by a slender branch twisted in the handle of the door, and stakes set against the window shutters; so that though a thief might get in with perfect ease, he would find some embarrassment in getting out;

an idea most probably borrowed from the mystery of an eel trap. The schoolhouse stood in a rather lonely but pleasant situation, just at the foot of a woody hill, with a brook running close by, and a formidable birch tree growing at one end of it. From here the low murmur of his pupils' voices, poring over their lessons, might be heard in a drowsy summer's day, like the hum of a beehive; interrupted now and then by the authoritative voice of the master, in the tone of menace or command; or, possibly, by the appalling sound of the birch as he urged some tardy loiterer along the flowery path of knowledge. Truth to say, he was a conscientious man, that ever bore in mind the golden maxim [MAX-imm]—"Spare the rod and spoil the child." Ichabod Crane's scholars certainly were not spoiled.

But when school hours were over, and on holiday afternoons, he would sometimes convoy some of the smaller pupils home, especially if they happened to have pretty sisters, or mothers noted for the comforts of the cupboard. Indeed it behooved him to keep on good terms with his pupils. The revenue arising from his school was small, and would have been scarcely sufficient to furnish him with daily bread, for he was a huge feeder, and though lank, had the dilating [DYE-lay-ting] powers of an anaconda; but, to help out his maintenance, he was, according to country custom in those parts, boarded and lodged at the houses of the farmers whose children he instructed. With these he lived successively a week at a time, assisting his hosts in the lighter labors of their farms; thus going the rounds of the neighborhood, with all his worldly effects tied up in a cotton handkerchief.

In addition to his other vocations, he was the singing-master of the neighborhood, and picked up many bright shillings by instructing the young folks in the art of singing psalms. It was a matter of no little vanity to him on Sundays, to take his station in front of the church gallery, with a band of chosen singers; and certain it was that his voice resounded far above all the rest of the congregation. Thus, by diverse little makeshifts, in that ingenious way which is commonly called "by hook and by crook," the worthy pedagogue [PEDD-uh-gahg] got on tolerably enough, and was thought, by all who understood nothing of the labor of head work, to have a wonderful easy life of it.

The schoolmaster is generally a man of some importance in

the female circle of a rural neighborhood; being considered a kind of idle gentlemanlike personage, of vastly superior taste and accomplishments to the rough country swains, and, indeed, inferior in learning only to the parson. His appearance, therefore, is apt to occasion some little stir at the tea table of a farmhouse, and the addition of some special cakes or other enticing treats. Our man of letters, therefore, was peculiarly happy in the smiles of all the country damsels. How he would figure among them in the churchyard, between services on Sundays! gathering grapes for them from the wild vines that overrun the surrounding trees; reciting for their amusement all the epitaphs on the tombstones; or sauntering, with a whole bevy of them, along the banks of the adjacent millpond; while the more bashful country bumpkins hung sheepishly back, envying his superior elegance and ease of speech.

From his half-itinerant [eye-TINN-er-ant] life, also, he was a kind of traveling gazette, carrying the whole budget of local gossip from house to house; so that his appearance was always greeted with satisfaction. He was, moreover, esteemed by the women as a man of great erudition [air-you-DIH-shun], for he had read several books quite through, and was a perfect master of Cotton Mather's *History of New England Witchcraft*, in which, by the way, he most firmly and potently believed.

He was, in fact, an odd mixture of small shrewdness and simple credulity [kredd-YOU-luh-tee]. His eagerness to hear tales of the unknown, and his willingness to believe each fantasy he was told, were equally extraordinary; and both had been increased by his residence in this spellbound region. No tale was too gross or monstrous for his capacious [ca-PAY-shus] swallow. It was often his delight, after his school was dismissed in the afternoon, to stretch himself on the rich bed of clover, bordering the little brook that whimpered by the schoolhouse, and there pore over old Mather's direful tales, until the gathering dusk of evening made the printed page a mere mist before his eyes. Then, as he wended his way, by swamp and stream and awful woodland, to the farmhouse where he happened to be quartered, every sound of nature, at that witching hour, fluttered his excited imagination: the moan of the whippoorwill from the hillside; the boding cry of the tree toad; the dreary hooting of the screech owl; or the sudden rustling in the thicket of birds frightened from their roost. The fireflies, too, which sparkled most vividly in the darkest places, now and then startled him, as one of uncommon brightness would stream across his path; and if, by chance, a flying beetle happened to blunder against him, the poor knave was ready to give up the ghost, with the idea that he had been struck by some sort of goblin or witch. His only resource on such occasions, either to drown thought, or drive away evil spirits, was to sing psalm tunes; and the good people of Sleepy Hollow, as they sat by their doors in the evening, were often filled with awe, at hearing his nasal melodies floating from the distant hill, or along the dusky road.

Another of his sources of fearful pleasure was to pass long winter evenings with the old Dutch wives, as they sat spinning by the fire, with a row of apples roasting and sputtering along the hearth, and listen to their marvelous tales of ghosts and goblins, and haunted fields, and haunted brooks, and haunted bridges, and haunted houses, and particularly of the headless horseman, or Galloping Hessian of the Hollow, as they sometimes called him. He would delight them equally by his anecdotes of witchcraft and of the direful omens which prevailed in the earlier times of Connecticut; and would frighten them woefully with speculations about comets and shooting stars; and with the alarming fact that the world did absolutely turn round, and that they were half the time upside down!

But if there was a pleasure in all this, while snugly cuddling in the chimney corner of a chamber that was all of a ruddy glow from the crackling wood fire, and where, of course, no specter dared to show its face, it was dearly purchased by the terrors of his subsequent walk homeward. What fearful shapes and shadows beset his path amid the dim and ghastly glare of a snowy night!—With what wistful look did he eye every trembling ray of light streaming across the waste fields from some distant window!—How often was he appalled by some shrub covered with snow, which looked like a hooded ghost waiting in his very path!—How often did he shrink with curdling awe at the sound of his own steps on the frosty crust beneath his feet; and dread to look over his shoulder, lest he should behold some uncouth being tramping close behind him!—and how often was he thrown into complete dismay by some rushing blast, howling among the trees, in the idea that it was the Galloping Hessian on one of his nightly rides.

All these, however, were mere terrors of the night, phantoms of the mind that walk in darkness; and though he had seen many specters in his time, and been more than once beset by Satan in diverse shapes in his lonely strolls, yet daylight put an end to all these evils; and he would have passed a pleasant life of it, in spite of the Devil and all his works, if his path had not been crossed by a being that causes more perplexity to mortal man than ghosts, goblins, and the whole race of witches put together, and that was—a woman.

Among the musical disciples who assembled one evening in each week, to receive his instructions in the singing of psalms, was Katrina Van Tassel, the daughter and only child of a substantial Dutch farmer. She was a blooming lass of fresh eighteen, ripe and melting and rosy-cheeked as one of her father's peaches, and universally famed, not merely for her beauty, but for the wealth she would one day inherit.

Ichabod Crane had a soft and foolish heart toward women; and it is not to be wondered at, that so tempting a morsel soon found favor in his eyes; more especially after he had visited her in her paternal mansion. Old Baltus Van Tassel was a perfect picture of a thriving, contented, liberal-hearted farmer. He was satisfied with his wealth, but prided himself upon the hearty abundance, rather than the style in which he lived. The pedagogue's mouth watered, as he looked upon the vast treasures of this rustic empire—the silos fairly bursting with grain, the troops of suckling pigs, squadrons of snowy geese, regiments of turkeys—this sumptuous promise of luxurious winter fare. In his devouring mind's eye, he pictured to himself every roasting pig running about with an apple in its mouth, and as the enraptured Ichabod fancied all this, and as he rolled his great green eyes over the fat meadow lands and the orchards burdened with ruddy fruit, his heart yearned after the damsel who was to inherit these domains.

From the moment Ichabod laid his eyes upon these regions of delight, the peace of his mind was at an end, and his only study was how to gain the affections of the peerless daughter of Van Tassel. In this enterprise, however, he had more real difficulties than generally fell to the lot of a knight-errant [AIR-ant] of yore, who seldom had anything but giants, enchanters, fiery dragons, and such easily conquered adversaries to contend with; and had to make his way merely through gates of iron and brass, and walls of stone, to the castle keep, where the lady of his heart was confined; all which he achieved as easily as a man would carve his way to the center of a Christmas pie, and then the lady gave him her hand as a matter of course. Ichabod, on the contrary, in order to win his way to the heart of this country coquette [ko-KETT] had to encounter a host of fearful adversaries of real flesh and blood: the numerous rustic admirers who beset every portal to her heart, keeping a watchful and angry eye upon each other, but ready to fly out in the common cause against any new competitor.

Among these the most formidable was a burly, roaring, roystering blade, of the name of Abraham, or, according to the Dutch abbreviation, Brom Van Brunt, the hero of the country round, which rung with his feats of strength and hardihood. He was broad-shouldered, with short curly black hair, and a bluff, but not unpleasant countenance, having a mingled air of fun and arrogance. From his Herculean [her-kyoo-LEE-an] frame and great powers of limb, he had received the nickname of Brom Bones, by which he was universally known. He was famed for great knowledge and skill in horsemanship, being as dexterous on horseback as a Tartar. He was always ready for either a fight or a frolick; had more mischief than ill-will in his composition; and with all his overbearing roughness, there was a strong dash of waggish good humor at bottom. He had three or four boon companions of his own stamp, who regarded him as their model, and at the head of whom he scoured the country, attending every scene of feud or merriment for miles round. Sometimes his crew would be heard dashing along past the farmhouses at midnight, with whoop and holler, like a troop of Cossacks; and the old dames, startled out of their sleep, would listen for a moment till the hurry-scurry had clattered by, and then exclaim, "Aye, there goes Brom Bones and his gang!" The neighbors looked upon him with a mixture of awe, admiration, and goodwill; and when any madcap prank, or rustic brawl, occurred in the vicinity, always shook their heads, and warranted Brom Bones was at the bottom of it.

This raucous local hero had for some time singled out the blooming Katrina for the object of his uncouth gallantries, and though his amorous toyings were something like the gentle caresses and endearments of a bear, yet it was whispered that she did not altogether discourage his hopes. Certain it is, his advances were signals for rival candidates to retire; so much so, that when his horse was seen tied to Van Tassel's fence, on a Sunday night (a sure sign that his master was courting, or, as it is termed, "sparking within"), all other suitors passed by in despair, and carried the war into other quarters.

Such was the formidable rival with whom Ichabod Crane had to contend, and, considering all things, a stouter man than he would have shrunk from the competition, and a wiser man would have despaired. He had, however, a happy mixture of pliability [ply-uh-BILL-ih-tee] and perseverance in his nature; he was in form and spirit like a supple jack pine—yielding, but tough; though he bent, he never broke; and though he bowed beneath the slightest pressure, yet the moment it was away— jerk! he was as erect, and carried his head as high as ever.

To have taken the field openly against his rival would have been madness. Ichabod, therefore, made his advances in a quiet and subtle manner. Under cover of his character of sing-ing-master, he made frequent visits at the farmhouse and car-ried on his suit with Katrina by the side of the spring under the great elm, or sauntering along in the twilight, that hour so favorable to the lover's eloquence. And, strange as it may seem, from the moment Ichabod Crane began his advances, the interests of Brom Bones evidently declined; his horse was no longer seen tied to the fence on Sunday nights, and a deadly feud gradually arose between him and the instructor of Sleepy Hollow.

Brom, who had a degree of rough chivalry in his nature, would rather have carried matters to open warfare, and have settled their pretensions to the lady according to the mode of those most concise and simple reasoners, the knights-errant of yore—by single combat; but Ichabod was too conscious of the superior might of his adversary to do physical battle against him; he had overheard the boast of Bones, that he would "dou-ble the schoolmaster up, and put him on a shelf," and he was too wary to give him an opportunity. There was something extremely provoking in Ichabod's nonviolence, for it left Brom no alternative but to draw upon the funds of rustic waggery in his disposition, and to play boorish practical jokes upon his rival. Ichabod became the object of whimsical persecution to Bones and his gang of rough riders; Brom especially seized all opportunities of turning him into ridicule in the presence of his mistress.

In this way matters went on for some time, without producing any material effect on the relative situations of the contending powers. On a fine autumnal afternoon, Ichabod, in pensive mood, sat enthroned in the schoolhouse, on the lofty stool whence he usually watched all the concerns of his little literary realm. The stillness was suddenly interrupted by the appearance of a Negro lad mounted on the back of a ragged, wild, half-broken colt, which he managed with a rope for a halter. He came clattering up to the school door with an invitation to Ichabod to attend a merrymaking, or "quilting frolic," to be held that evening at Mynheer [mine-HAIR] Van Tassel's, and having delivered his message with an air of importance and fine language, he dashed over the brook, and was seen scampering away up the hollow, full of the importance and hurry of his mission.

All was now bustle and hubbub in the formerly quiet schoolroom. The scholars were hurried through their lessons, without stopping at trifles; books were flung aside, without being put away on the shelves; inkstands were overturned; benches thrown down; and the whole school was turned loose an hour before the usual time, bursting forth like a legion of young imps, yelping and racketing about the green, in joy at their early emancipation.

The gallant Ichabod now spent at least an extra half-hour primping himself, brushing and furbishing up his best, and indeed his only suit of rusty black, and arranging his looks by a bit of broken looking-glass that hung up in the schoolhouse. That he might make his appearance before his mistress in the true style of a cavalier, he borrowed a horse from the farmer with whom he was staying, an old Dutchman, of the name of Hans Van Ripper, and thus gallantly mounted, issued forth like a knight-errant in quest of adventures. The animal he bestrode was a broken-down plow horse, that had outlived almost everything but his viciousness. He was gaunt and shagged, with a thin neck and a head like a hammer; his rusty mane and tail were tangled and knotted with burrs; one eye had lost its pupil, and was glaring and ghostly; but the other had the gleam of a genuine devil in it. Still he must have had fire and mettle in his day, if we may judge from his name, which was Gunpowder. He had, in fact, been a favorite steed of his master's, who was a furious rider, and had infused, very probably, some of his own spirit into the animal; for, old and broken down as he looked, there was more lurking deviltry in him than in any young filly in the country.

Ichabod was a suitable figure for such a steed. He rode with short stirrups, which brought his knees nearly up to the pommel of the saddle; his sharp elbows stuck out like grasshoppers'; he carried his whip perpendicularly in his hand, like a scepter, and as the horse jogged on, the motion of his arms was not unlike the flapping of a pair of wings. Such was the appearance of Ichabod and his steed, as they shambled out of the gate of Hans Van Ripper, and it was altogether such an apparition as is seldom to be met with in broad daylight.

It was, as I have said, a fine autumnal day; the sky was clear and serene, and nature wore that rich and golden livery which we always associate with the idea of abundance. The forests had put on their sober brown and yellow, while some trees of the tenderer kind had been pinned by the frosts into brilliant dyes of orange, purple, and scarlet. Streaming files of wild ducks began to make their appearance high in the air; the bark of the squirrel might be heard from the groves of beech and hickory nuts, and the sad whistle of the quail at intervals from the neighboring stubble field.

The sun gradually wheeled his broad disk down into the west. The wide bosom of the Tappaan Zee lay motionless and glassy, excepting that here and there a gentle undulation waved and prolonged the blue shadow of the distant mountain. A few amber clouds floated in the sky, without a breath of air to move them. The horizon was of a fine golden tint, changing gradually into a pure apple green, and from that into the deep blue of the mid-heaven. A slanting ray lingered on the woody crests of the precipices [PRESS-ih-pih-sez] that overhung some parts of the river, giving greater depth to the dark gray and purple of their rocky sides. A sloop was loitering in the distance, dropping slowly down with the tide, her sail hanging uselessly against the mast; and as the reflection of the sky gleamed along the still water, it seemed as if the vessel was suspended in air.

It was toward evening that Ichabod arrived at the castle of Baltus Van Tassel, which he found thronged with the pride and flower of the adjacent country. Old farmers in homespun coats and breeches [BRICH-ez], blue stockings, huge shoes, and magnificent pewter buckles. Their brisk, withered little dames in close crimped caps, long-waisted short gowns, and homespun petticoats. Buxom lasses, almost as antiquated as their mothers, excepting where a straw hat, a fine ribbon, or perhaps a white frock, gave symptoms of city innovations. The sons, in short square-skirted coats with rows of stupendous brass buttons, and their hair generally queued [KYOOD] in the fashion of the times.

Brom Bones, however, was the hero of the scene, having come to the gathering on his favorite steed, Daredevil, a creature, like himself, full of mettle and mischief, and which no one but himself could manage. He was, in fact, noted for preferring vicious animals, given to all kinds of tricks, which kept the rider in constant risk of his neck, for he held a tractable [TRACK-tuh-bull] well-broken horse as unworthy of a lad of spirit.

Ichabod surveyed the luxurious display of cakes, and pies, and hams, and roasted chickens—all the delights of a genuine Dutch table in the sumptuous time of autumn, and he did justice to every heaped-up platter. For he was a kind and thankful toad, whose heart dilated in proportion as his skin was filled with good cheer; and whose spirits rose with eating, as some men's do with drink. He could not help, too, rolling his large eyes round him as he ate, and chuckling with the possibility that he might one day be lord of all this scene of almost unimaginable luxury and splendor. Then, he thought, how soon he'd turn his back upon the old schoolhouse; snap his fingers in the face of Hans Van Ripper, and every other miserly patron; and kick any itinerant pedagogue out of doors that should dare to call him comrade!

And now the sound of the music from the common room, or

hall, summoned to the dance. Ichabod prided himself upon his dancing as much as upon his vocal powers. Not a limb, not a fiber about him was idle, and to have seen his loosely hung frame in full motion, and clattering about the room, you would have thought St. Vitus himself, that blessed patron of the dance, was figuring before you in person. How could the flogger of urchins be otherwise than animated and joyous; the lady of his heart was his partner in the dance, and smiled graciously in reply to all his amorous oglings; while Brom Bones, sorely smitten with love and jealousy, sat brooding by himself in one corner.

When the dance was at an end, Ichabod was attracted to a knot of the sager folks, who, with old Van Tassel, sat smoking at one end of the porch, gossiping over former times, and drawling out long stories about the war and especially about the ghosts and apparitions that were known to inhabit the local area. Such fantastic legends and superstitions thrive best in these sheltered, long-settled retreats; but are trampled underfoot by the shifting throng that forms the population of most of our country places. This is perhaps the reason why we so seldom hear of ghosts except in our long-established Dutch communities.

The immediate cause, however, of the prevalence of supernatural stories in these parts, was doubtless owing to the vicinity of Sleepy Hollow. There was a contagion in the very air that blew from that haunted region; it breathed forth an atmosphere of dreams and fancies infecting all the land. Several of the Sleepy Hollow people were present at Van Tassel's, and, as usual, were doling out their wild and wonderful legends. Many dismal tales were told about funeral trains, and mournful cries and wailings heard and seen about the great tree where the unfortunate Major André was taken, and which stood in the neighborhood. Some mention was made also of the woman in white, that haunted the dark glen at Raven Rock, and was often heard to shriek on winter nights before a storm, having perished there in the snow. The chief part of the stories, however, turned upon the favorite specter of Sleepy Hollow, the headless horseman, who had been heard several times of late, patrolling the country; and, it was said, tethered his horse nightly among the graves in the churchyard.

The sequestered situation of this church seems always to have made it a favorite haunt of troubled spirits. It stands on a knoll, surrounded by locust trees and lofty elms, from among which its decent, whitewashed walls shine modestly forth, like Christian purity, beaming through the shades of retirement. On one side of the church extends a wide woody dell, along which raves a large brook among broken rocks and trunks of fallen trees. Over a deep black part of the stream, not far from the church, was formerly thrown a wooden bridge; the road that led to it, and the bridge itself, were thickly shaded by overhanging trees, which cast a gloom about it, even in the daytime; but occasioned a fearful darkness at night. Such was one of the favorite haunts of the headless horseman, and the place where he was most frequently encountered. The tale was told of old Brouwer, an ardent disbeliever in ghosts, and how he met the horseman returning from one of his raids into Sleepy Hollow, and how he got up behind him on the horse; how they galloped over bush and brake, over hill and swamp, until they reached the bridge; when the horseman suddenly turned into a skeleton, threw old Brouwer into the brook, and sprang away over the treetops with a clap of thunder.

The story was immediately matched by a thrice marvelous adventure of Brom Bones, who made light of the Galloping Hessian as an outright jockey. Bones declared that, on returning one night from a neighboring village, he had been overtaken by this midnight trooper; that he had offered to race with him for a bowl of punch, and should have won it, too, for Daredevil beat the goblin horse all hollow, but just as they came to the church bridge, the Hessian bolted, and vanished in a flash of fire.

All these tales, told in that drowsy undertone with which men talk in the dark, the faces of the listeners only now and then receiving a casual gleam from the glare of a pipe, sunk deep in the mind of Ichabod. He repaid them in kind with large extracts from his invaluable author, Cotton Mather, and added many very marvelous events that had taken place in his native state of Connecticut, and fearful sights which he had seen in his nightly walks about Sleepy Hollow.

The revel now gradually broke up. The old farmers gathered together their families in their wagons, and were heard for some time rattling along the hollow roads, and over the distant hills; the sounds gradually died away and the late scene of noise and frolick was all silent and deserted. Ichabod only lingered behind, according to the custom of country lovers, to have a tête-à-tête [tay-tah-TAY] with the heiress, fully convinced that he was now on the high road to success. What passed at this interview I will not pretend to say, for in fact I do not know. Something, however, I fear me, must have gone wrong, for he certainly sallied forth, after no very great interval, with an air quite desolate and chopfallen. Could that girl have been playing off any of her coquettish tricks?—Was her encouragement of the poor pedagogue all a mere sham, to secure her conquest of his rival?—Heaven only knows, not I! —Let it suffice to say, Ichabod stole forth with the air of one who had been sacking a hen roost, rather than a fair lady's heart. Without looking to the right or left to notice the scene of rural wealth, on which he had so often gloated, he went straight to the stable, and with several hearty cuffs and kicks, roused his steed most uncourteously from the comfortable quarters in which he was soundly sleeping.

It was the very witching time of night that Ichabod, heavy-hearted and crestfallen, pursued his travel homeward, along the sides of the lofty hills which rose above Tarry Town, and which he had traversed so cheerily in the afternoon. The hour was as dismal as himself. In the dead hush of midnight, he could even hear the barking of the watchdog from the opposite shore of the Hudson; but it was so vague and faint as only to give an idea of his distance from this faithful companion of man. No signs of life occurred near him, but occasionally the melancholy chirp of a cricket, or perhaps the guttural twang of a bullfrog, from a neighboring marsh, as if sleeping uncomfortably, and turning suddenly in his bed.

All the stories of ghosts and goblins that he had heard in the afternoon now came crowding upon his recollection. The night grew darker and darker; the stars seemed to sink deeper in the sky, and driving clouds occasionally hid them from his sight. He had never felt so lonely and dismal. He was, moreover, approaching the very place where many of the scenes of the ghost stories had been laid. In the center of the road stood an enormous tulip tree, which towered like a giant above all the other trees of the neighborhood, and formed a kind of land-mark. Its limbs were gnarled [NARR-uld], and fantastic, large enough to form trunks for ordinary trees, twisting down almost to the earth, and rising again into the air. It was connected with the tragical story of the unfortunate André, who had been taken prisoner near there; and was universally known by the name of Major André's tree. The common people regarded it with a mixture of respect and superstition, partly out of sympathy for the fate of its ill-starred namesake, and partly from the tales of strange sights, and doleful lamentations, told concerning it.

As Ichabod approached this fearful tree, he began to whistle; he thought his whistle was answered—it was but a blast sweeping sharply through the dry branches. As he approached a little nearer, he thought he saw something white, hanging in the midst of the tree—he paused and ceased whistling; but on looking more narrowly, perceived that it was a place where the tree had been scathed by lightning, and the white wood laid bare. Suddenly he heard a groan—his teeth chattered, and his knees smote against the saddle: it was but the rubbing of one huge bough upon another, as they were swayed about by the breeze. He passed the tree in safety, but new perils lay before him.

About two hundred yards from the tree a small brook crossed the road, and ran into a marshy and thickly wooded glen, known by the name of Wiley's Swamp. A few rough logs, laid side by side, served for a bridge over this stream. On that side of the road where the brook entered the wood, a group of oaks and chestnuts, matted thick with wild grapevines, threw a cavernous gloom over it. To pass this bridge was the severest trial. It was at this identical spot that the unfortunate André was captured, and under the cover of those chestnuts and vines were the sturdy yeomen concealed who surprised him. This has ever since been considered a haunted stream, and fearful are the feelings of the schoolboy who has to pass it alone after dark.

As he approached the stream, his heart began to thump; he summoned up, however, all his resolution, gave his horse half a score of kicks in the ribs, and attempted to dash briskly across the bridge; but instead of starting forward, the perverse old animal made a lateral movement, and ran broadside against the fence. Ichabod, whose fears increased with the delay, jerked the reins on the other side, and kicked lustily with the opposite foot: It was all in vain; his steed started, it is true, but it was only to plunge to the opposite side of the road into a thicket of brambles and elderbushes. The schoolmaster now bestowed both whip and heel upon the starveling ribs of old Gunpowder, who dashed forward, snuffing and snorting, but came to a stand just by the bridge with a suddenness that had nearly sent his rider sprawling over his head. Just at this moment a plashy tramp by the side of the bridge caught the sensitive ear of Ichabod. In the dark shadow of the grove, on the margin of the brook he beheld something huge, misshapen, black and towering. It stirred not, but seemed gathered up in the gloom, like some gigantic monster ready to spring upon the traveler.

The hair of the affrighted pedagogue rose upon his head with terror. What was to be done? To turn and fly was now too late; and besides, what chance was there of escaping ghost or goblin, if such it was, which could ride upon the wings of the wind? Summoning up, therefore, a show of courage, he demanded in stammering accents—"Who are you?" He received no reply. He repeated his demand in a still more agitated voice. Still there was no answer. Once more he pounded the sides of the inflexible Gunpowder, and shutting his eyes, broke forth with involuntary fervor into a psalm tune. Just then the shadowy object of alarm put itself in motion, and with a scramble and a bound, stood at once in the middle of the road. Though the night was dark and dismal, yet the form of the unknown might now in some degree be ascertained. He appeared to be a horseman of large dimensions, and mounted on a black horse of powerful frame. He made no offer of molestation or sociability, but kept aloof on one side of the road, jogging along on the blind side of old Gunpowder, who had now got over his fright and waywardness.

Ichabod, who had no relish for this strange midnight companion, and bethought himself of the adventure of Brom Bones with the Galloping Hessian, now quickened his steed, in hopes of leaving him behind. The stranger, however, quickened his horse to an equal pace. Ichabod pulled up, and fell into a walk, thinking to lag behind—the other did the same. His heart began to sink within him; he endeavored to resume his psalm tune, but his parched tongue clove to the roof of his mouth, and he could not utter a note. There was something in the moody and dogged silence of this persistent companion that was mysterious and appalling. It was soon fearfully accounted for. On mounting a rising ground, which brought the figure of his fellow-traveler in relief against the sky, gigantic in height, and muffled in a cloak, Ichabod was horror-struck, on perceiving that he was headless!—but his horror was still more increased, on observing that the head, which should have rested on his shoulders, was carried before him on the pommel of his saddle! His terror rose to desperation; he rained a shower of kicks and blows upon Gunpowder, hoping, by a sudden movement, to give his companion the slip—but the specter started full jump with him. Away then they dashed, through thick and thin; stones flying, and sparks flashing, at every bound. Ichabod's flimsy garments fluttered in the air, as he stretched his long lank body away over his horse's head, in the eagerness of his flight.

They had now reached the road which turns off to Sleepy Hollow; but Gunpowder, who seemed possessed with a demon, instead made an opposite turn, and plunged headlong downhill to the left. This road leads through a sandy hollow shaded by trees for about a quarter of a mile, where it crosses the bridge famous in goblin story, and just beyond swells the green knoll on which stands the whitewashed church.

As yet the panic of the steed had given his unskillful rider an apparent advantage in the chase; but just as he had got halfway through the hollow, the girths of the saddle gave way, and he felt it slipping from under him. He seized it by the pommel, and endeavored to hold it firm, but in vain; and had just time to save himself by clasping old Gunpowder round the neck, when the saddle fell to the earth, and he heard it trampled underfoot by his pursuer. For a moment the terror of Hans Van Ripper's wrath passed across his mind—for it was his Sunday saddle; but this was no time for petty fears: the goblin was hard on his haunches; and (unskillful rider that he was!) he had much-ado to maintain his seat; sometimes slipping on one side, sometimes on another, and sometimes jolted on the high ridge of his horse's backbone, with a violence that he verily feared would cleave him in two.

An opening in the trees now cheered him with the hopes that the church-bridge was at hand. The wavering reflection of a silver star in the bosom of the brook told him that he was not mistaken. He saw the walls of the church dimly glaring under the trees beyond. He recollected the place where Brom Bones's ghostly competitor had disappeared. "If I can but reach that bridge," thought Ichabod, "I am safe." Just then he heard the black steed panting and blowing close behind him; he fancied that he felt his hot breath. Another convulsive kick in the ribs, and old Gunpowder sprung upon the bridge; he thundered over the resounding planks; he gained the opposite side; and now Ichabod cast a look behind to see if his pursuer should vanish, according to rule, in a flash of fire and brimstone. Just then he saw the goblin rising in his stirrups, and in the very act of hurling his head at him. Ichabod endeavored to dodge the horrible missile, but too late. It encountered his cranium [CRAY-nee-um] with a tremendous crash—he was tumbled headlong into the dust, and Gunpowder, the black steed, and the goblin rider, passed by like a whirlwind.

The next morning the old horse was found without his saddle, and with the bridle under his feet, soberly cropping the grass at his master's gate. Ichabod did not make his appearance at breakfast—dinner hour came, but no Ichabod. The boys assembled at the schoolhouse, and strolled idly about the banks of the brook; but no schoolmaster. Hans Van Ripper now began to feel some uneasiness about the fate of poor Ichabod, and his saddle. An inquiry was set on foot, and after diligent investigation they came upon his traces. In one part of the road leading to the church was found the saddle trampled in the dirt; the tracks of horses' hoofs deeply dented in the road, and evidently at furious speed, were traced to the bridge, beyond which, on the bank of a broad part of the brook, where the water ran deep and black, was found the hat of the unfortunate Ichabod, and close beside it a shattered pumpkin.

The brook was searched, but the body of the schoolmaster was not to be discovered. Hans Van Ripper, as executor of his estate, examined the bundle which contained all his worldly effects. They consisted of two shirts and a half; two stocks for the neck; a pair or two of worsted stockings; an old pair of corduroy trousers; a rusty razor; a book of psalm tunes; and a broken pitch-pipe. As to the books and furniture of the school-house, they belonged to the community, excepting Cotton Mather's *History of New England Witchcraft*, a *New England Almanac*, and a book of dreams and fortune telling; in which last was a sheet of paper much scribbled and blotted in several fruitless attempts to make a copy of verses in honor of the heiress of Van Tassel. These magic books and the poetic scrawl were forthwith consigned to the flames by Hans Van Ripper, who from that time forward determined to send his children no more to school; observing, that he never knew any good come of this same reading and writing. Whatever money the schoolmaster possessed, and he had received his quarter's pay but a day or two before, he must have had about his person at the time of his disappearance.

The mysterious event caused much speculation at the church on the following Sunday. Knots of gazers and gossips were collected in the churchyard, at the bridge, and at the spot where the hat and pumpkin had been found. The stories of Brouwer, of Bones, and many others, were called to mind; and when they had diligently considered them all, and compared them with the symptoms of the present case, they shook their heads, and came to the conclusion that Ichabod had been carried off by the Galloping Hessian. As he was a bachelor, and in nobody's debt, nobody troubled his head anymore about him; the school was moved to a different quarter of the hollow, and another pedagogue reigned in his stead.

It is true, an old farmer, who had been down to New York on a visit several years after, and from whom this account of the ghostly adventure was received, brought home the news that Ichabod Crane was still alive; that he had left the neighborhood partly through fear of the goblin and Hans Van Ripper, and partly in mortification at having been suddenly dismissed by the heiress; that he had moved to a distant part of the country; had taught school and studied law at the same time; had been admitted to the bar, turned politician, electioneered, written for the newspapers, and finally had been made a Justice of the Small Claims Court. Brom Bones, too, who, shortly after his rival's disappearance, conducted the blooming

Katrina in triumph to the altar, was observed to look exceedingly knowing whenever the story of Ichabod was related, and always burst into a hearty laugh at the mention of the pumpkin; which led some to suspect that he knew more about the matter than he chose to tell.

The old country wives, however, who are the best judges of these matters, maintain to this day that Ichabod was spirited away by supernatural means; and it is a favorite story often told about the neighborhood round the winter evening fire. The bridge became more than ever an object of superstitious awe, and that may be the reason why the road has been altered of late years, so as to approach the church by the border of the millpond. The schoolhouse being deserted, soon fell to decay, and was reported to be haunted by the ghost of the unfortunate pedagogue; and the plowboy, loitering homeward of a still summer evening, has often fancied his voice at a distance, chanting a melancholy psalm tune among the tranquil solitudes of Sleepy Hollow.

THANKSGIVING

"A Prayer of Thanksgiving"
by
ROBERT LOUIS STEVENSON

Lord, behold our family here assembled.
We thank thee
For this place in which we dwell;
For the peace accorded us this day,
For the hope with which we expect tomorrow;
For the health, the work, the food
And the bright skies that make our lives delightful,
For our friends in all parts of the earth, and our friendly
  helpers . . .
Let peace abound in our small company.

"Ezra's Thanksgivin' Out West"

by
EUGENE FIELD

About the story:
Ah, the good old days, when Thanksgiving rituals cen-
tered on the home and hearth. Ezra's days in Massachu-
setts are very old, to be sure, but perhaps they will call
to mind holiday activities that you enjoyed as a child,
but that somehow got lost along the way. What memo-
ries will your children have about Thanksgiving Day and
its attendant joys? Will they, like Ezra, look fondly back
on our present as "the good old days"?

Suggested reading level: All ages
Approximate reading time: 19 minutes
Pronunciation and vocabulary guide:
> **gamboled** [GAMM-buld]: leaped about; frolicked
> **daguerreotype** [duh-GAIR-uh-tipe]: an early photo-
> graphic process
> **didoes** [DYE-doze]: antics, pranks
> **meeting-house:** church
> **meeting:** a church service
> **Psalmody** [SALM-uh-dee]: a book of psalms
> **Common:** an open area or community park
> **Tartars** [TAR-turz]: ferocious, violent-tempered people;
> like Mongolian warriors
> **dyspepsia** [diss-PEP-see-ah]: indigestion
> **pippins, russets, bellflowers:** types of apples

*E*zra had written a letter to the home folks, and in it he
had complained that never before had he spent such a
weary, lonesome day as this Thanksgiving Day had
been.

Having finished this letter, he sat for a long time gazing idly
into the open fire that snapped cinders all over the hearthstone

and sent its red forks dancing up the chimney to join the winds that frolicked and gamboled [GAMM-buld] across the Kansas prairies that raw November night.

It had rained hard all day, and was cold; and although the open fire made every honest effort to be cheerful, Ezra, as he sat in front of it in the wooden rocker and looked down into the glowing embers, experienced a dreadful feeling of loneliness and homesickness.

"I'm sick o' Kansas," said Ezra to himself. "Here I've been in the plaguey country for goin' on a year, and—yes, I'm sick of it, powerful sick of it. What a miser'ble Thanksgivin' is out this way. I wish I was back in ol' Mass'chusetts—that's the country for *me*, and they hev the kind o' Thanksgivin' I like!"

Musing in this strain, while the rain went patter-patter on the windowpanes, Ezra saw a strange sight in the fireplace— yes, right among the embers and the crackling flames Ezra saw a strange, beautiful picture unfold and spread itself out like a panorama.

"How very wonderful!" murmured the young man. Yet he did not take his eyes away, for the picture soothed him and he loved to look upon it.

"It is a pictur' of long ago," said Ezra softly. "I had like to forgot it, but now it comes back to me as nat'ral-like as an ol' friend. An' I seem to be a part of it, an' the feelin' of that time comes back with the pictur', too."

Ezra did not stir. His head rested upon his hand, and his eyes were fixed upon the shadows in the firelight.

"It is a pictur' of the ol' home," said Ezra to himself. "I am back there in Belchertown, with the Holyoke hills up north an' the Berkshire Mountains a-loomin' up gray an' misty-like in the western horizon.

"Seems as if it wuz early mornin'; everything is still, and it is so cold when we boys crawl out o' bed that, if it wuzn't Thanksgivin' mornin', we'd crawl back again an' wait for Mother to call us. But it *is* Thanksgivin' mornin', and we're goin' skatin' down on the pond.

"The squealin' o' the pigs has told us it is five o'clock, and we must hurry; we're goin' to call by for the Dickerson boys an' Hiram Peabody, an' we've got to hyper! Brother Amos gets on about half o' my clothes, and I get on 'bout half o' his, but it's all the same; they are stout, warm clo'es, and they're big enough to fit any of us boys—Mother looked out for that when she made 'em.

"When we go downstairs, we find the girls there, all bundled up nice an' warm—Mary an' Helen an' Cousin Irene. They're going with us, an' we all start out tiptoe and quiet-like so's not to wake up the ol' folks. The ground is frozen hard; we stub our toes on the frozen ruts in the road. When we come to the minister's house, Laura is standin' on the front stoop a-waitin' for us.

"Laura is the minister's daughter. She's a friend o' Sister Helen's—pretty as a daguerreotype [duh-GAIR-uh-tipe], an' gentle-like and tender. Laura lets me carry her skates, an' I'm glad of it, although I have my hands full already with the lantern, the skates, and the rest.

"Hiram Peabody keeps us waitin', for he has overslept himself, an' when he comes trottin' out at last the girls make fun of him—all except Sister Mary, an' she sort o' sticks up for Hiram, an' we're all so 'cute we kind o' calc'late we know the reason why.

"And now," said Ezra softly, "the pictur' changes: seems as if I could see the pond. The ice is like a black lookin'-glass, and Hiram Peabody slips up the first thing, an' down he comes, lickety-split, an' we all laugh—except Sister Mary, an' *she* says it is very imp'lite to laugh at other folks' misfortunes.

"Ough! How cold it is, and how my fingers ache with the frost when I take off my mittens to strap on Laura's skates! But, oh, how my cheeks burn! And how careful I am not to hurt Laura, an' how I ask her if that's 'tight enough,' an' how she tells me 'jist a little tighter' and how we two keep foolin' along till the others hev gone an' we are left alone!

"An' how quick I get my *own* skates strapped on—none o' your new-fangled skates with springs an' plates an' clamps an' such, but honest, ol'-fashioned wooden ones with steel runners that curl up over my toes an' have a bright brass button on the end! How I strap 'em and lash 'em and buckle 'em on! An' Laura waits for me an' tells me to be sure to get 'em on tight enough—why, bless me! after I once got 'em strapped on, if them skates hed come off, the feet wud ha' come with 'em!

"An' now away we go—Laura and me. Around the bend—near the medder where Si Baker's dog killed a woodchuck last summer—we meet the rest. We forget all about the cold. We run races an' play snap the whip, an' cut all sorts o' didoes [DYE-doze], an' we never mind the pick'rel weed that is froze in on the ice an' trips us up every time we cut the outside edge; an' then we boys jump over the air holes, an' the girls stan' by an' scream an' tell us they know we're agoin' to drownd ourselves.

"So the hours go, an' it is sunup at last, an' Sister Helen says we must be gettin' home. When we take our skates off, our feet feel as if they were wood. Laura has lost her scarf; I lend her mine, and she kind o' blushes. The old pond seems glad to have us go, and the willer tree waves us goodbye. Laura promises to come over to our house in the evenin', and so we break up.

"Seems now," continued Ezra musingly, "seems now as if I could see us all at breakfast. The race on the pond has made us hungry, and Mother says she never knew anybody else's boys that had such capac'ties as hers.

"It is the Yankee Thanksgivin' breakfast—sausages an' fried potatoes, an' buckwheat cakes, an' syrup—maple syrup, mind ye, for Father has his own sugar bush, and there was a big run o' sap last season. Mother says, 'Ezry an' Amos, won't you never get through eatin'? We want to clear off the table, fer there's pies to make, and nuts to crack, and land sakes alive! The turkey's got to be stuffed yet!'

"Then how we all fly around! Mother sends Helen up into the attic to get a squash while Mary's makin' the piecrust. Amos an' I crack the walnuts—they call 'em hickory nuts out in this pesky country of sagebrush and pasture land. The walnuts are hard, and it's all we can do to crack 'em.

"Ev'ry once'n a while one of 'em slips outer our fingers and goes dancin' over the floor or flies into the pan Helen is squeezin' pumpkin into through the col'nder. Helen says we're shif'-less an' good for nothin' but frivolin'; but Mother tells us how to crack the walnuts so's not to let 'em fly all over the room, an' so's not to be all jammed to pieces like the walnuts was down at the party at the Peasleys' last winter.

"An' now here come Tryphena Foster, with her gingham

gown an' muslin apron on; her folks have gone up to Amherst for Thanksgivin', an' Tryphena has come over to help our folks get dinner. She thinks a great deal o' Mother, 'cause Mother teaches her Sunday-school class an' says Tryphena oughter marry a missionary.

"There is bustle everywhere, the rattle uv pans an' the clatter of dishes; an' the new kitchen stove begins to warm up an' git red, till Helen loses her wits and is flustered, an' sez she never could git the hang o' that stove's dampers.

"An' now," murmured Ezra gently, as a tone of deeper reverence crept into his voice, "I can see Father sittin' all by himself in the parlor. Father's hair is very gray, and there was wrinkles on his honest old face. He is lookin' through the winder at the Holyoke hills over yonder, and I can guess he's thinkin' of the time when he wuz a boy like me an' Amos, an' uster climb over them hills an' kill rattlesnakes an' hunt partridges.

"Or doesn't his eyes quite reach the Holyoke hills? Do they fall kind o' lovingly but sadly on the little buryin' ground jest beyond the village? Ah, Father knows that spot, an' he loves it, too, for there are treasures there whose memory he wouldn't swap for all the world could give.

"So, while there is a kind o' mist in Father's eyes, I can see he is dreamin'-like of sweet an' tender things, and a-communin' with memory—hearin' voices I never heard, an' feelin' the touch of hands I never pressed; an' seein' Father's peaceful face I find it hard to think of a Thanksgivin' sweeter than Father's is.

"The pictur' in the firelight changes now," said Ezra, "an' seems as if I wuz in the old frame meetin'-house. The meetin'-house is on the hill, and meetin' begins at half-pas' ten. Our pew is well up in front—seems as if I could see it now. It has a long red cushion on the seat, and in the hymn-book rack there is a Bible an' a couple of Psalmodies [SALM-uh-deez].

"We walk up the aisle slow, and Mother goes in first; then comes Mary, then me, then Helen, then Amos, and then Father. Father thinks it is jest as well to have one o' the girls set in between me an' Amos.

"The meetin'-house is full, for everybody goes to meetin' Thanksgivin' Day. The minister reads the proclamation an' makes a prayer, an' then he gives out a psalm, an' we all stan' up an' turn 'round an' join the choir. Sam Merritt has come up from Palmer to spend Thanksgivin' with the ol' folks, an' he is singin' tenor today in his ol' place in the choir. Some folks say he sings wonderful well, but *I* don't like Sam's voice. Laura sings soprano in the choir, and Sam stands next to her an' holds the book.

"Seems as if I could hear the minister's voice, full of earnestness an' melody, comin' from way up in his little round pulpit. He is tellin' us why we should be thankful, an', as he quotes Scriptur', we boys wonder how anybody can remember so much of the Bible.

"Then I get nervous and worried. Seems to me the minister was never comin' to lastly, and I find myself wonderin' whether Laura is listenin' to what the preachin' is about, or is writin' notes to Sam Merritt in the back of the tune book. I get thirsty, too, and I fidget about till Father looks at me, and Mother nudges Helen, and Helen passes it along to me with interest.

"An' then," continues Ezra in his revery, "when the last hymn is given out an' we stan' up again an' join the choir, I am glad to see that Laura is singin' outer the book with Miss Hubbard, the alto. An' goin' out o' meetin' I kind of edge up to Laura and ask her if I kin have the pleasure of seein' her home.

"An' now we boys all go out on the Common to play ball. The Enfield boys have come over, and, as all the Hampshire County folks know, they are tough fellers to beat. Gorham Polly keeps tally, because he has got the newest jackknife— oh, how slick it whittles the old broom handle Gorham picked up in Packard's store an' brought along jest to keep tally on! It is a great game of ball; the bats are broad and light, and the ball is small and soft.

"But the Enfield boys beat us at last; leastwise they make seventy tallies to our fifty-eight, when Heman Fitts knocks the ball over into Aunt Dorcas Eastman's yard, and Aunt Dorcas comes out an' picks up the ball an' takes it into the house, an' we have to stop playin'. Then Phineas Owen allows he can flop any boy in Belchertown, an' Moses Baker takes him up, an' they wrassle like two Tartars [TAR-turz], till last Moses tuckers Phineas out an' downs him as slick as a whistle.

"Then we all go home, for Thanksgivin' dinner is ready. Two

long tables have been made into one, and one of the big table-cloths Gran'ma had when she set up housekeepin' is spread over 'em both. We all set round—Father, Mother, Aunt Lydia Holbrook, Uncle Jason, Mary, Helen, Tryphena Foster, Amos, and me. How big an' brown the turkey is, and how good it smells!

"There are bounteous dishes of mashed potatoes, turnip, an' squash, and the celery is very white and cold, the biscuits are light and hot, and the stewed cranberries are red as Laura's cheeks. Amos and I get the drumsticks; Mary wants the wish-bone to put over the door for Hiram, but Helen gets it. Poor Mary, she always *did* have to give up to 'rushin' Helen,' as we call her.

"The pies—oh, what pies Mother makes; no dyspepsia [diss-PEP-see-ah] in 'em, but good nature an' good health an' hos-pitality! Pumpkin pies, mince, an' apple, too, and then a big dish of pippins an' russets an' bellflowers, an', last of all, wal-nuts with cider from the Zebrina Dickerson farm!

"I tell ye, there's a Thanksgivin' dinner for ye! that's what we get in old Belchertown; an' that's the kind of livin' that makes the Yankees so all-fired good an' smart.

"But the best of all," said Ezra very softly to himself, "oh, yes, the best scene in all the pictur' is when evenin' comes, when all the lamps are lit in the parlor, when the neighbors come in, and when there is music and singin' an' games. An' it's this part o' the pictur' that makes me homesick now and fills my heart with a longin' I never had before; an' yet it sort o' mellows and comforts me, too.

"Miss Serena Cadwell, whose beau was killed in the war, plays on the melodeon, and we all sing—all of us: men, wom-enfolks, an' children. Sam Merritt is there, and he sings a tenor song about love. The women sort of whisper round that he's goin' to be married to a Palmer lady nex' spring, an' I think to myself I never heard better singin' than Sam's.

"Then we play games—proverbs, buzz, clap-in-clap-out, coperhagen, fox-an'-geese, button-button-who's-got-the-but-ton, spin-the-platter, go-to-Jerusalem, my-ship's-come-in; and all the rest.

"The ol' folks, play with the young folks just as nat'ral as can be; and we all laugh when Deacon Hosea Cowles hez to mea-

sure six yards of love ribbon with Miss Hepsey Newton, and
cut each yard with a kiss; for the deacon hez been sort o' pur-
rin' round Miss Hepsy for goin' on two years.

"Then, aft'r a while, when Mary and Helen bring in the
cookies, nutcakes, cider, an' apples, Mother says, 'I don't believe we're goin' to hev enough apples to go round; Ezry, I
guess I'll have to get you to go down to the cellar for some
more.' Then I says, 'All right, Mother, I'll go, providin' someone'll go along an' hold the candle.'

"An' when I say this I look right at Laura, an' she blushes.
Then Helen, jest for meanness, says, 'Ezry, I s'pose you ain't
willin' to have your fav'rite sister go down to the cellar with
you and catch her death o' cold?' But Mary, who hez been
showin' Hiram Peabody the phot'graph album for more'n an
hour, comes to the rescue an' makes Laura take the candle,
and she shows Laura how to hold it so it won't go out.

"The cellar is warm an' dark. There are cobwebs all between
the rafters an' everywhere else except on the shelves where
Mother keeps the butter an' eggs an' other things that would
freeze in the pantry upstairs. The apples are in bar'ls up against
the wall, near the potater bin. How fresh an' sweet they smell!

"Laura thinks she sees a mouse, an' she trembles an' wants
to jump up on the pork bar'l, but I tell her that there shan't no
mouse hurt her while I'm around; and I mean it, too, for the
sight of Laura a-tremblin' makes me as strong as one of Father's steers.

" 'What kind of apples do you like best, Ezry?' asks Laura,
'russets or greenin's or crow-eggs or bellflowers or Baldwins or
pippins?'

" 'I like the Baldwins best,' says I, ' 'coz they got red cheeks
just like yours!'

" 'Why, Ezry Thompson! how you talk!' says Laura. 'You
oughter be ashamed of yourself!'

"But when I get the dish filled up with apples there ain't a
Baldwin in all the lot that can compare with the bright red of
Laura's cheeks. An' Laura knows it, too, an' she sees the
mouse again, an' screams, and then the candle goes out, and
we are in a dreadful stew.

"But I, bein' almost a man, contrive to bear up under it, and
knowin' she is an orph'n, I comfort an' encourage Laura the

best I know how, and we are almost upstairs when Mother comes to the door and wants to know what has kep' us so long. Jest as if Mother doesn't know! Of course she does; an' when Mother kisses Laura goodbye that night there is in the act a tenderness that speaks more sweetly than even Mother's words.

"It is so like Mother," mused Ezra; "so like her with her gentleness an' clingin' love. Hers is the sweetest picture of all, and hers the best love."

Dream on Ezra; dream of the old home with its dear ones, its holy influences, and its precious inspiration!—Mother.

Dream on in the faraway firelight; and as the angel hand of memory unfolds these sacred visions, with thee and them shall abide, like a Divine Comforter, the spirit of Thanksgiving.

CHRISTMAS

"A Visit from St. Nicholas"
by
CLEMENT CLARKE MOORE

Suggested listening level: I
Approximate reading time: 5 minutes
Pronunciation and vocabulary guide:
   coursers: a swift or spirited horse
   droll: humorous or whimsical
   ere [AIR]: before

'Twas the night before Christmas, when all through the house
Not a creature was stirring, not even a mouse;
The stockings were hung by the chimney with care,
In hopes that St. Nicholas soon would be there;

The children were nestled all snug in their beds,
While visions of sugarplums danced in their heads;
And Mamma in her kerchief, and I in my cap,
Had just settled our brains for a long winter's nap—

When out on the lawn there arose such a clatter,
I sprang from my bed to see what was the matter.
Away to the window I flew like a flash,
Tore open the shutters and threw up the sash.

The moon on the breast of the new-fallen snow
Gave a luster of midday to objects below;
When what to my wondering eyes should appear,
But a miniature sleigh and eight tiny reindeer,
With a little old driver, so lively and quick
I knew in a moment it must be St. Nick.

More rapid than eagles his coursers they came,
And he whistled and shouted, and called them by name:

"Now, Dasher! now, Dancer! now, Prancer and Vixen!
On, Comet! on, Cupid! on, Donder and Blitzen!
To the top of the porch, to the top of the wall!
Now dash away, dash away, dash away all!"

As dry leaves that before the wild hurricane fly,
When they meet with an obstacle, mount to the sky,
So up to the housetop the coursers they flew,
With the sleigh full of toys—and St. Nicholas, too.

And then in a twinkling I heard on the roof
The prancing and pawing of each little hoof.
As I drew in my head, and was turning around,
Down the chimney St. Nicholas came with a bound.

He was dressed all in fur from his head to his foot,
And his clothes were all tarnished with ashes and soot;
A bundle of toys he had flung on his back,
And he looked like a peddler just opening his pack.

His eyes, how they twinkled! his dimples, how merry!
His cheeks were like roses, his nose like a cherry;
His droll little mouth was drawn up like a bow,
And the beard on his chin was as white as the snow.

The stump of a pipe he held tight in his teeth,
And the smoke it encircled his head like a wreath.
He had a broad face and a little round belly
That shook, when he laughed, like a bowl full of jelly.

He was chubby and plump—a right jolly old elf;
And I laughed, when I saw him, in spite of myself.
A wink of his eye and a twist of his head
Soon gave me to know I had nothing to dread.

He spoke not a word, but went straight to his work,
And filled all the stockings; then turned with a jerk,

And laying a finger aside of his nose,
And giving a nod, up the chimney he rose.

He sprang to his sleigh, to his team gave a whistle,
And away they all flew like the down of a thistle;
But I heard him exclaim, ere [AIR] he drove out of sight,
"Happy Christmas to all, and to all a good night!"

"The Gift of the Magi"

by

O. HENRY

About the story:

O. Henry was the name adopted by William Sidney Porter during his three-year stay in a Texas prison for the crime of embezzlement. When his sentence was up, he moved to New York City and began to churn out brilliant stories for local newspapers and magazines at a furious pace. His vignettes about the lives of commonplace New Yorkers were collected in **The Trimmed Lamp** *and* **The Four Million,** *from which "The Gift of the Magi" is taken.*

Many of O. Henry's stories make excellent oral reading, as this one and "The Ransom of Red Chief" should demonstrate. However, the vocabulary in some of the works, though rich and rewarding, can also be troublesome for listeners as well as readers. Therefore, it is advisable to read over any selections you choose and make whatever substitutions are necessary before presenting them aloud.

Suggested listening level: II
Approximate reading time: 15 minutes
Pronunciation and vocabulary guide:

> **Magi** [MAY-jye]: the wise men from the East who paid homage to the infant Jesus
> **flat:** an apartment
> **vestibule** [VESS-tih-byool]: a small entrance hall
> **longitudinal** [lawn-jih-TOO-dihn-ul]: running lengthwise
> **Mme. or Madame** [meh-DAM]
> **metaphor** [MET-uh-fore]: a figure of speech in which one idea is used in place of another
> **chaste:** pure
> **patent** [PAY-tent]: obvious, plain

One dollar and eighty-seven cents. That was all. And sixty cents of it was in pennies. Pennies saved one and two at a time by bulldozing the grocer and the vegetable man and the butcher until one's cheeks burned with the silent accusation of stinginess that such close dealing implied. Three times Della counted it. One dollar and eighty-seven cents. And the next day would be Christmas.

There was clearly nothing to do but flop down on the shabby little couch and cry. So Della did it. Which supports the moral observation that life is made up of sobs, sniffles, and smiles, but mostly of sniffles.

While the mistress of the home is gradually sinking from the first stage to the second, take a look at the home. A furnished flat renting for $8 per week. Now that amount will certainly not provide much in the way of splendor, and in this case it provided none at all.

In the vestibule [VESS-tih-byool] below was a letter-box into which no letter would go, and an electric button from which no mortal finger could coax a ring. Beneath the button was a card bearing the name "Mr. James Dillingham Young."

The "Dillingham" had been more proudly and frequently displayed during a former period of prosperity when its possessor was being paid $30 per week. Now, when the income was shrunk to $20, the letters of "Dillingham" looked blurred, as though they were thinking seriously of contracting to a modest and unassuming D. But whenever Mr. James Dillingham Young came home and reached his flat above, he was called "Jim" and greatly hugged by Mrs. James Dillingham Young, already introduced to you as Della. Which is all very good.

Della finished her cry and touched up her cheeks with a powder puff. She stood by the window and looked out dully at a gray cat walking a gray fence in a gray backyard. Tomorrow would be Christmas Day, and she had only $1.87 with which to buy Jim a present. She had been saving every penny she could for months, with this result. Twenty dollars a week doesn't go far. Expenses had been greater than she had calculated. They always are. Only $1.87 to buy a present for Jim. Her Jim. Many a happy hour she had spent planning for something nice for him. Something fine and rare and sterling—

something just a little bit near to being worthy of the honor of being the wife of Mr. James Dillingham Young.

There was a looking glass between the windows of the room. Perhaps you have seen a looking glass in an $8 flat. A very thin and very agile person may, by observing his reflection in a rapid sequence of longitudinal [lawn-jih-TUDE-inn-all] strips, obtain a fairly accurate conception of his looks. Della, being slender, had mastered the art.

Suddenly she whirled from the window and stood before the glass. Her eyes were shining brilliantly, but her face had lost its color within twenty seconds. Rapidly she pulled down her hair and let it fall to its full length.

Now, there were two possessions of the James Dillingham Youngs in which they both took a mighty pride. One was Jim's gold watch that had been his father's and his grandfather's. The other was Della's hair. Had the Queen of Sheba lived in the flat across the airshaft, Della would have let her hair hang out the window someday to dry just to depreciate her Majesty's jewels and gifts. Had King Solomon been the janitor, with all his treasures piled up in the basement, Jim would have pulled out his watch every time he passed, just to see him pluck at his beard from envy.

So now Della's beautiful hair fell about her, rippling and shining like a cascade of brown waters. It reached below her knee and made itself almost a garment for her. And then she did it up again nervously and quickly. Once she faltered for a minute and stood still while a tear or two splashed on the worn red carpet.

On went her old brown jacket; on went her old brown hat. With a whirl of skirts and with the brilliant sparkle still in her eyes, she fluttered out the door and down the stairs to the street.

Where she stopped the sign read: "Mme. [meh-DAM] Sofronie. Hair Goods of All Kinds." One flight up Della ran, and collected herself, panting. Madame, large, too white, chilly, hardly looked like one named "Sofronie."

"Will you buy my hair?" asked Della.

"I buy hair," said Madame. "Take yer hat off and let's have a sight at the looks of it."

Down rippled the brown cascade.

"Twenty dollars," said Madame, lifting the mass with a practiced hand.

"Give it to me quick," said Della.

Oh, and the next two hours tripped by on rosy wings. Forget the hashed metaphor [MET-uh-fore]. She was ransacking the stores for Jim's present.

She found it at last. It surely had been made for Jim and no one else. There was no other like it in any of the stores, and she had turned all of them inside out. It was a platinum fob chain, simple and chaste in design, properly proclaiming its value by substance alone and not by gaudy ornamentation—as all good things should do. It was even worthy of The Watch. As soon as she saw it she knew that it must be Jim's. It was like him. Quietness and value—the description applied to both. Twenty-one dollars they took from her for it, and she hurried home with the 87 cents. With that chain on his watch Jim might be properly anxious about the time in any company. Grand as the watch was, he sometimes looked at it on the sly on account of the old leather strap that he used in place of a chain.

When Della reached home her intoxication gave way a little to prudence and reason. She got out her curling irons and lighted the gas and went to work repairing the ravages made by generosity added to love. Which is always a tremendous task, dear friends—a mammoth task.

Within forty minutes her head was covered with tiny, close-lying curls that made her look very much like a truant schoolboy. She looked at her reflection in the mirror long, carefully, and critically.

"If Jim doesn't kill me," she said to herself, "before he takes a second look at me, he'll say I look like a Coney Island chorus girl. But what could I do—oh! what could I do with a dollar and eighty-seven cents?"

At seven o'clock the coffee was made and the frying pan was on the back of the stove hot and ready to cook the chops.

Jim was never late. Della doubled the fob chain in her hand and sat on the corner of the table near the door that he always entered. Then she heard his step on the stair away down on the first flight, and she turned white for just a moment. She had a habit of saying little silent prayers about the simplest everyday things, and now she whispered, "Please God, make him think I am still pretty."

The door opened and Jim stepped in and closed it. He looked thin and very serious. Poor fellow, he was only twenty-two— and to be burdened with a family! He needed a new overcoat and he was without gloves.

Jim stopped inside the door, as immovable as a setter at the scent of quail. His eyes were fixed upon Della, and there was an expression in them that she could not read, and it terrified her. It was not anger, nor surprise, nor disapproval, nor horror, nor any of the sentiments that she had been prepared for. He simply stared at her fixedly with that peculiar expression on his face.

Della wriggled off the table and went for him.

"Jim, darling," she cried, "don't look at me that way. I had my hair cut off and sold it because I couldn't have lived through Christmas without giving you a present. It'll grow out again—you won't mind, will you? I just had to do it. My hair grows awfully fast. Say 'Merry Christmas!' Jim, and let's be happy. You don't know what a nice—what a beautiful, nice gift I've got for you."

"You've cut off your hair?" asked Jim, laboriously, as if he had not arrived at that patent [PAY-tent] fact yet even after the hardest mental labor.

"Cut it off and sold it," said Della. "Don't you like me just as well, anyhow? I'm me without my hair, ain't I?"

Jim looked about the room curiously.

"You say your hair is gone?" he said, with an air almost of idiocy.

"You needn't look for it," said Della. "It's sold, I tell you— sold and gone, too. It's Christmas Eve, boy. Be good to me, for it went for you. Maybe the hairs of my head were numbered," she went on with a sudden serious sweetness, "but nobody could ever count my love for you. Shall I put the chops on, Jim?"

Out of his trance Jim seemed quickly to wake. He enfolded his Della. For ten seconds let us discreetly look away and politely focus on something else. Eight dollars a week or a million a year—what is the difference? A mathematician or a wit would give you the wrong answer. The magi brought valuable gifts, but that was not among them. This dark assertion will be illuminated later on.

Jim drew a package from his overcoat pocket and threw it upon the table.

"Don't make any mistake, Dell," he said, "about me. I don't think there's anything in the way of a haircut or a shave or a shampoo that could make me like my girl any less. But if you'll unwrap that package you may see why you had me going awhile at first."

White fingers and nimble tore at the string and paper. And then an ecstatic scream of joy; and then, alas! a quick feminine change to hysterical tears and wails, necessitating the immediate employment of all the comforting powers of the lord of the flat.

For there lay The Combs—the set of combs, side and back, that Della had worshiped for long in a Broadway window. Beautiful combs, pure tortoiseshell, with jeweled rims—just the shade to wear in the beautiful vanished hair. They were expensive combs, she knew, and her heart had simply craved and yearned over them without the least hope of possession. And now, they were hers, but the tresses that should have adorned the coveted adornments were gone.

But she hugged them to her bosom, and at length she was able to look up with dim eyes and a smile and say, "My hair grows so fast, Jim!"

And then Della leaped up like a singed cat and cried, "Oh, oh!"

Jim had not yet seen his beautiful present. She held it out to him eagerly upon her open palm. The dull precious metal seemed to flash with a reflection of her bright and ardent spirit.

"Isn't it a dandy, Jim? I hunted all over town to find it. You'll have to look at the time a hundred times a day now. Give me your watch. I want to see how it looks on it."

Instead of obeying, Jim tumbled down on the couch and put his hands under the back of his head and smiled.

"Dell," said he, "let's put our Christmas presents away and keep 'em a while. They're too nice to use just at present. I sold the watch to get the money to buy your combs. And now suppose you put the chops on."

The magi, as you know, were wise men—wonderfully wise

men—who brought gifts to the Babe in the manger. They invented the art of giving Christmas presents. Being wise, their gifts were no doubt wise ones, possibly bearing the privilege of exchange in case of duplication. And here I have lamely related to you the uneventful chronicle of two foolish children in a flat who most unwisely sacrificed for each other the greatest treasures of their house. But in a last word to the wise of these days let it be said that of all who give gifts these two were the wisest. Of all who give and receive gifts, such as they are wisest. Everywhere they are wisest. They are the magi.

"A Christmas Carol"

by
CHARLES DICKENS

About the story:

Here is a true classic that has become a tradition in many families. Whether it is read on Christmas Eve, Christmas morning, or any other time during the Christmas season, this story will never fail to inspire the imaginations of young and old alike.

Although the story has been shortened somewhat to make it possible to read aloud in one sitting, younger children may still wander off occasionally, which is all quite natural and good. As they grow and come to anticipate the telling of this story at Christmastime, their attention will lengthen and they will become thoroughly involved in the story, not in spite of—but because of— the fact that they know it by heart.

Traditions—healthy, productive, family traditions— are getting hard to come by these days, and so I offer up this one for your approval with the knowledge that this was Mr. Dickens's intention for the tale all along.

Suggested listening level: All ages
Approximate reading time: 60 minutes
Pronunciation and vocabulary guide:
  covetous [CUV-eh-tuss]: greedy
  morose [more-OSE]: gloomy, melancholy
  tacitly [TASS-it-lee]: implied but not spoken
  irresolution [ear-rezz-oh-LEW-shun]: uncertainty, indecisiveness
  cravat [krah-VAT]: necktie
  inexplicable [inn-ex-PLICK-uh-bull]: unexplainable
  apparition [app-uh-RISH-on]: a ghost or specter
  fettered [FETT-erd]: chained
  incessant [inn-SESS-ant]: without interruption, unceasing

prodigiously [pro-DIDGE-ous-lee]: enormously, extraordinarily
bade [BAD]: past tense of bid
ogre [OH-ger]: a monster
almshouse: poorhouse
feign [FANE]: pretend, disguise
malady [MAL-uh-dee]: a disease or ailment

*M*arley was dead, to begin with. There is no doubt whatever about that. The register of his burial was signed by the clergyman, the clerk, the undertaker, and by Scrooge himself. Old Marley was as dead as a doornail.

Scrooge and he had been partners for I don't know how many years. Scrooge was his sole executor, his sole administrator, his sole assign, his sole heir, his sole friend, and sole mourner. And even Scrooge was not so dreadfully cut up by the sad event but that he was an excellent man of business on the very day of the funeral, and solemnized it with an undoubted bargain.

Scrooge had never painted out Old Marley's name. There it stood, years afterward, about the warehouse door: Scrooge and Marley. The firm was known as Scrooge and Marley. Sometimes people new to the business called Scrooge Scrooge, and sometimes Marley, but he answered to both names. It was all the same to him.

Oh! but he was a tight-fisted hand at the grindstone, Scrooge! a squeezing, wrenching, grasping, scraping, clutching, covetous [CUV-eh-tuss] old sinner! Hard and sharp as flint; secret, and self-contained, and solitary as an oyster. The cold within him froze his old features, nipped his pointed nose, shriveled his cheek, stiffened his gait; made his eyes red, his thin lips blue; and spoke out shrewdly in his grating voice.

External heat and cold had little influence on Scrooge. No warmth could warm, no wintry weather chill him. No wind that blew was bitterer than he, no falling snow was more intent upon its purpose, no pelting rain less open to entreaty. Nobody ever stopped him in the street to say, with gladsome looks, "My dear Scrooge, how are you? When will you come to see me?" No beggars implored him to bestow a trifle, no children asked him what it was o'clock, no man or woman ever once in all his life inquired the way to such and such a place, of Scrooge. Even the blind men's dogs appeared to know him; and, when they saw him coming on, would tug their owners into doorways and up courts; and then would wag their tails as though they said, "No eye at all is better than an evil eye, dark master!" But what did Scrooge care? It was the very thing he liked.

Once upon a time—of all the good days in the year, on Christmas Eve—old Scrooge sat busy in his countinghouse. It was cold, bleak, biting weather. The fog came pouring in at every chink and keyhole, and was so dense without, that, although the court was of the narrowest, the houses opposite were mere phantoms.

The door of Scrooge's countinghouse was open, that he might keep his eye upon his clerk, who in a dismal little cell beyond, a sort of tank, was copying letters. Scrooge had a very small fire, but the clerk's fire was so very much smaller that it looked like one coal. But he couldn't replenish it, for Scrooge kept the coal-box in his own room; and so the clerk was forced to put on his white comforter, and try to warm himself at the candle; in which effort, not being a man of strong imagination, he failed.

"A Merry Christmas, Uncle! God save you!" cried a cheerful voice. It was the voice of Scrooge's nephew.

"Bah!" said Scrooge. "Humbug!"

He had so heated himself with rapid walking in the fog and frost, this nephew of Scrooge's, that he was all in a glow; his face was ruddy and handsome; his eyes sparkled, and his breath smoked again.

"Christmas a humbug, Uncle?" said Scrooge's nephew. "You don't mean that, I am sure!"

"I do," said Scrooge. "Merry Christmas! What right have you to be merry? What reason have you to be merry? You're poor enough."

"Come, then," returned the nephew gaily. "What right have you to be dismal? What reason have you to be morose [more-OSE]? You're rich enough."

Scrooge, having no better answer ready on the spur of the moment, said, "Bah!" again; and followed it up with "Humbug!"

"Don't be cross, Uncle!" said the nephew.

"What else can I be," returned the uncle, "when I live in such a world of fools as this? Merry Christmas! Out upon Merry Christmas! What's Christmastime to you but a time for paying bills without money; a time for finding yourself a year older, and not an hour richer? If I could work my will," said Scrooge indignantly, "every idiot who goes about with 'Merry Christmas' on his lips should be boiled with his own pudding, and buried with a stake of holly through his heart. You keep Christmas in your own way, and let me keep it in mine."

"Keep it!" repeated Scrooge's nephew. "But you don't keep it."

"Let me leave it alone, then," said Scrooge. "Much good may it do you! Much good it has ever done you!"

"There are many things from which I might have derived good, by which I have not profited, I dare say," returned the nephew, "Christmas among the rest. But I am sure I have always thought of Christmastime as a good time; a kind, forgiving, charitable, pleasant time; the only time I know of, in the long calendar of the year, when men and women seem to open their shut-up hearts freely, and to think of people below them as if they really were fellow-passengers to the grave, and not another race of creatures bound on other journeys. And therefore, Uncle, though it has never put a scrap of gold or silver in my pocket, I believe that it *has* done me good and *will* do me good; and I say, God bless it!"

The clerk in the tank involuntarily applauded. Becoming immediately sensible of the impropriety, he poked the fire, and extinguished the last frail spark forever.

"Let me hear another sound from *you*," said Scrooge, "and you'll keep your Christmas by losing your job!"

"Don't be angry, Uncle. Come! Dine with us tomorrow."

Scrooge dismissed the invitation at once and attempted to halt all further conversation with an icy "Good afternoon!"

"I am sorry, with all my heart," said the nephew, "to find you so resolute. We have never had any quarrel to which I have been a party. But I have made the trial in homage to

Christmas, and I'll keep my Christmas humor to the last. So a Merry Christmas, Uncle!"

"Good afternoon," said Scrooge.

"And a Happy New Year!" added the nephew.

"Good afternoon!" said Scrooge.

His nephew left the room and stopped at the outer door to bestow the greetings of the season on the clerk, who, cold as he was, was warmer than Scrooge; for he returned them cordially.

"There's another fellow," muttered Scrooge, who overheard him. "My clerk, with fifteen shillings a week, and a wife and family, talking about a Merry Christmas. It's madness!"

As the nephew went out the door, two portly gentlemen came in, carrying some books and papers; they removed their hats and bowed to Scrooge.

"At this festive season of the year, Mr. Scrooge," said one of the gentlemen, taking up a pen, "it is more than usually desirable that we should make some slight provision for the poor and destitute, who suffer greatly at the present time. Many thousands are in want of common necessaries; hundreds of thousands are in want of common comforts, sir."

"Are there no prisons?" asked Scrooge.

"Plenty of prisons," said the gentleman, laying down the pen again.

"And the union workhouses?" demanded Scrooge. "Are they still in operation?"

"They are. Still," returned the gentleman, "I wish I could say they were not."

"Oh! I was afraid, from what you said at first, that something had occurred to stop them in their useful course," said Scrooge. "I am very glad to hear it."

"Under the impression that they scarcely furnish Christian cheer of mind or body to the multitude," returned the gentleman, "a few of us are endeavoring to raise a fund to buy the Poor some meat and drink, and means of warmth. We choose this time, because it is a time, of all others, when Want is keenly felt, and Abundance rejoices. What shall we put you down for?"

"Nothing!" Scrooge replied.

"You wish to be anonymous?" asked the gentleman.

"I wish to be left alone," said Scrooge. "Since you ask me what I wish, gentlemen, that is my answer. I don't make merry myself at Christmas, and I can't afford to make idle people merry. I help to support the establishments I have mentioned —they cost enough; and those who are badly off must go there."

"Many can't go there; and many would rather die," the gentleman responded.

"If they would rather die," said Scrooge, "they had better do it, and decrease the surplus population."

Seeing clearly that it would be useless to pursue their point, the gentlemen withdrew, and Scrooge resumed his labors. Not long afterward, he was distracted from his work by the sound of a small boy who, cold as he was, stooped down at Scrooge's keyhole to regale him with a Christmas carol; but, at the first sound of

"God rest you, merry gentlemen,
Let nothing you dismay!"

Scrooge seized his ruler with such energy of action that the singer fled in terror.

At length the hour of shutting up the countinghouse arrived. With an ill-will Scrooge dismounted from his stool, and tacitly [TASS-it-lee] admitted the fact to the expectant clerk in the tank, who instantly snuffed his candle out, and put on his hat.

"You'll want all day tomorrow, I suppose?" said Scrooge.

"If quite convenient, sir," replied the clerk meekly.

"It's not convenient," said Scrooge, "and it's not fair. If I docked you half-a-crown for it, you'd think yourself ill used, I suppose?"

The clerk smiled faintly.

"And yet," said Scrooge, "you don't think *me* ill used when I pay a day's wages for no work."

The clerk observed that it was only once a year.

"A poor excuse for picking a man's pocket every twenty-fifth of December!" said Scrooge, buttoning his coat to the chin. "But I suppose you must have the whole day. Be here all the earlier next morning."

The clerk promised that he would; and Scrooge walked out with a growl.

Scrooge lived in the house that once belonged to his deceased partner, Marley. It was a dreary place, and nobody lived in it but Scrooge, the other rooms being all let out as offices.

Now it is a fact that there was nothing at all particular about the knocker on the door, except that it was very large. It is also a fact that Scrooge had seen it, night and morning, during his whole residence in that place. And then let any man explain to me, if he can, how it happened that Scrooge, having his key in the lock of the door, saw in the knocker—not a knocker, but Marley's face. It looked at Scrooge as Marley used to look; with ghostly spectacles turned up on its ghostly forehead; and, though the eyes were wide open, they were perfectly motionless.

As Scrooge stared at this phenomenon, it was a knocker again.

To say that he was not startled would be untrue, but he put his hand upon the key he had relinquished, turned it sturdily, walked in, and lighted his candle.

He *did* pause, with a moment's irresolution [ear-rezz-oh-LEW-shun], before he shut the door; and he *did* look cautiously behind it first, as if he half expected to be terrified with the sight of Marley's pigtail sticking out into the hall. But there was nothing on the back of the door, except the screws and nuts that held the knocker on, so he said, "Pooh, pooh!" and closed it with a bang, the sound resounding through the house like thunder.

Up the wide, dark flight of stairs he went to his bedroom, and locked himself in; double-locked himself in, which was not his custom. Thus secured against surprise, he took off his cravat [krah-VAT]; put on his dressing gown and slippers, and his nightcap; and sat down before the very small fire.

As he threw his head back in the chair, his glance happened to rest upon a bell, a disused bell, that hung in the room, and communicated, for some purpose now forgotten, with a chamber in the highest story of the building. It was with great astonishment, and with a strange, inexplicable [inn-ex-PLICK-uh-bull] dread, that, as he looked, he saw this bell begin to swing. It swung so softly in the outset that it scarcely made a sound; but soon it rang out loudly, and so did every bell in the house.

This might have lasted half a minute, or a minute, but it seemed an hour. The bells ceased, as they had begun, together. They were succeeded by a clanking noise deep down below as if some person were dragging a heavy chain over the casks in the wine-merchant's cellar. Scrooge then remembered to have heard that ghosts in haunted houses were described as dragging chains.

The cellar door flew open with a booming sound, and then he heard the noise much louder on the floors below; then coming up the stairs; then coming straight toward his door.

"It's a humbug still!" said Scrooge. "I won't believe it."

His color changed, though, when, without a pause, it came on through the heavy door and passed into the room before his eyes. Upon its coming in, the dying flame leaped up, as though it cried, "I know him! Marley's Ghost," and fell again.

The same face: the very same. Marley in his pigtail, usual waistcoat, tights, and boots. The chain he drew was clasped about his middle. It was long, and wound about him like a tail; and it was made (for Scrooge observed it closely) of cashboxes, keys, padlocks, ledgers, deeds, and heavy purses wrought in steel. His body was transparent: so that Scrooge, observing him, and looking through his waistcoat, could see the two buttons on his coat behind.

"How now!" said Scrooge, caustic and cold as ever. "What do you want with me?"

"Much!"—Marley's voice; no doubt about it.

"Who are you?" demanded Scrooge.

"Ask me who I *was*," the specter replied.

"Who *were* you, then?" said Scrooge, raising his voice.

"In life I was your partner, Jacob Marley," said the Ghost, sitting down on the opposite side of the fireplace. "You don't believe in me," observed the Ghost.

"I don't," said Scrooge.

"Why do you doubt your senses?" asked the Ghost.

"Because," said Scrooge, "a little thing affects them. A slight disorder of the stomach makes them cheats. You may be an undigested bit of beef, a blot of mustard, a crumb of cheese, a fragment of an underdone potato. There's more of gravy than of grave about you, whatever you are!"

At this the spirit raised a frightful cry, and shook its chain with such a dismal and appalling noise, that Scrooge held on tight to his chair, to save himself from falling in a swoon. But how much greater was his horror when the phantom, taking off the bandage round his head, as if it were too warm indoors, its lower jaw dropped down upon its breast!

Scrooge fell upon his knees, and clasped his hands before his face.

"Mercy!" he said. "Dreadful apparition [app-uh-RISH-on], why do you trouble me?"

"It is required of every man," the Ghost returned, "that the spirit within him should walk abroad among his fellow-men, and travel far and wide; and, if that spirit goes not forth in life, it is condemned to do so after death. It is doomed to wander through the world—oh, woe is me!—and witness what it cannot share, but might have shared on earth, and turned to happiness!"

Again the specter raised a cry, and shook its chain and wrung its shadowy hands.

"You are fettered [FETT-erd]," said Scrooge, trembling. "Tell me why?"

"I wear the chain I forged in life," replied the Ghost. "I made it link by link, and yard by yard; I girded it on of my own free will, and of my own free will I wore it. Is its pattern strange to you?"

Scrooge trembled more and more.

"Or would you know," pursued the Ghost, "the weight and length of the strong coil you bear yourself? It was full as heavy and as long as this seven Christmas Eves ago. You have labored on it since. It is a ponderous chain!"

Scrooge glanced about him on the floor, in the expectation of finding himself surrounded by hundreds of feet of iron cable; but he could see nothing.

"Jacob!" he said imploringly. "Old Jacob Marley, tell me more! Speak comfort to me, Jacob!"

"I have none to give," the Ghost replied. "Nor can I tell you what I would like to. A very little more is all that is permitted to me. I cannot rest, I cannot stay, I cannot linger anywhere. Seven years dead and traveling all the time, on the wings of the wind; no rest, no peace. Incessant [inn-SESS-ant] torture of remorse."

"But you were always a good man of business, Jacob," faltered Scrooge.

"Business!" cried the Ghost, wringing his hands again. "Mankind was my business; charity, mercy, forbearance, and benevolence were all my business. Why did I walk through crowds of fellow-beings with my eyes turned down, and never raise them to that blessed star which led the Wise Men to a poor abode? Were there no poor homes to which its light would have conducted *me*?

"Hear me!" cried the Ghost. "My time is nearly gone. I am here tonight to warn you that you have yet a chance and hope of escaping my fate. You will be haunted by Three Spirits."

Scrooge's countenance fell.

"Is that the chance and hope you mentioned, Jacob?" he demanded in a faltering voice.

"It is," the Ghost replied.

"I—I think I'd rather not," said Scrooge.

"Without their visits," said the Ghost, "you cannot hope to shun the path I tread. Expect the first tomorrow when the bell tolls one. Expect the second on the next night at the same hour. The third, upon the next night when the last stroke of twelve has ceased to vibrate. Look to see me no more; and look that, for your own sake, you remember what has passed between us!"

The apparition walked backward from Scrooge; and, at every step it took, the window raised itself a little, so that, when the specter reached it, it was wide open, and the specter floated out upon the bleak, dark night.

Scrooge followed to the window, desperate in his curiosity. He looked out.

The air was filled with phantoms, wandering hither and thither in restless haste, and moaning as they went. Every one of them wore chains like Marley's Ghost. Many had been personally known to Scrooge in their lives. These creatures and their spirit voices faded together into the mist, and the night became as it had been when he walked home.

Scrooge closed the window, and examined the door by which the Ghost had entered. It was double-locked, as he had locked it with his own hands, and the bolts were undisturbed. He tried to say "Humbug!" but stopped at the first syllable and, thoroughly exhausted, fell asleep in bed without undressing.

When Scrooge awoke it was pitch-dark. He heard the chimes of a neighboring church sound the quarter-hours, so he lay in bed listening till it tolled the hour. To his great astonishment, the heavy bell rang twelve times. Twelve! It was past two when he went to bed. The clock must be wrong.

"Why, it isn't possible," said Scrooge, "that I can have slept through a whole day and far into another night. It isn't possible that anything has happened to the sun, and this is twelve at noon!"

Scrooge thought, and thought, and thought it over and over, and could make nothing of it. Marley's Ghost still bothered him exceedingly. Every time he resolved within himself that it was all a dream, his mind flew back again, like a strong spring released, and presented the same problem to be worked all through, "Was it a dream or not?"

Scrooge lay in this state until the chime had gone three-quarters more, when he suddenly remembered that the Ghost had warned him of a visitation when the bell tolled one. He resolved to lie awake until the hour was passed.

"Ding, dong!"

"A quarter-past," said Scrooge, counting.

"Ding, dong!"

"Half-past," said Scrooge.

"Ding, dong!"

"A quarter to it," said Scrooge.

"Ding, dong!"

"The hour itself," said Scrooge triumphantly, "and nothing else!"

He spoke before the hour bell sounded, which it now did with a deep, dull, hollow, melancholy ONE. Light flashed up in the room upon the instant, and Scrooge found himself face to face with an unearthly visitor—as close to it as I am now to you.

It was a strange figure—like a child; yet not so like a child as like an old man; yet the face had not a wrinkle in it, and the tenderest bloom was on the skin. It held a branch of fresh green holly in its hand. But the strangest thing about it was, that from the top of its head there sprang a bright clear jet of light, by which all this was visible; and which was doubtless extinguished by the cap, which it now held under its arm. Its belt, too, sparkled and glittered now in one part and now in another, and what was light one instant at another time was dark, so the figure itself fluctuated in its distinctness.

"Are you the Spirit, sir, whose coming was foretold to me?" asked Scrooge.

"I am!"

The voice was soft and gentle. Singularly low, as if, instead of being so close behind him, it were at a distance.

"Who and what are you?" Scrooge demanded.

"I am the Ghost of Christmas Past."

"Long past?" inquired Scrooge.

"No. Your past."

Scrooge then made bold to inquire what business brought him there.

The Ghost replied, "Your welfare. Your reclamation. Take heed!"

It put out its strong hand as it spoke, and clasped him gently by the arm.

"Rise! and walk with me!"

He rose; but, finding that the Spirit made toward the window, clasped its robe and begged, "I am mortal," Scrooge pleaded, "and liable to fall."

"Bear but a touch of my hand *there*," said the Spirit, laying it upon his heart, "and you shall be upheld in more than this!"

As the words were spoken, they passed through the wall, and stopped upon an open country road, with fields on either hand. The city had entirely vanished.

"Good Heaven!" said Scrooge, clasping his hands together, as he looked about him. "I was bred in this place. I was a boy here!"

"You recollect the way?" inquired the Spirit.

"Remember it!" cried Scrooge with fervor. "I could walk it blindfolded."

They walked along the road, Scrooge recognizing every gate, and post, and tree, until some shaggy ponies now were seen trotting toward them with boys upon their backs. Other boys appeared, too, all in great spirits and full of merry music.

Scrooge knew and named them every one. Why did his cold eye glisten, and his heart leap up as they went past? Why was he filled with gladness when he heard them give each other Merry Christmas? What was Merry Christmas to Scrooge? Out upon Merry Christmas! What good had it ever done to him?

"The school is not quite deserted," said the Ghost. "A solitary child, neglected by his friends, is left there still."

Scrooge said he knew it. And he sobbed.

They soon approached, by a well-remembered lane, a large house, but one of broken fortunes; the spacious offices were little used, their walls were damp and mossy, and their windows broken, and their gates decayed. In a long, bare melancholy room near the back was a lonely boy reading near a feeble fire; and Scrooge sat on one of the writing desks and wept to see his poor forgotten self as he had used to be.

"Poor boy!" Scrooge sobbed. "I wish," he said, drying his eyes with his cuff, "but it's too late now."

"What is the matter?" asked the Spirit.

"Nothing," said Scrooge. "Nothing. There was a boy singing a Christmas carol at my door last night. I should like to have given him something; that's all."

The Ghost smiled thoughtfully, and waved its hand, saying as it did so, "Let us see another Christmas!"

Scrooge's former self grew larger at the words, and the room became a little darker and more dirty. He was not reading now, but walking up and down despairingly. The door opened, and a little girl, much younger than the boy, came darting in, and putting her arms about his neck, and often kissing him, addressed him as her "dear, dear brother."

"I have come to bring you home, dear brother!" said the child, clapping her tiny hands, and bending down to laugh. "Father is so much kinder than he used to be, that home's like heaven!"

"Always a delicate creature, whom a breath might have withered," said the Ghost. "But she had a large heart!"

"So she had," cried Scrooge. "You're right. I will not deny it, Spirit. God forbid!"

"She died a woman," said the Ghost, "and had, as I think, children."

"One child," Scrooge returned.

"True," said the Ghost. "Your nephew!"

The scene quickly changed to the heart of the city. It was plain enough, by the dressing of the shops, that here, too, it was Christmastime again; but it was evening, and the streets were lighted up.

The Ghost stopped at a certain warehouse door, and asked Scrooge if he knew it.

"Know it!" said Scrooge. "I was apprenticed here!"

They went in. At sight of an old gentleman in a Welsh wig, sitting behind a high desk, Scrooge cried in great excitement—

"Why, it's old Fezziwig! Bless his heart!"

Old Fezziwig laid down his pen, and looked up at the clock, which pointed to the hour of seven.

"Yo ho, there! Ebenezer! Dick!" he cried.

Scrooge's former self, now a grown young man, came briskly in, accompanied by his fellow apprentice.

"Dick Wilkins, to be sure!" said Scrooge to the Ghost. "Bless me, yes. There he is. He was very much attached to me, was Dick. Poor Dick! Dear, dear!"

"Yo ho, my boys!" said Fezziwig. "No more work tonight. Christmas Eve, Dick. Christmas Eve, Ebenezer!"

"He gives a Christmas Eve party for all his employees and friends of his family every year, doesn't he," said the Ghost. "And they love him for it, though he spends only a few pounds on the affair each year."

"It isn't that," said Scrooge. "He has the power to render us happy or unhappy; to make our service light or burdensome; a pleasure or a toil. Say that his power lies in words and looks; in things so slight and insignificant that it is impossible to add and count 'em up—what then? The happiness he gives is quite as great as if it cost a fortune."

He felt the Spirit's glance, and stopped.

"What is the matter?" asked the Ghost.

"Nothing particular," said Scrooge. "I should like to be able to say a word or two to my clerk just now. That's all."

He turned upon the Ghost, and seeing that it looked upon him with a face, in which in some strange way there were fragments of all the faces it had shown him, wrestled with it.

"Leave me! Take me back! Haunt me no longer!" he cried.

In the struggle, if it can be called a struggle, Scrooge seized the Spirit's cap and pressed it down upon its head to extinguish its light. He was conscious of being exhausted, and overcome by an irresistible drowsiness; and, further, of being in his own bedroom. He sank into a heavy sleep.

Awaking in the middle of a prodigiously [pro-DIDGE-ouslee] tough snore, and sitting up in bed to get his thoughts together, Scrooge had no need to be told that the bell was again upon the stroke of one. He was ready for a broad field of strange appearances; nothing between a baby and a rhinoceros would have astonished him very much. When the bell struck one, he perceived a blaze of ruddy light that appeared to emanate from the adjoining room. He got up softly, and shuffled in his slippers to the door. The moment Scrooge's hand was on the lock, a strange voice called him by his name, and bade [BAD] him enter. He obeyed.

There he beheld a jolly Giant, glorious to see; who bore a glowing torch, high up, to shed its light on Scrooge as he came peeping round the door.

"Come in!" exclaimed the Ghost. "Come in! and know me better, man!"

Scrooge entered timidly, and hung his head before this Spirit. He was not the dogged Scrooge he had been; and though the Spirit's eyes were clear and kind, he did not like to meet them.

"I am the Ghost of Christmas Present," said the Spirit. "Look upon me!"

Scrooge reverently did so. It was clothed in one simple deep green robe, or mantle, bordered with white fur. This garment hung so loosely on the figure, that its broad chest was bare. Its feet, observable beneath the ample folds of the garment, were also bare; and on its head it wore no other covering than a holly wreath, set here and there with shining icicles.

"Spirit," said Scrooge submissively, "conduct me where you will. I went forth last night on compulsion, and I learned a lesson which is working now. Tonight if you have something to teach me, let me profit by it."

"Touch my robe!" the Ghost commanded.

Scrooge did as he was told, and held it fast.

They stood in the city streets on Christmas morning, where

people scurried about to the poulterers' shops, the fruiterers', and the grocers' before the steeples called them all to church and chapel. The sight of these poor revelers appeared to interest the Spirit very much, for he stood with Scrooge beside him in a baker's doorway, and sprinkled incense on their purchases from his torch. And it was a very uncommon kind of torch, for once or twice, when there were angry words between some shoppers who had jostled each other, he shed a few drops of water on them from it, and their good humor was restored directly. For they said, it was a shame to quarrel upon Christmas Day. And so it was! God love it, so it was!

And they went on, invisible, as they had been before, into the suburbs of the town, and straight to Scrooge's clerk's shabby four-room house. On the threshold of the door the Spirit smiled, and stopped to bless Bob Cratchit's dwelling with the sprinklings of his torch.

Then up rose Mrs. Cratchit, Bob's wife, dressed out but poorly in a twice-turned gown, but brave in ribbons, which are cheap, and make a goodly show for sixpence; and she laid the tablecloth, assisted by Belinda Cratchit, second of her daughters, also brave in ribbons; while Master Peter Cratchit tended a saucepan of potatoes.

"What has ever got your precious father, then?" said Mrs. Cratchit. "And your brother, Tiny Tim, and your sister, Martha?"

"Here they come, Mother!" cried the two young Cratchits. "Hurrah!"

And in the door came little Bob, the father, with his threadbare clothes darned up and brushed to look seasonable, and Tiny Tim upon his shoulder. Alas for Tiny Tim, he bore a little crutch, and had his limbs supported by an iron frame!

"And how did little Tim behave?" asked Mrs. Cratchit when Bob had hugged his family to his heart's content.

"As good as gold," said Bob, "and better. Somehow, he gets thoughtful, sitting by himself so much, and thinks the strangest things you ever heard. He told me, coming home, that he hoped the people saw him in the church, because he was a cripple, and it might be pleasant to them to remember upon Christmas Day who made lame beggars walk and blind men see."

Bob's voice was trembling when he told them this, and trembled more when he said that Tiny Tim was growing strong and hearty.

They all dined on their small, but flavorful Christmas goose, which, when accompanied by apple sauce, mashed potatoes, and Christmas pudding, was a sufficient dinner for the whole family.

At last the dinner was all done, the cloth was cleared, the hearth swept, and the fire made up. A shovel full of chestnuts was put on the fire, and all the Cratchit family drew round the hearth in what Bob Cratchit called a circle, meaning half a one, to toast the season with tumblers of hot spiced cider, which Bob served out with beaming looks, while the chestnuts on the fire sputtered and cracked noisily. Then Bob proposed:

"A Merry Christmas to us all, my dears. God bless us!"

Which all the family reechoed.

"God bless us every one!" said Tiny Tim, the last of all.

He sat very close to his father's side, upon his little stool. Bob held his withered little hand to his, as if he loved the child, and wished to keep him by his side, and dreaded that he might be taken from him.

"Spirit," said Scrooge, with an interest he had never felt before, "tell me if Tiny Tim will live."

"I see a vacant seat," replied the Ghost, "in the poor chimney corner, and a crutch without an owner, carefully preserved. If these shadows remain unaltered by the Future, the child will die."

"No, no," said Scrooge. "Oh, no, kind Spirit! say he will be spared."

"What is it to you?" returned the Ghost. "If he be like to die, he had better do it, and decrease the surplus population."

Scrooge hung his head to hear his own words quoted by the Spirit, and was overcome with penitence and grief.

"Will you decide what men shall live, what men shall die?" asked the Ghost. "It may be that, in the sight of Heaven, you are more worthless and less fit to live than millions like this poor man's child."

Scrooge bent before the Ghost's rebuke, and, trembling, cast his eyes upon the ground. But he raised them speedily on hearing his own name.

"Mr. Scrooge!" said Bob. "I'll give you Mr. Scrooge, the Founder of the Feast!"

"The Founder of the Feast, indeed!" cried Mrs. Cratchit, reddening. "I wish I had him here. I'd give him a piece of my mind to feast upon, and I hope he'd have a good appetite for it."

"My dear," said Bob, "the children! Christmas Day."

"It should be Christmas Day, I am sure," said she, "on which one drinks the health of such an odious, stingy, hard, unfeeling man as Mr. Scrooge. You know he is, Robert! Nobody knows it better than you do, poor fellow!"

"My dear!" was Bob's mild answer. "Christmas Day."

"I'll drink his health for your sake and the day's," said Mrs. Cratchit, "not for his. Long life to him! A Merry Christmas and a Happy New Year! He'll be very merry and very happy, I have no doubt!"

The children drank the toast after her. It was the first of their proceedings which had no heartiness in it. Tiny Tim drank it last of all, but he didn't care twopence for it. Scrooge was the ogre [OH-ger] of the family. The mention of his name cast a dark shadow on the party, which was not dispelled for full five minutes.

By this time it was getting dark, and snowing pretty heavily. Scrooge and the Spirit left the Cratchits and went along the streets, the brightness of the roaring fires in kitchens, parlors, and all sorts of rooms was wonderful. Scrooge was surprised to hear his own nephew's hearty laugh and to find himself in a bright, gleaming room, with the Spirit standing by his side.

"Ha, ha!" laughed Scrooge's nephew, holding his sides, rolling his head, and twisting his face into the most extravagant contortions. "He said that Christmas was a humbug, as I live! And he believed it, too!"

"More shame for him, Fred!" said Scrooge's niece, by marriage.

"He's a comical old fellow," said Scrooge's nephew, "that's the truth; and not so pleasant as he might be. However, his offenses carry their own punishment, and I have nothing to say against him. His wealth is of no use to him. He doesn't do any good with it. He doesn't make himself comfortable with it."

"I have no patience with him," observed Scrooge's niece. Scrooge's niece's sisters, and all the other ladies who were there, expressed the same opinion.

"Oh, I have!" said Scrooge's nephew. "I am sorry for him; I couldn't be angry with him if I tried. Who suffers by his ill whims? Himself always. Here he takes it into his head to dislike us, and he won't come and dine with us. What's the consequence? He loses some pleasant moments, which could do him no harm. I mean to give him the same chance every year, whether he likes it or not, for I pity him. He may rail at Christmas till he dies, but he can't help thinking better of it—I defy him—if he finds me going there, in good temper, year after year, and saying, "Uncle Scrooge, how are you?' "

They all laughed and passed around goblets of mulled wine. Afterward there was music and games of all sorts, some of which made fun of Scrooge, and made everyone laugh uproariously.

"He has given us plenty of merriment, I am sure," said Fred, "and it would be ungrateful not to drink his health. Here is a glass of mulled wine ready to our hand at the moment; and I say, 'Uncle Scrooge!' "

"Well! Uncle Scrooge!" they cried.

"A Merry Christmas and a Happy New Year to the old man, whatever he is!" said Scrooge's nephew. "He wouldn't take it from me, but may he have it, nevertheless. Uncle Scrooge!"

Uncle Scrooge had imperceptibly become so gay and light of heart, that he would have joined in the toast, and thanked them in an inaudible speech, if the Ghost had given him time. But the whole scene passed off in the breath of the last word spoken by his nephew; and he and the Spirit were again upon their travels.

Much they saw, and far they went, and many homes they visited, but always with a happy end. The Spirit stood beside sickbeds, and they were cheerful; on foreign lands, and they were close at home; by struggling men, and they were patient in their greater hope; by poverty, and it was rich. In almshouse, hospital, and jail, in misery's every refuge, where vain man in his little brief authority had not made fast the door and barred the Spirit out, he left his blessing and taught Scrooge his precepts.

It was almost midnight when Scrooge noticed something strange protruding from under the Spirit's robe.

"Is it a foot or a claw?" he asked.

From under the folds the Spirit brought forth two children, wretched, abject, frightful, hideous, miserable. They knelt down at its feet, and clung upon the outside of its garment. They were a boy and a girl. Yellow, meager, ragged, scowling, wolfish; no change, no degradation, no perversion of humanity in any grade, through all the mysteries of wonderful creation, has monsters half so horrible and dread. Scrooge started back, appalled.

"Spirit! are they yours?" Scrooge could say no more.

"They are Man's," said the Spirit, looking down upon them. "This boy is Ignorance. This girl is Want. Beware of them both, and all of their degree, but most of all beware of this boy, for on his brow I see that written which is Doom, unless the writing be erased."

"Have they no refuge or resource?" cried Scrooge.

"Are there no prisons?" said the Spirit, turning on him for the last time with his own words. "Are there no workhouses?"

The bell struck twelve.

Scrooge looked about him for the Ghost, and saw it not. As the last stroke ceased to vibrate, he remembered the prediction of old Jacob Marley, and, lifting up his eyes, beheld a solemn Phantom, draped and hooded, coming like a mist along the ground toward him.

The Phantom slowly, gravely, silently approached. When it came near him, Scrooge bent down upon his knee; for in the very air through which this Spirit moved it seemed to scatter gloom and mystery.

It was shrouded in a deep black garment, which concealed its head, its face, its form, and left nothing of it visible, save one outstretched hand. But for this, it would have been difficult to detach its figure from the night, and separate it from the darkness by which it was surrounded.

"I am in the presence of the Ghost of Christmas Yet to Come?" said Scrooge.

The Spirit answered not, but pointed onward with its hand.

"You are about to show me shadows of the things that have not happened, but will happen in the time before us," Scrooge pursued. "Is that so, Spirit?"

Although well used to ghostly company by this time, Scrooge feared the silent shape so much that his legs trembled beneath him, and he found that he could hardly stand when he prepared to follow it.

"Ghost of the Future!" he exclaimed, "I fear you more than any specter I have seen. But as I know your purpose is to do me good, and as I hope to live to be another man from what I was, I am prepared to bear your company, and do it with a thankful heart. Will you not speak to me?"

It gave him no reply. The hand was pointed straight before them.

"Lead on!" said Scrooge. "Lead on! The night is waning fast, and it is precious time to me, I know. Lead on, Spirit!"

The Phantom moved away as it had come toward him. Scrooge followed in its shadow, which seemed to carry him along. They were soon in the heart of the city, among the merchants and traders, who chinked the money in their pockets, and conversed in groups, and looked at their watches, as Scrooge had seen them often.

The Spirit stopped beside one little knot of businessmen. Observing that the hand was pointed to them, Scrooge advanced to listen to their talk.

"No," said a great fat man with a monstrous chin, "I don't know much about it either way. I only know he's dead."

"When did he die?" inquired another.

"Last night, I believe," returned the fat man.

"Why, what was the matter with him?" asked a third, taking a vast quantity of snuff out of a very large snuffbox. "I thought he'd never die."

"God knows," said the first, with a yawn.

"It's likely to be a very cheap funeral," said another, "for, upon my life, I don't know of anybody to go to it. Suppose we make up a party, and volunteer?"

"I don't mind going if a lunch is provided," one of the men replied, which was received with a general laugh.

Scrooge knew these men. They were men of business: very wealthy, and of great importance. He had made a point always of standing well in their esteem in a business point of view, that is, strictly in a business point of view.

Scrooge looked toward the Spirit for an explanation. He was at first inclined to be surprised that the Spirit should attach importance to conversations apparently so trivial; but feeling assured that they must have some hidden purpose, he set himself to consider what it was likely to be.

Quiet and dark, beside him stood the Phantom, with its outstretched hand.

"Spirit!" said Scrooge, shuddering from head to foot. "I see, I see. The case of this unhappy man might be my own. My life tends that way now. Merciful heaven, what is this?"

He recoiled in terror, for the scene had changed, and now he almost touched a bed—a bare bed on which, beneath a ragged sheet, there lay a something covered up, which, though it was dumb, announced itself in awful language. A pale light, rising in the outer air, fell straight upon the bed; and on it, plundered and bereft, unwatched, unwept, uncared for, was the body of this man.

Scrooge glanced toward the Phantom. Its steady hand was pointed to the head. The cover was so carelessly adjusted that the slightest raising of it, the motion of a finger upon Scrooge's part, would have disclosed the face. He thought of it, felt how easy it would be to do, and longed to do it; but he had no more power to withdraw the veil than to dismiss the specter at his side.

The body lay in the dark, empty house, with not a man, a woman, or a child to say he was kind to me in this or that, and for the memory of one kind word I will be kind to him. A cat was tearing at the door, and there was a sound of gnawing rats beneath the hearthstone. What *they* wanted in the room of death, and why they were so restless and disturbed, Scrooge did not dare to think.

"Spirit!" he said, "this is a fearful place. In leaving it, I shall not leave its lesson, trust me. Let us go!"

Still the Ghost pointed with an unmoved finger to the head.

"I understand you," Scrooge returned, "and I would do it if I could. But I have not the power, Spirit. I have not the power."

The Phantom spread its dark robe before him for a moment, like a wing; and conducted him through several streets familiar to his feet. As they went along, Scrooge looked here and there to find himself, but nowhere was he to be seen. They entered poor Bob Cratchit's house; the dwelling he had visited before; and found the mother and the children seated round the fire.

The mother laid her sewing upon the table, and put her hand up to her face.

"My eyes are weak from working in the candlelight," she said, "and I wouldn't show weak eyes to your father when he comes home for the world. It must be near his time."

"Past it rather," Peter answered, shutting up the book he was reading. "But I think he has walked a little slower than he used, these last few evenings, Mother."

They were very quiet again. At last she said, and in a steady, cheerful voice, that only faltered once:

"I have known him walk with—I have known him walk with Tiny Tim upon his shoulder very fast indeed."

"And so have I," cried Peter. "Often."

"And so have I," exclaimed another. So had all.

"But he was very light to carry," she resumed, "and his father loved him so, that it was no trouble, no trouble. And there is your father at the door!"

She hurried out to meet him; and little Bob in his threadbare clothes came in. The two young Cratchits got upon his knees, and laid, each child, a little cheek against his face, as if they said, "Don't mind it, Father. Don't be grieved!"

"You went today, then, Robert?" said his wife.

"Yes, my dear," returned Bob. "I wish you could have gone. It would have done you good to see how green a place it is. But you'll see it often. I promised him that I would walk there every Sunday. My little, little child!" cried Bob. "My little child!"

He broke down all at once. He couldn't help it. If he could have helped it, he and his child would have been farther apart, perhaps, than they were.

"However and whenever we part from one another," he said to his family, "I am sure we shall none of us forget poor Tiny Tim—shall we—or this first parting that there was among us?"

"Never, Father!" cried they all.

"And I know," said Bob, "I know, my dears, that when we recollect how patient and how mild he was; although he was a little, little child; we shall not quarrel easily among ourselves, and forget poor Tiny Tim in doing it."

"No, never, Father!" they all cried again.

"I am very happy," said little Bob, "I am very happy!"

"Specter," said Scrooge, "something informs me that our parting moment is at hand. I know it but I know not how. Tell me what man that was whom we saw lying dead?"

The Ghost of Christmas Yet to Come pointed as before, and Scrooge accompanied it until they reached an iron gate. He paused to look round before entering.

A churchyard. Here, then, the wretched man, whose name he had now to learn, lay underneath the ground. The Spirit stood among the graves, and pointed down to one. He advanced toward it trembling.

"Before I draw nearer to that stone to which you point," said Scrooge, "answer me one question. Are these the shadows of the things that *will* be, or are they shadows of the things that *may* be only?"

Still the Ghost pointed downward to the grave by which it stood.

Scrooge crept toward it, trembling as he went; and, following the finger, read upon the stone of the neglected grave his own name, EBENEZER SCROOGE.

"Am *I* that man who lay upon the bed?" he cried upon his knees.

The finger pointed from the grave to him, and back again.

"No, Spirit! Oh, no, no!"

The finger was still there.

"Spirit!" he cried, tight clutching at its robe, "hear me! I am not the man I was. I will not be the man I must have been. Why show me this, if I am past all hope?"

For the first time the hand appeared to shake.

"Good Spirit," he pursued, as down upon the ground he fell before it. "Assure me that I yet may change these shadows you have shown me by an altered life. I will honor Christmas in my heart, and try to keep it all the year. I will live in the Past, the Present, and the Future. The Spirits of all three shall strive within me. I will not shut out the lessons that they teach. Oh, tell me I may sponge away the writing on this stone!"

Holding up his hands in a last prayer to have his fate reversed, he saw an alteration in the Phantom's hood and dress. It shrunk, collapsed, and dwindled down into a bedpost.

Yes! and the bedpost was his own. The bed was his own, the room was his own. Best and happiest of all, the Time before him was his own, to make amends in!

"I will live in the Past, the Present, and the Future!" Scrooge repeated as he scrambled out of the bed. "The Spirits of all three shall strive within me. O Jacob Marley! Heaven and Christmastime be praised for this! I say it on my knees, old Jacob; on my knees!"

He was so fluttered and so glowing with his good intentions, that his broken voice would scarcely answer to his call. He had been sobbing violently in his conflict with the Spirit, and his face was wet with tears.

"I am here!" he cried. "The shadows of the things that would have been may be dispelled. They will be. I know they will!"

His hands were busy with his garments all this time: turning them inside out, putting them on upside down, tearing them, mislaying them, making them parties to every kind of extravagance.

"I don't know what to do!" cried Scrooge, laughing and crying in the same breath. "I am as light as a feather, I am as happy as an angel, I am as merry as a schoolboy, I am as giddy as a drunken man. A Merry Christmas to everybody! A Happy New Year to all the world! Hello here! Whoop! Hello!"

He frisked through the house, noting the door by which the Ghost of Jacob Marley entered; the corner where the Ghost of Christmas Present sat; the window from which he saw the wandering Spirits.

"It's all right, it's all true, it all happened," he cried with glee. "Ha, ha, ha!"

Really, for a man who had been out of practice for so many years, it was a splendid laugh, a most illustrious laugh.

"I don't know what day of the month it is," said Scrooge. "I don't know how long I have been among the Spirits. I don't know anything. I'm quite a baby. Never mind. I don't care. I'd rather be a baby. Hello! Whoop! Hello here!"

He was struck by the sound of churchbells ringing out the

lustiest peals he had ever heard. Running to the window, he opened it, and put out his head. No fog, no mist; clear, bright, jovial, stirring, cold; golden sunlight; heavenly sky; sweet fresh air; merry bells. Oh, glorious! Glorious!

"What's today?" cried Scrooge, calling downward to a boy in Sunday clothes, who perhaps had loitered to look about him.

"Eh?" returned the boy with all his might of wonder.

"What's today, my fine fellow?" said Scrooge.

"Today!" replied the boy. "Why, *Christmas Day.*"

"It's Christmas Day!" said Scrooge to himself. "I haven't missed it. The Spirits have done it all in one night. They can do anything they like. Of course they can. Of course they can. Hello, my fine fellow!"

"Hello!" returned the boy.

"Do you know the poulterer's in the next street at the corner?" Scrooge inquired.

"I should hope I did," replied the lad.

"An intelligent boy!" said Scrooge. "Do you know whether they've sold the prize turkey that was hanging up there?"

"What! the one as big as me?" returned the boy. "It's hanging there now."

"Go and buy it, and tell 'em to bring it here, that I may give them the directions where to take it. Come back with the man, and I'll give you a shilling. Come back with him in less than five minutes, and I'll give you half-a-crown!"

The boy was off like a shot.

"I'll send it to Bob Cratchit's," whispered Scrooge, rubbing his hands, and splitting with a laugh. "He shan't know who sends it. It's twice the size of Tiny Tim."

The hand in which he wrote the address was not a steady one; but write it he did, somehow, and went downstairs to open the street door, ready for the coming of the poulterer's man. As he stood there, waiting his arrival, the knocker caught his eye.

"I shall love it as long as I live," cried Scrooge, patting it with his hand. "I scarcely ever looked at it before. What an honest expression it has in its face! It's a wonderful knocker!—Here's the turkey. Hello! Whoop! How are you! Merry Christmas!"

He dressed himself "all in his best," and at last got out into the streets. The people were by this time pouring forth, as he had seen them with the Ghost of Christmas Present; and, walking with his hands behind him, Scrooge regarded every one with a delighted smile. He looked so irresistibly pleasant, in a word, that three or four good-humored fellows said, "Good morning, sir! A Merry Christmas to you!"

He had not gone far when, coming on toward him, he beheld the portly gentleman who had walked into his counting-house the day before seeking a donation for the poor.

"My dear sir," said Scrooge, quickening his pace, and taking the old gentleman by both his hands, "how do you do? I hope you succeeded yesterday. It was very kind of you. A Merry Christmas to you, sir!"

"Mr. Scrooge?" the startled man inquired.

"Yes," said Scrooge. "That is my name, and I fear it may not be pleasant to you. Allow me to ask your pardon. And will you have the goodness—" Here Scrooge whispered in his ear.

"Lord bless me!" cried the gentleman, as if his breath were taken away. "My dear Mr. Scrooge, are you serious?"

"If you please," said Scrooge. "Not a farthing less. A great many back payments are included in it, I assure you. Will you do me the favor?"

"My dear sir," said the other, shaking hands with him, "I don't know what to say to such munifi—"

"Don't say anything, please," retorted Scrooge. "Come and see me. Will you come and see me?"

"I will!" cried the old gentleman. And it was clear he meant to do it.

"Thankee," said Scrooge. "I am much obliged to you. I thank you fifty times. Bless you!"

That afternoon he turned his steps toward his nephew's house. He passed the door a dozen times before he had the courage to go up and knock. But he made a dash and did it.

"Is your master at home, my dear?" said Scrooge to the girl. "Nice girl! Very."

"Yes, sir," replied the girl.

"Where is he, my love?" said Scrooge.

"He's in the dining room, sir, along with mistress. I'll show you upstairs, if you please."

"Thankee. He knows me," said Scrooge, with his hand already on the dining room lock. "I'll go in here, my dear."

He turned it gently, and poked his face in round the door.

"Fred!" said Scrooge.

"Why, bless my soul!" cried Fred, "who's that?"

"It's I. Your Uncle Scrooge. I have come to dinner. Will you let me in, Fred?"

Let him in! It is a mercy he didn't shake his arm off. He was at home in five minutes. Nothing could be heartier. His niece looked just the same. So did everyone when they arrived. Wonderful party, wonderful games, won-der-ful happiness!

But he was early at the office next morning. Oh, he was there early! If he could only be there first, and catch Bob Cratchit coming late! That was the thing he had set his heart upon.

And he did it; yes, he did! The clock struck nine. No Bob. A quarter-past. No Bob. He was full eighteen minutes and a half behind his time. Scrooge sat with his door wide open, that he might see him come into the tank.

His hat was off before he opened the door. He was on his stool in a jiffy, driving away with his pen, as if he were trying to overtake nine o'clock.

"Hello!" growled Scrooge in his accustomed voice as near as he could feign [FANE] it. "What do you mean by coming here at this time of day?"

"I am very sorry, sir," said Bob. "I *am* behind my time. It's only once a year, sir," pleaded Bob, appearing from the tank. "It shall not be repeated. I was making rather merry yesterday, sir."

"Now, I'll tell you what, my friend," said Scrooge. "I am not going to stand this sort of thing any longer. And therefore," he continued, leaping from his stool, and giving Bob such a dig in the waistcoat that he staggered back into the tank again, "and therefore I am about to raise your salary!"

Bob trembled, and got a little nearer to the ruler. He had a momentary idea of knocking Scrooge down with it, holding him, and calling to the people in the street for help and a strait-jacket.

"A Merry Christmas, Bob!" said Scrooge, with an earnest-ness that could not be mistaken, as he clapped him on the back. "A Merrier Christmas, Bob, my good fellow, than I have given you for many a year! I'll raise your salary, and endeavor to assist your struggling family, and we will discuss your af-fairs this very afternoon, Bob Cratchit!"

Scrooge was better than his word. He did it all, and infinitely more; and to Tiny Tim, who did NOT die, he was a second father. He became as good a friend, as good a master, and as good a man as the good old city knew. Some people laughed to see the alteration in him, but he let them laugh, and little heeded them; for he was wise enough to know that nothing ever happened on this globe, for good, at which some people did not have their fill of laughter in the outset; and knowing that such as these would be blind anyway, he thought it quite as well that they should wrinkle up their eyes in grins as have the malady [MAL-uh-dee] in less attractive forms. His own heart laughed, and that was quite enough for him.

He had no further dealings with Spirits, but lived upon the total abstinence principle ever afterward; and it was always said of him that he knew how to keep Christmas well, if any man alive possessed the knowledge. May that be truly said of us, and all of us! And so, as Tiny Tim observed, God bless us, every one!

Afterword

Throughout this book I have suggested additional materials for you to read aloud to your children. Now let me suggest that you encourage your children to satisfy their own particular literary interests by reading other stories of a favorite author or by reading the complete novel from which a favorite selection has been taken and presented here.

One final caution is appropriate. Don't think that a book must be either *one to read aloud* or *one for your children's own silent reading. There is absolutely nothing wrong with having your children bring home a Dickens novel, let's say, from which you read aloud one chapter while they read another on their own. But let's keep* Classics to Read Aloud to Your Children *in its own category—a special book that your children associate with those valuable moments they share with you. Let it be a book that will encourage outside exploration but that will also provide a safe harbor for return and renewal. Our children need that and so do we.*